THE STRATEGIC DRUCKER

Growth Strategies and Marketing Insights from The Works of Peter Drucker

THE STRATEGIC DRUCKER

Growth Strategies and Marketing Insights from The Works of Peter Drucker

Robert W. Swaim

Student, Colleague and Friend of
Peter F. Drucker for 30 Years

JOSSEY-BASS™
An Imprint of
⟨W⟩**WILEY**

Jossey-Bass

Contents

Acknowledgments

I wish to extend my appreciation to the following individuals who played a significant role in helping me develop Peter Drucker's teachings for China that eventually led to the writing of this book.

Les Charlton, the Associate Editor of *Business Beijing Magazine* who encouraged me to write the *Drucker Files* series of over 20 articles that became the foundation for significant parts of this book.

Xueying "Penny" Peng, my researcher in China who eventually knew more about Drucker than I did and whom Peter also admired.

J. Michael Marks, a friend of over 30 years who was kind enough to provide his creative insight in the editing of this book.

Thomas W. Zimmerer, former Dean of the Saint Leo University School of Business, who worked with me to create nine fully accredited Drucker MBA courses that became an integral part of the Saint Leo University–Peter Drucker MBA Program for China.

Professor Joseph Maciariello, at the Drucker School, who was my content expert in my development of Peter Drucker's works for the China Drucker MBA and Executive Development Programs to ensure I did not put words in Peter's mouth.

Peter F. Drucker, who was my teacher, colleague and friend for close to 30 years and always had time to share his insights with me.

Preface

Peter F. Drucker (1909–2005)

THE FATHER OF MODERN MANAGEMENT

Peter F. Drucker is known throughout the world as the *Father of Modern Management,* and countless articles have been written since he passed away in 2005, relative to his extensive contributions to management and society. I had the good fortune of knowing Peter first as a teacher, then as a colleague and also as a friend for almost 30 years. I also devoted nearly five years to working with Peter to develop the Drucker MBA and Drucker Executive Development Programs that are now offered in China. The programs I eventually developed and taught in many cities in China included nine fully US-accredited MBA courses that were based on the nearly 40 books and thousands of articles he had written on management and other related topics. The reader will therefore find a number of references to China in this book; however, the concepts presented will apply nearly everywhere.

In working together, we had numerous conversations in which he shared additional insight on a number of topics that he had previously not written about. Many of these pertained to his views on strategy and, in particular, on sales and marketing. I therefore feel uniquely qualified to share some additional insight relating to his work as well as to some of his omissions, or what I call "Drucker gaps". Also, we have to go beyond Drucker to implement a number of these concepts today.

The Strategic Drucker and Beyond

One of the Drucker MBA courses I developed was "*Strategy and the Purpose of a Business*" and was based on his views on strategy, marketing and other related topics that were contained in, sometimes sandwiched in, his numerous books and countless articles. Throughout Peter Drucker's many books he discussed the importance of strategy; however, he never devoted an entire book to the subject although he claimed, "I developed the first book on what is now called 'strategy,' *Managing for Results*, which appeared in 1964."[1] To this day, he is still not known to be a strategist like more notable contributors such as Michael Porter, known in particular for his "*Five Competitive Forces Model*" as described in his 1980 book *Competitive Strategy*[2] and Henry H. Mintzberg of McGill University in Montreal, who has written extensively on the subject.[3]

Richard Koch in his 1995 book, *The Financial Times Guide to Strategy,* commented, "Considering his long innings and large tally of books, and the appropriately high esteem in which he is held, it is salutary to reflect that Drucker actually says remarkably little about strategy. His main contribution is the idea of the *Theory of the Business.* The fit of this theory with the business environment—that is, the degree to which the firm's theory of the business strikes a market and economic chord—may be as important to the firm's success as the strength of its core competencies or its market position. Drucker did not exactly say this but he would have done, had he ever deigned to write a book on strategy."[4]

I would disagree with Koch's observations that Drucker's main contribution to strategy was his *Theory of the Business*, and furthermore this book suggests that there actually is no "theory" in the *Theory of the Business*. However, Drucker's views on the Purpose of a Business, the importance of Mission and Vision, his focus on the Customer, Non-customers and Going Outside (known today as the Voice of the Customer), and on what he considered to be the two most important functions of the organization, Marketing and Innovation, are far more significant contributions than the "theory." However, Koch is correct in suggesting that Drucker never wrote a book that was entirely devoted to strategy. On the other hand, contained in many of his 39 books and thousands of articles are *possibly* the critical ingredients for such a book. This book therefore attempts to consolidate many of Drucker's observations and writings on strategy and other topics related to business growth, such as sales, marketing, innovation, mergers and acquisitions, and strategic alliances into one source, just as I had to do when conducting the research for the development of the Drucker Strategy Course. Even then, the reader will find in a number of cases Drucker's views to be incomplete, leaving omissions or gaps that need to be filled. Also, to understand the application of a number of his concepts today, or if they are still valid, we must sometimes go beyond Drucker.

What Are Drucker Gaps?

Peter Drucker was very good at describing *what* should be done, often suggesting the right questions management should be asking itself (Drucker's Strategic Thinking), as will be seen in the chapter, "Strategy and the Purpose of a Business," but he often neglected to mention *how* to do it. I have therefore included my observations on a number of Drucker's concepts on strategy and related topics. Although I am not the first to identify these gaps, perhaps I am among the first to attempt to close them, at least in the area of strategy, with this book. As an example, William Clarkson, a former CEO of Graphic Controls, a subsidiary of Times-Mirror, in calling attention to the gap between academic theory and its practical application, wrote in 1985, "Yet a major gap exists between academia's theoretical and conceptual understanding of management and industry's ability to use this body of knowledge in a practical, relevant, and cost-effective way." In reference to Drucker, he added, "On one side of the gap, we have Drucker, the seer. On the other side of the gap, we have the US manager, knowing that the Management Bible (Drucker's 1973 classic book, *Management: Tasks, Responsibilities, Practices*) has been written by Drucker, but not quite knowing how to have this knowledge become a part of her or his behavior and practice. His writings have been read by more managers than those of any other single author, living or dead. Yet there is that troubling gap between his theory and the practice of US managers."[5]

This book therefore also includes *practical guidelines* on how some of these gaps can be closed and how a number of Drucker's concepts on strategy can be applied in one's own organization. This is largely accomplished by referencing and including the work of other contributors to strategy and the other disciplines Drucker commented on that are required to fully understand the application of his concepts. The reader will also find a number of application tools included in Appendix A.

A Focus on Growth

This book will focus on Drucker's views on strategies to achieve business growth, both organically through sales and marketing, and innovation; and then external growth through mergers, acquisitions, and strategic alliances. Drucker's Strategic Thinking Process will also be covered in detail, outlining the essential steps that must be taken in order to arrive at the appropriate strategies for growth. Chapter 2, "Strategy and the Purpose of a Business," will cover most of Drucker's views on strategy and marketing in a unique hypothetical setting: Your company has retained him to provide you with advice on how to compete more effectively in the global economy. The interview you and your management team will have with him and the topics discussed and the questions asked by him lay the foundation for the other chapters that follow. This chapter illustrates Drucker's Strategic Thinking Approach to strategy and illustrates the right questions that need to be asked—according to Drucker.

His views on the key roles that senior management and planners must play in the strategic planning process are also reviewed as well as the importance of executive decision making. Drucker's observations on changing demographics and global trends in society that offer opportunities for innovation and growth help to reinforce some of his views on marketing and marketing research.

Summary: Who Was Drucker?

Nearly 30 years ago, I asked Peter, "How would you classify yourself—as a Professor of Management?"

He replied, "No Bob, I am a social scientist."[6]

Some 20 years later, he apparently rebranded himself as a social ecologist in *The Daily Drucker* (2004): "I consider myself a 'social ecologist,' concerned with man's man-made environment the way the natural ecologist studies the biological environment. The term 'social ecology' is my own coinage."[7] In *The Daily Drucker* he also cited a reference to *The Age of Discontinuity*, a book he wrote in 1969 as the first time he wrote about social ecology"[8] Webster's

New World Dictionary defines "ecology" from a sociology perspective as, "*Sociology* the study of the relationship and adjustment of human groups to their geographic environment."[9] Drucker did not see himself as a visionary, but rather as an astute observer of society, hence his initial classification as a social scientist. He did not predict the future, but called attention to what was happening today that would impact the future. As an example, he was ahead of most in identifying the issues of declining birthrates, aging populations, and shrinking populations, particularly in the developed world—trends to assist us in identifying possible opportunities for innovation and growth.

My descriptions of Drucker gaps are not intended to be a criticism of his work, but merely to provide some additional tools for the implementation of many of his concepts and teachings. In other cases, where his concepts were incomplete, the contributions of others were included to close the loop. Drucker wrote in his 1986 book, *The Frontiers of Management,* "I have never slighted techniques in my teaching, writing, and consulting. Techniques are tools; without tools, there is no 'practice,' only preaching."[10] I have taken the position that although this might have been the case, there were situations where more than tools were necessary to close some gaps— it was necessary to go beyond Drucker enlisting the contributions from experts (I have called them pundits) in various disciplines such as strategy, marketing and innovation.

Needless to say, it was a pleasure to have known and worked with Peter. Working with Peter on the China Programs was one of the highlights of my career.

Robert W. Swaim
Beijing, China

Endnotes

1. Peter F. Drucker, "Drucker on Drucker," *New Management* 2, no. 3 (Winter 1985): 7.
2. Michael Porter, *Competitive Strategy: Techniques for Analyzing Industries and Competitors* (New York: The Free Press, 1980).
3. Henry Mintzberg, "Crafting Strategy," *Harvard Business Review* 65, no. 4 (July-August 1987); and Henry Minztberg, Bruce Ahlstrand, and Joseph Josepel, *Strategy Safari: A Guided Tour Through the Wilds of Strategic Management* (New York: Free Press, 1998).
4. Richard Koch, *The Financial Times Guide to Strategy: How to Create and Deliver a useful Strategy,* 2nd ed. (London: Pearson Education Limited, 2000), 147–148.

5. William Clarkson, "Drucker: Closing the Theory/Practice Gap," *New Management* 2, no. 3 (Winter 1985): 21–23.
6. Rosabeth Moss Kanter, "Drucker: The Unsolved Puzzle," *New Management* 2, no. 3 (Winter 1988); and Thomas J. Peters, "The Other Half of the Message," *New Management* 2, no. 3 (Winter 1985).
7. Drucker's response to my question at the Claremont Graduate School during the fall of 1977. Drucker held the position of the Clarke Professor of Social Science during his entire tenure at the Claremont Graduate University, not as a "social ecologist."
8. Peter F. Drucker, *The Daily Drucker: 366 Days of Insight and Motivation for Getting the Right Things Done* (New York: HarperCollins Publishers, Inc., 2004).
9. Peter F. Drucker, *The Age of Discontinuity: Guidelines to our Changing Society* (London: William Heinemann, Ltd., 1969).
10. Peter F. Drucker, *The Frontiers of Management* (New York: Truman Talley Books, 1986), 220–227.

Drucker on Managing Growth

THE NEED FOR BUSINESS GROWTH AND STRATEGY

Growth will continue to be a desirable and indeed a necessary business objective.[1]

Peter F. Drucker*

I start the journey of exploring Peter Drucker's views on strategy and strategic management with a discussion of growth. After all, what is the purpose of developing a strategy if it is not to provide the direction for the future growth of the firm? As Drucker stated in *Management* (1973), "Growth will continue to be a desirable and indeed a necessary business objective." He went on to add, "In a growing economy there is plenty of room. Industries that have passed their peak decline slowly and are being held up by the overall buoyancy of the economy. New industries can grow well and grow more by accident than by management. But when the economy as such does not grow, changes in the economy are bound to be abrupt and sharp. Then indeed a company or an industry that does not grow will decline. Then there is even more need for a strategy that enables a management to plan for growth and to manage growth."[2] Needless to say, the banking and mortgage industries need a strategy.

---

* All chapter opening quotes are from Peter Drucker unless noted otherwise.

In his discussions of the need for marketing, Drucker also spoke about what contributed to a growth company. The quotation below is just one aspect of what Drucker suggested needed to be asked of customers and non-customers. (Non-customers is a term he came up with to describe those who are not buying from your company.)

Management has to ask which of the customer's wants are not adequately satisfied by the products or services offered him today. The ability to ask this question and to answer it correctly usually makes the difference between a growth company and one that depends on the rising tide of the economy or of the industry. But whoever contents himself to rise with the tide will also fall with it.[3]

Peter F. Drucker[*]

The Falling Tide

As the first decade of the 21st century draws to a close, the US economy can be best described as having no growth, or only marginal growth, depending on whose numbers we are given, or as Drucker once commented on statistics, "Tell me what you want to prove and I will develop the numbers."[4] This lack of economic growth can be attributed to many factors including the credit crisis as a result of the greed and stupidity of those who ventured into the subprime mortgage market (as lenders, investors and customers)—compounded by the collapse of the housing market and the highest number of home loan foreclosures since the Great Depression; oil; the falling value of the dollar against most currencies; the huge national debt increasing every day with the cost of US military commitments in Iraq and Afghanistan, and a volatile capital market witnessing triple digit swings in the stock markets depending on what day it is, to name but a few factors.

Despite the weak economy, the "Street" (the Wall Street analysts) is still ever critical of the companies that do not meet their growth expectations. Take as an example a report by Reuters (April 25, 2008) with the headline, "3M revenue growth disappoints, shares

---

[*] All quotes are from Peter F. Drucker unless noted otherwise.

fall." The article cited 3M's first-quarter growth increased 8.9 percent of which foreign currency translation accounted for 6.1 percent. According to Adam Fleck, a Morningstar analyst, "A lot of the growth of this quarter was from currency translation. That's positive for the company but not as positive as true organic growth."[5] The article went on to add that 3M's first-quarter net income was $988 million, or $1.38 per share, beating analysts' average forecast of $1.35 per share. Despite these results Reuters concluded that although "3M reported better-than-expected quarterly profit on Thursday, its shares fell amid investor concern that the weak dollar accounts for too much of the company's growth." 3M shares did fall 86 cents in that afternoon's trading to $79.95, down 17 percent from their 52-week high of $97.

In this article we see the typical short-term expectations of the "analysts." Although the company (3M) beat its first-quarter 2008 net income expectations of $1.35 per share with actual results of $1.38 per share, analysts were disappointed with the firm's "organic growth" of only 2.8 percent compared with 6.1 percent in currency translation, or a total of 8.9 percent. Can you place yourself in the 3M headquarters conference room the following Monday morning when the chairman states to all the executives present, "We beat the quarterly sales forecast by 2.8 percent and earnings per share expectations by 2 percent. What are we going to do in the second quarter?" Never mind discussing whether the strategy is appropriate for the current environment and asking some of Drucker's key questions, which we will review in the next chapter. Who is the competition here—the analysts?

Dimensions of Business Growth

The following is a brief description of the elements of a business that can contribute to growth. These include both Organic and External Growth Dimensions.

Organic Growth Dimension: An increase in sales revenues attributed to sales and marketing, including price increases, and innovative efforts of the firm in developing new products or services. This will be covered in Chapters 2 through 5.

> *External Growth Dimension:* An increase in sales revenues as a result of mergers and acquisitions. Horizontal acquisitions include expanding geographically or acquiring new products to complement the firm's present product line. Backward vertical acquisitions involve acquiring a source of supply, while forward vertical acquisitions involve acquiring a part of the marketing channel to reduce sales and marketing expenses as well as get closer to the customer. Strategic alliances, both formal and informal, also provide opportunities for growth. Divestitures will show a temporary increase in revenues as a result of a business unit's sale but will also result in a decline of product sales of that business unit. M&A and alliances as a growth strategy will be covered in Chapter 6.
>
> *Other External Dimension:* Currency Translations will result in a gain or loss in revenues depending on the exchange rate between local currencies the firm is charging for its products and the eventual exchange into US dollars.

Table 1.1 is a snapshot of 3M's 2007 SEC 10-K Report and the *Dimensions of Business Growth* as reported by the company. This is an excellent example of being able to quickly ascertain how the company is growing in each of these dimensions.

As can be seen in Table 1.2, a significant percentage of the firm's growth was attributed to currency translations as a result of a weaker dollar compared to the euro in the EU, the pound in the UK and the yen in Japan.

The reported *Dimensions of Business Growth* for the firm coupled with the criticism from the "analysts" forced George Buckley, the chairman and CEO of the firm to respond with the following statements at the firm's May 13, 2008 shareholder's meeting.

"The US is by far the largest single market for us. And so it's obvious that for 3M to meet its long-term growth aspirations, the US business has to grow faster. It's increasingly clear to all of us that driving growth in the United States will continue to be challenging in the near term."[6] To achieve this growth, Buckley commented that "3M will try harder to differentiate its products from competition, innovate more, and improve service to squeeze growth out of its US markets." The article went on to comment on 3M's international business that comprised 63 percent of its sales in 2007 and could be 70 percent by 2010. Also, of this, 30 percent, or $7 billion,

Table 1.1   3M Results of Operations

Net Sales	US	International	Worldwide
Net sales (US$ millions)	$8,987	$15,475	$24,462
% of worldwide sales	36.7%	63.3%	
Components of net sales change:			
Volume: organic	1.6%	7.4%	5.1%
Volume: acquisitions	3.1	2.1	2.4
Price	1.0	(1.1)	(0.2)
Local currency sales (including acquisitions)	5.7	8.4	7.3
Divestitures	(4.2)	(3.6)	(3.8)
Translation	–	5.2	3.2
Total sales change	1.5%	10.0%	6.7%

Source: 2007 SEC 10-K Report

Table 1.2   3M Dimensions of Business Growth

Dimensions of Growth	Component	Results	% Total Company
Organic Growth	Sales & Marketing	Increase Sales	5.1
		Price Increases	(0.2)
	Innovation	New Products & Services	
External Growth	Mergers & Acquisitions	Horizontal Acquisitions (expand geographically, product extensions)	2.4
		Vertical Acquisitions (backward— acquire source of supply; forward— acquire channel to become closer to customer)	
	Strategic Alliances	Formal Alliances (joint ventures, license & patent agreements)	
	Strategic Alliances	Informal Alliances (marketing & distribution agreements)	
	Divestitures	Loss of Unit's Sales	(3.8)
Other External	Currency Translation	Gain/Loss on Conversion of Local Currency to US dollars	3.2
Total Growth			6.7%

Source: Developed by Robert W. Swaim (2006)

came from emerging markets where sales were growing at nearly 20 percent per year. The article added that, "3M shares fell 49 cents to $77.18 Tuesday."

As an added note, 3M was selected as an example in our discussion of growth since 63.3 percent of its total revenues were derived from outside the US, the firm reports its growth in accordance with the *Dimensions of Business Growth,* it is a Fortune 500 company, and also a component of the firms that comprise the Dow Jones Industrial Average. The chairman's comments in the last article on the need for differentiation and innovation tie directly into Drucker's views on the two most important functions of the organization, *marketing* and *innovation,* and will be covered in detail in this book.

Despite the chairman's positive outlook relative to the firm's future growth opportunities, apparently the "analysts" were not impressed, and the firm's shares price declined. The question here is—does 3M need a better investor relations manager or a better strategy? Drucker's and others' views on the important role the CEO plays in strategy and strategic planning is covered in more detail as well.

Drucker on Growth

Growth is the result of success.
A company grows because it is doing a good job.
Its products meet with increasing demand.[7]

In Drucker's earlier writings, his discussions on growth were directed more on the *size* of the organization and how it transitioned from the small entrepreneurial organization to the larger organization. This also included his views on the need to change the attitude and behavior of top-management people, including the structure of management and very often, to replace the owner-founder with professional management. A short discussion of organizational lifecycle theory is included in this book, since it presents a more comprehensive strategic approach and a less anecdotal approach than Drucker's to complement this important element of business strategy.

Growth is not automatic. It does not follow from success.[8]

Approximately 20 years later, Drucker changed his views on what contributed to growth and in particular, he no longer believed that success was a contributing factor. How to sort out these different views?

The Need for Growth Objectives

Drucker commented in *Management* (1973) that "It is not enough for a management to say, 'We want growth.' Management needs a rational growth policy."[9] He stressed that management needs to establish a rational growth policy with both *minimum* and *optimum* objectives. He also stressed that "growth in the context of a business is an economic rather than a physical term. Volume by itself is irrelevant." He added, "A business grows in economic performance and economic results. To want to be a "billion-dollar company" is not a rational growth objective. Growth objectives have to be economic objectives rather than volume objectives."[10] Unfortunately in *Management,* and what will be a recurring theme throughout this book, Drucker did not provide us with any insight on how to establish *optimum objectives.* He did, however go on to expand on this in *Managing in Turbulent Times* (1980) with a rule that "any growth which, within a short period of time, results in the overall increase in the total productivities [not defined] of the enterprise's resources is healthy growth."[11]

Drucker on the Need for Management

The normal cause of business growth is able and competent management.[12]

The above quote by Drucker, although made over 50 years ago in *The Practice of Management* (1954), is still directly applicable in today's environment and focuses more on success or business performance and results rather than size. Matthew Kirdahy writes in a *Forbes.com* article, "A snapshot of recent corporate history shows that CEOs have always been in danger of losing their jobs in a heartbeat. These days, it's proven that they are spending less time in the office because of an intense business environment and super-competitive global marketplace. It's the kind of job that doesn't appeal to everyone, despite the fantastic paycheck. As it stands, the average tenure is about six years; however, there are those who haven't even hit that short mark, whether it was their choice or not."[13] This short tenure as described by Kirdahy can largely be attributed to the often conflicting demands being placed on the CEO for short-term results in the form of quarterly earnings per share and the longer-term strategic direction of the business.

Porter on the Need for Leadership

Michael E. Porter is known as one of the major contributors on strategy and a number of his views, as well as those of others, are included in this book when it is felt we need to go "beyond Drucker" on a key point. Here, Porter speaks of the need for leadership, not management in terms of crafting the business's strategy.

> *In many companies, leadership had degenerated into orchestrating operational improvements and making deals.*[14]
>
> Michael E. Porter

Porter expanded on the above quote by stressing the need for executive leadership to define and communicate the business's strategy, identify which industry changes and customer needs the company will respond to, which target customers the company should serve, and so forth, as well as making choices of what the business will not do. The role of the CEO and others in strategic planning will be addressed in this book including the views of Drucker and other contributors such as Porter.

An Opposing View: "The Growth Trap"

In his *Harvard Business Review* article, "What Is Strategy?" (1996), Porter also took a somewhat different view on the importance of growth when he wrote, "Among all other influences, the desire to grow has perhaps the most perverse effect on strategy."[15] What did Porter mean by this and what kind of growth is desirable?

His more recent views on strategy describe the importance of strategic positioning, making trade-offs, and forging a fit among activities. He also differentiated between operational effectiveness and strategic positioning by stating, "Operational effectiveness means performing similar activities better than rivals perform them (obtaining efficiency and the use of such tools as: Best Practices, Total Quality Management, Zero Defects, and Six Sigma). In contrast, strategic positioning means performing different activities from rivals or performing similar activities in different ways." Porter commented that operational effectiveness cannot be used as a basis of competition over an extended period of time since competitors can quickly imitate management techniques, new technologies, input improvements to the company's value chain, and so forth.

Porter commented, "Competitive strategy is about being different and deliberately choosing a different set of activities to deliver a unique mix of value." This he considered to be the essence of strategy. According to Porter, "the essence of strategic positioning is to choose activities that are different from rivals." He then identified the sources of where the firm might choose to be different: *variety-based positioning* (based on the choice of product or service varieties and distinctive sets of activities, rather than customer segments); *needs-based positioning* (a more traditional approach of targeting a segment of customers with different needs), and *access-based positioning* (segmenting customers that are accessible in different ways—geography, customer scale—or of anything that requires a different set of activities to reach customers in the same way).[16]

With respect to strategic positioning, Porter also stressed that it requires trade-offs, that is, one cannot be all things to all people. Senior management/leadership, as previously noted, needs to make clear they are choosing to compete in one way and not another. Here he stated, "Trade-offs are essential to strategy. They create the need for choice and purposefully limit what a company offers." Porter also discussed the importance of "fit" or how activities relate to each other and considered it as a central component of competitive strategy. Drucker also spoke of the importance of "fit" in his discussion of "The Theory of the Business," although he places it in a different perspective than Porter, which will be covered in the next two chapters. Porter classified "fit" as first-order fit or *simple consistency* between each activity (function) and the overall strategy. Second-order fit is when *activities are reinforcing* with consistency in the firm's functions while third-order fit is classified as *optimizing of effort*, such as coordination and exchange of information across activities to eliminate redundancy and minimize wasted effort. Porter then went on to emphasize that fit among many activities is fundamental to both competitive advantage and the sustainability of that advantage. Here he also stressed that, "Strategic positions should have a horizon of a decade or more, not of a single planning cycle." This he attributed to fit among a company's activities, which also creates pressure to improve operational effectiveness thus contributing to continuity and sustainability. Drucker disagrees with this view in his discussion of "What will our business be?" since it is impacted by changes that take place in the organization's external environment requiring adjustments to the organization's strategy. This will be covered in the next two chapters.

Returning to the issue of growth, Porter described the "growth trap" as consisting of management's concern that trade-offs appear to constrain growth (serving one group of customers and excluding others) and places a real or imagined limit on revenue growth. As such, management is tempted to abandon the business's strategic position. Porter felt that "compromises and inconsistencies in the pursuit of growth will erode the competitive advantage a company had with its original varieties or target customers." He added that attempting to compete in several ways at once creates confusion and undermines the organizational focus. This will essentially result in decreasing profits with more revenue (growth) seen as the answer, often leading to more acquisitions. Positive growth on the other hand can be achieved by concentrating on deepening a strategic position rather than broadening and compromising it. Deepening according to Porter means making the company's activities more distinctive, strengthening fit, and communicating the strategy better to those customers who should value it. He went on to add that "a company can often grow faster—and far more profitably—by penetrating needs and varieties where it is distinctive than by slugging it out in potentially higher growth arenas in which the company lacks uniqueness."[17]

Rather than just offering theory, Porter provided some potential solutions to achieving growth, such as through globalization, that are consistent with strategy and open up large markets (such as China and India) for a focused a strategy. He contrasted this with companies seeking growth through broadening domestically. He did suggest, however, that seeking domestic growth within their industry, such as our example of 3M, can overcome some of the risks to strategy by creating stand-alone units, each with its own brand name and tailored activities.

At general management's core is strategy: defining a company's position, making trade-offs, and forging fit among activities.[18]

Michael E. Porter

Porter later attempted to reconcile this newer version of strategy as compared to his original "generic" strategies, which will be covered later in Chapter 3.

Chapter Summary

The focus of this chapter is on the need for growth that can be achieved through "organic growth" attributed to sales, marketing, and innovation, and "external growth" through mergers and acquisitions and strategic alliances. Another perspective on growth was also presented based on Michael Porter's views. His views on strategy were introduced early in the book to illustrate how other contributors build on Drucker's concepts and often go "beyond Drucker."

Endnotes

1. Peter F. Drucker, *Management: Tasks, Responsibilities, Practices* (New York: Harper & Row 1973), 773.
2. Ibid., 773.
3. Ibid., 91.
4. Comment made by Drucker during a Ph.D. class at the Claremont Graduate School during the Fall of 1978.
5. "3M revenues growth disappoints, shares fall," Reuters, April 25, 2008.
6. "CEO Says 3M Will Aim to Spur Its US Growth," Associated Press News, May 13, 2008.
7. Peter F. Drucker, *Management: Tasks, Responsibilities, Practices* (New York: Harper & Row, 1973), 765.
8. Ibid., 774.
9. Ibid., 775.
10. Peter F. Drucker, *The Practice of Management* (New York: Harper & Row, 1954), 251.
11. Peter F. Drucker, *Managing in Turbulent Times* (New York: Harper Publishing, 1980), 48.
12. Peter F. Drucker, *The Practice of Management* (New York: Harper & Row, 1954), 251.
13. Matthew Kirdahy, "Quick Succession," *Forbes.com*, March 13, 2008.
14. Michael E. Porter, "What Is Strategy?" *Harvard Business Review* (November–December 1996), 77.

15. Ibid., 75–77.
16. Ibid., 65–68.
17. Ibid., 75–77.
18. Ibid., 77.

Strategy and the Purpose
of a Business

The purpose of a business is to create a customer.[1]

Part One: Drucker Visits Your Company

Introduction

Strategy and the Purpose of a Business really defines Drucker's approach to business strategy and marketing. Although Drucker said there are only two functions in an organization that contribute to results, *Marketing* and *Innovation,* he never really devoted an entire book to marketing as he did for innovation in his book, *Innovation and Entrepreneurship* (1985). Drucker's *Managing for Results* (1964) did address numerous topics contained in contemporary marketing texts as well as those on strategy, but it still comes up short of being a comprehensive discussion of the discipline. You will therefore find that this chapter probably comes closest to anything Drucker had written on strategy and marketing in one source.

The reader will also get a firm grasp of Drucker's approach, of knowing the right questions to ask, or Drucker's Strategic Thinking. Of course, knowing what to do and how to do it after one answers the questions is part of closing the Drucker gap. The content of this chapter was originally written as an article for *Business Beijing* magazine and then served as a reading assignment for our Chinese MBA students, so the reader will see several references to the Chinese environment.[2] Whether the reader is in China or other parts of the world, the key questions Drucker asks you to answer are applicable anywhere. Therefore, as you review this chapter, consider how you would respond to Drucker's questions relative to your own organization. And then ask not only "what do I do", but "how do I do it"?

A Meeting With Peter F. Drucker[3]

You are about to engage the world's foremost authority on management and a recipient of the 2002 Presidential Medal of Freedom (the highest award for a civilian in the United States), Peter F. Drucker, to spend a day at your company with you and your management team. You want to gain some insight and advice from him as to the direction your company should take and what is the best strategy to consider. You are concerned about how your company can compete in a dynamic and rapidly changing global economy and you are uncertain as to what China's entry into the World Trade Organization will mean to your company.

You contact some of the companies he has consulted with, such as General Electric and other Fortune 500 companies, and they suggest that you will not be disappointed in bringing Drucker to China. They tell you he will not provide you with any answers, but with the *right questions* you and your management team should be asking yourselves—then you will have the answers. He will not give a lecture, but he will provide you with insight on a number of important issues for your company's management to consider such as, what do we know and not know about the future, and what this might mean for your business strategy? Are you ready for his visit?

The Morning Session of Drucker's Visit with You

You and your management team are in the conference room, Drucker enters and after introductions, he asks you, "What is the purpose of your business?" How would you answer him?

If you said, to make a profit, he laughs and says, "You don't know anything about business," and adds, "The answer is not only false, it is irrelevant." He then goes on to explain to you that "THE PURPOSE OF A BUSINESS IS TO CREATE A CUSTOMER."[4] This chapter will explain what Drucker means by this definition of the Purpose of a Business and what he has written on the subject, including the key questions that management needs to ask in order to formulate strategies to create and retain customers. We will not ignore your most likely answer to his question, "to make a profit," as Drucker puts profit into its proper perspective later in the interview.

The Three Key Questions Drucker Asks You in the Morning Meeting   Drucker goes on with the meeting. "Ladies and Gentlemen, at the end of today's meeting you will want to be able to determine how you are going to answer the following three key questions:

1. What is our business?
2. What will our business be?
3. What should our business be?"

What Is Our Business?

The question deals with defining the Mission of the business. And the first and most critical question to be asked in defining the Mission of the business is, "Who is the customer?"[5] Drucker adds "that there are usually two or more types of customers. As an example, for a business involved in branded consumer products, the grocer is one customer, getting shelf space in his stores and the consumer is the other customer; will she buy your product when she is in the store? Each customer defines a different business, has different expectations and values, and buys something different."[6]

Drucker continues, "We need to look outside from the point of view of the customer and market. Any serious attempt to state, 'What is our business?' must start with the customer's realities, his situation, his behavior, his expectations and values. To satisfy the customer is the Mission and Purpose of every business." Other key questions that also need to be answered include "Where is the customer?" and "What does the customer buy?" These last two questions deal with market segmentation. Drucker later rephrased the last question to "What is value to the customer?"[7]

According to Drucker, every organization operates on a Theory of the Business. That is, a set of assumptions about:

- What its business is
- What its objectives are

- How it defines results
- Who its customers are
- What the customers value and pay for

Drucker goes on in the meeting, "Let us reflect on what I call the Theory of the Business and the Three Pillars of Assumptions that comprise the Theory of the Business."[8] These are:

1. The environment—markets, clients, distribution channels, competition, etc.
2. The business's core competencies, that consist of the different capabilities of the organization
3. The assumptions about the future Vision and Current Mission of the organization

Let's review each of these.

Assumptions About the Market and Key Questions   First of all, it is important to stop saying, "We know," and instead say, "Let's ask":

- What do we assume about the market?
- Is the market still what we think it is?
- Who is our customer?
- Who is our distribution channel? What do they pay for?
- Non-customers: Why don't they buy from us? What are they willing to pay for? What is value to them?

Drucker has coined the term "non-customers" to describe those people who do not buy from you. As an example, your business may have a 20 percent market share in your industry. On the other hand, 80 percent are not buying from you—they are "non-customers," and Drucker stresses that you need to find out why they are not buying from you.

Drucker asks, "When was the last time you talked to your non-customers to find out why they are not buying from you? What did you learn?" How would you answer him?

Assumptions About Core Competencies and Key Questions   Drucker goes on to point out other key questions you need to ask relative to your organization's core competencies. These include:

- What are we good at?
- What are the abilities and knowledge we depend on in order to conquer and maintain our leadership in the market?

- What are the things we know how to do better than our competitors and with less effort?
- In what areas are we really excellent, and in what areas would we have to be?

Drucker asks, "How would you respond to these four questions?"

Assumptions About Mission   Drucker stresses that the organization's Mission needs to be reviewed and updated as your environment changes. Key questions to ask here include:

- What is our Mission?
- What should it have to be?
- What results are we trying to achieve?
- How are we going to measure them, or at least value them?

Drucker adds "that in asking the question, 'What is our business?', the organization should not wait until the business or industry is in trouble. The question should be asked at the inception of the business, and particularly for a business that has ambitions to grow. The most important time to ask, "what is our business?" is when a company has been successful."[9]

In defining the organization's Mission then, it should include the following key elements:

- Customer Needs—*WHAT is being satisfied?*
- Customer Groups—*WHO is being satisfied?*
- Technologies Used, Functions Performed and Unique Capabilities (Core Competencies)—*HOW customer needs are being satisfied.*[10]

Drucker then asks you in the meeting, "Does your company have a Mission Statement that includes the above key elements?"

We cannot overemphasize the importance of defining the organization's Mission and revisiting the Mission on a regular basis. As an example, at one time the SCM Corporation was one of the largest manufacturers of electric typewriters in the world and had a significant market share. The company viewed its Mission as making electric typewriters while customers were changing to word processors and eventually PCs. When was the last time your company bought an electric typewriter? SCM failed to ask the important questions about its Mission, and was ultimately declared bankrupt.

Drucker and the Two Most Important Functions of a Business

According to Drucker, "A business enterprise has two basic functions, *Marketing* and *Innovation*."[11] The following are Drucker's comments to you on the Marketing Function.

"True marketing starts out with the customer, his demographics, his realities, his needs, his values. Marketing does not ask, what do we want to sell?—It asks, what does the customer want to buy? Marketing does not say, this is what our product does—it says, these are the satisfactions the customer looks for, values and needs."[12]

With respect to the Innovative Function, Drucker comments, "It is not enough for the business to provide just any economic goods and services; it must provide better and more economical ones. The most productive innovation is a different product or service creating a new potential or satisfaction, rather than an improvement." Drucker continues, "Managers must convert society's needs into opportunities for profitable business."

We will expand on Drucker's views on and the importance of innovation in another chapter in this book. Briefly, Drucker states "that organizations who do not innovate will not survive."

What Will Our Business Be?

In your meeting, Drucker now turns to the second important question you have to ask, "What will our business be?" He points out that this "aims at adaptation to anticipated changes. It aims at modifying, and developing the ongoing business." Drucker goes on, "There are four major factors that will determine what your business will be. These are:

- Market Potential and Market Trend
- Changes in Market Structure
- Innovation
- The Consumer"[13]

He expands on these four factors with some additional insight and other questions for you to answer.

Market Potential and Market Trends

- How large can we expect the market for our business to be in five or 10 years—assuming no basic changes in market structure or technology?
- What will be the factors that will determine this development?

Changes in Market Structure

- What changes in market structure are to be expected as the result of economic developments, changes in fashion or taste, or moves by competitors?

Innovation

- What innovations will change the customer's wants, create new ones, extinguish old ones, create new ways of satisfying his wants, change his concepts of value, or make it possible to give him greater value satisfaction?

Drucker asks you, "What innovations are taking place in your industry?"

The Consumer

- What wants does the consumer have that are not being adequately satisfied by the products or services offered to him today?

What Should Our Business Be?

Drucker continues asking the question, "What should our business be?" which involves developing a Vision for the future. One does this by answering the following questions:

- What changes in the environment can be observed that have an impact on characteristics, Mission and Purpose of the business?
- What opportunities are opening up or can be created to fulfill the Purpose and Mission of the business by making it into a different business?
- How to build these anticipations into the Theory of the Business, into objectives, strategies and work assignments?

According to Drucker, "The market, its potential and its trends are the starting point. Changes in demographics are the only events regarding the future for which true prediction is possible. Management needs to anticipate changes in market structure, fashion or taste and moves from competition. Also, which of the consumer's wants are not adequately satisfied by the products or services offered today?"

Drucker adds, "The ability to ask these questions (consumer's wants) makes the difference between a growth company and one that depends for its development on the rising tide of the economy or industry. Whoever is content to rise with the tide will also fall with it."[14]

The Importance of Strategic Vision

Just as Drucker stresses the importance of a Mission Statement, the business also needs a Vision Statement. According to Drucker, "The characteristics of Strategic Vision include:

- It charts an organization's future strategic course—defines the business composition in three to five years.
- It identifies business activities to be pursued.
- It defines the business's future market position.
- It defines its future customer focus.
- It defines the kind of organization the business wants to become."

Drucker points out "that Mission and Vision Statements guide managerial decision making (where are we going and what is important?). It also arouses employee motivation and commitment (instills confidence in senior management—they know where the organization is going and how to get there). It prepares the organization for the future and the establishment of long-term objectives. The Vision is not to make a profit—the real Mission and Vision are what we will do to make a profit?"

Drucker asks you, "Does your business have a Vision Statement?"

The Concept of Planned Abandonment and Key Questions to Ask

In addition to having a Vision for the future, Drucker stresses "that management needs to make a systematic analysis of its present businesses and products. The old that no longer fits the Purpose and Mission of the business, no longer conveys satisfaction to the customers, and no longer makes a superior contribution. All existing products, services, processes, markets, end uses and distribution channels need to be assessed."[15] This is Drucker's "Concept of Planned Abandonment" and needs to be implemented, even if the existing but aging product is still making money. Key questions that need to be asked relative to the abandonment of the old include:

- Are they still viable?
- Are they likely to remain viable?
- Do they still give value to the customer?
- Are they likely to do so tomorrow?
- Do they still fit the realities of population and markets, of technology and economy?
- If not, how can we best abandon them—or at least stop pouring in further resources and efforts?

Drucker asks, "Have you made an assessment of your present products or businesses to determine if they should be abandoned?" How would you answer him?

We will cover Drucker's Concept of Planned Abandonment in more detail in Chapter 6, "Getting Rid of Yesterday."

Drucker on Strategy and Certainties on Which to Base Strategies

According to Drucker, "The purpose of strategy is to enable the organization to achieve its desired results in an unpredictable environment and allows the organization to be purposefully opportunistic. Strategy is also the test of the Theory of the Business. Failure of strategy to produce the desired results is usually the first serious indication that the Theory of the Business needs to be thought through again. Also, unexpected successes are often the first indication that the Theory of Business needs to be rethought."

Drucker points out that "there are five certainties or assumptions on which to base strategy. These include:

1. The Collapsing Birthrate in the Developed World and The Aging Population.
2. Shifts in the Distribution of Disposable Income.
3. Defining Performance.
4. Global Competitiveness.
5. The Growing Incongruence Between Economic Globalization and Political Splintering."[16]

Because of the time constraints of your meeting with Drucker, he will only discuss some of these certainties. Those interested in learning more about his views should refer to his book, *Management Challenges for the 21st Century.*

The Collapsing Birthrate in the Developed World and the Aging Population   "The most important new certainty—if only because there is no precedent for it in all of history—is the collapsing birthrate in the developed world. In Central Europe and in Japan, the birthrate has already fallen well below the rate needed to reproduce the population. By the end of the 21st century, the population in Italy may be 20 million people, down from 60 million; Japan may be 50 or 55 million, down from the present 125 million." Drucker goes on, "More important than absolute numbers is the age distribution within the population. Of those 20-odd million Italians by the year 2080, a very small number will be under 15, and a very large number—at least one-third of the population will be over 60 years old. The same trends will be seen in other parts of the world including China. In 2002 there were 130 million people over 65 years old in China. By 2040 or sooner, there will be 400 million, or almost one-third of the population over 65 years old in China. What are the implications for Chinese companies?"[17]

Drucker poses the following questions for you to consider:

- Will the steady growth in the number of older people continue to provide market opportunities—and for how long?
- Will their income still be high (developed countries) or go down?
- Will they continue to spend as freely as they have been doing?
- Will they continue to want to be "young" and spend accordingly?

Drucker asks you to consider these questions. He asks, "What opportunities might this present for Chinese companies? What industries?" How would you respond to him?

Shifts in the Distribution of Disposable Income   Another certainty Drucker describes is the Distribution of Income. He points out that "shifts in disposable income are the most reliable foundation of strategy. Trends in the distribution of disposable income that go to a certain product category or service category tend, once established, to persist for a long period of time and are impervious to business cycles." He suggests, "Watch for changes in trend and a change within a trend (a switch from one kind of product or service within a category to another product or service within the same category." He adds, "Within the first decades of the 21st century, there will be both changes in the trends and changes within the trends."[18]

Drucker then asks, "Have you observed shifts in disposable income in China and what does this mean for your business? What trends have you observed or are anticipating will take place in the future?"

Global Competitiveness   Another certainty to base business strategy on is Global Competitiveness. Drucker comments during the meeting that "the world economy is increasingly becoming global and all institutions will have to make global competitiveness a strategic goal. Businesses can no longer define their scope in terms of national economies and national boundaries. They will have to define their scope in terms of industries and services worldwide. That no institution can hope to survive, let alone succeed, unless it measures up to the standards set by the leaders in its field, anyplace in the world."

Drucker asks, "What is the scope of your business in terms of its global competitiveness?"

Drucker predicts that "we will face a protectionist wave throughout the world in the next few decades as the first reaction to a period of turbulence is to try to build a wall that shields one's garden from the cold winds outside." The tariffs imposed on steel imports by the United States are a classical example of this protectionist wave that Drucker describes here. On the other hand, he comments that "such walls no longer protect institutions—and especially businesses that do not perform up to world standards. It will only make them more vulnerable."[19]

Drucker asks you, "What protectionist policies exist in China that may change as a result of China's membership of the World Trade Organization (WTO), and what impact will this have on your company?"

Summary of Key Questions to Answer

If you were taking notes during the morning meeting, these are the key questions you and your management team should now begin to develop information on in order to answer:

1. What is our business? (Mission)
2. What will our business be? (The changing environment that we are certain about)
3. What should our business be? (Vision)

We will have another meeting with Drucker in the afternoon. Topics Drucker will address in the afternoon session will include the importance of objectives and the kind of objectives that are needed, as well as putting profit into perspective.

Part Two: The Afternoon Meeting With Drucker

In Part Two we will first review the process you will need to go through in order to be able to answer his three key questions. Drucker will then focus on the importance of objectives, and finally put profit into perspective.

The Strategic Management Process and the Drucker Gap

Before you can answer the three key questions and formulate a strategy, it is necessary to perform an assessment of your external environment and of your own internal environment or your organization's capabilities, core competencies, and strengths and weaknesses. Figure 2.1, Drucker's Strategic Thinking Approach, outlines the key elements of the "Process" and questions that need to be asked. (*Note:* Drucker did not provide this tool, and it was necessary to add it to close the Drucker gap.)

Mission and Purpose of the Business

- What is the Mission of the business?
- Is the Mission appropriate for the current environment or does it need to be redefined?

You may not be able to answer these questions until you have completed your External Environment, Industry and Internal Environment Assessments.

Short-Term Objectives

- Are we meeting our short-term objectives (marketing, innovation, financial, etc.)? If not, is there something wrong with our Mission or strategy?

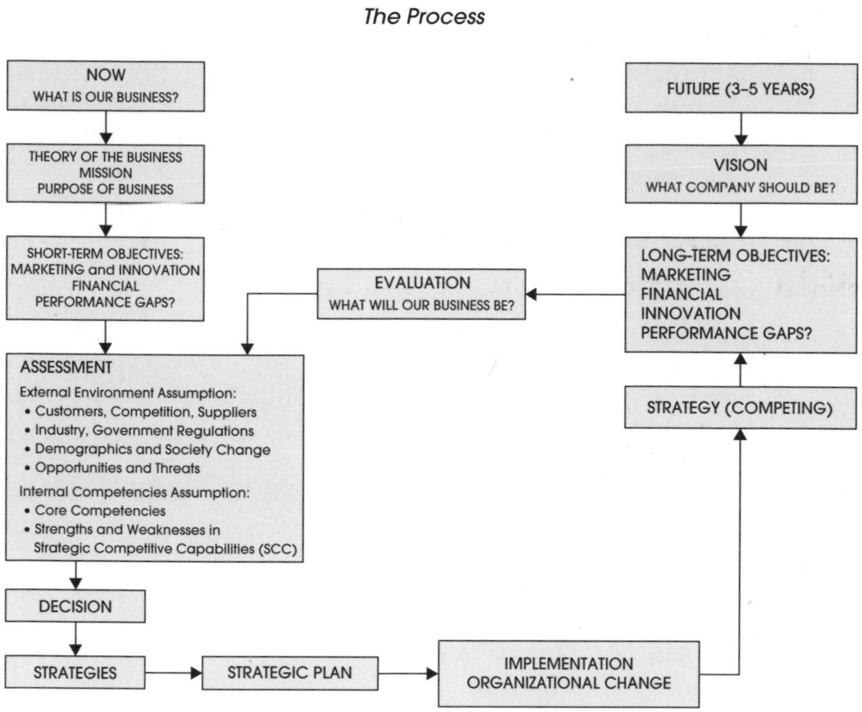

The Process

Figure 2.1   Drucker's Strategic Thinking Approach
Source: Developed by Robert W. Swaim (2003)

What Will Our Business Be?

- What changes have taken place or are taking place in the environment that will have an impact on our present customers, products and services, and industry?

Industry Analysis

- Should we be in this or another industry?
- Is the industry growing, stable, or declining?
- How easy or difficult is it for others to enter or leave the industry?
- Knowing what we know now, would we do this?

Vision for the Future

- What should our business be?

Long-Term Objectives

- What Financial, Marketing, Innovation and other Long-Term Objectives need to be established to achieve the Vision? (Drucker comments on the type of objectives needed later in the meeting.)

External Environment Assessment

- What changes are taking place or will take place in the following areas: Customers and Non-customers (changing needs), Competitors (competitive analysis), Technology, Suppliers, Government Regulations, Demographics and Society Changes, other, etc.?

Assessment of Innovative Opportunities and Potential Risks

- Based on the External Environment Assessment, what Innovative Opportunities should the organization prioritize and pursue?
- What "Risks or Threats" should the organization be aware of and attempt to minimize?

Internal Assessment (Core Competencies and Capabilities)

- Do we have the resources (capabilities) to compete?
- What other resources are needed and when?
- What weaknesses do we have in key competitive areas that we need to address?
- What strengths (core competencies) do we have that we should take advantage of?

Establishment of Long-Term Objectives (Three to Five Years)

- What Long-Term Objectives need to be established now in order to achieve our Vision?

Strategic Alternatives and Decision

- What is the best competitive strategy that will allow us to accomplish our objectives and achieve our Vision?
- What are the competitive strategies to consider?

Strategic Plan

- How are we going to document how we will get there (the Strategic Plan)?
- What resources will we need, how will we be organized?
- Who should do this?

Implementation of the Plan and Leading Change

- What changes may be necessary in the organization?
- Who will plan, lead and implement Organizational Change?
- Are we achieving our objectives?
- Are we receiving the right information when we need it for decision making?

Once again, Drucker asks, "Do you perform this Process, how often, and who does it in your organization?" How would you respond to him?

Drucker on Establishing Objectives

The following are some important comments by Drucker on the need for establishing objectives and the type of objectives that are needed. Drucker was the *first* to advocate the establishment of objectives many years ago in *The Practice of Management*.[20] According to Drucker, "The basic definitions of the business, and of its Purpose and Mission, have to be translated into objectives. Otherwise they remain insights, and good intentions that never become achievement. Objectives must be derived from the three key areas, *what our business is, what it will be, and what it should be.*" Drucker adds that, "Objectives are not fate; they are directions. They are not commands; they are commitments. They do not determine the future; they are a means to mobilize the resources and energies of the business for making the future."[21]

The following are some guidelines from Drucker on objectives:

- Objectives represent the fundamental strategy of a business.
- Objectives must be operational (converted into specific targets and assignments).
- Objectives must make possible concentration of resources and efforts (human resources, capital, physical facilities, etc.).

- There need to be multiple objectives—not one right objective (balance a variety of needs and goals).
- Objectives are needed in all areas of which the survival of the business depends.

The Need for Multiple Objectives

Drucker advocates that the following categories of objectives need to be established by the business: Marketing, Innovation, Human Resources, Financial Resources, Physical Resources, Productivity, Social Responsibility and Profit Requirements. We will focus on two key functions of a business Drucker stressed—*Marketing* and *Innovation*.

Marketing Objectives These allow management to make *two key decisions*; what part of the market to concentrate on, and what market and product lines the business should desire to be a leader in. The following are the key areas for Marketing Objectives:[22]

- *Existing products* and services in *existing markets*—the desired standing of existing products in their present market, expressed in the local currency, and percentage points, and measured against both direct and indirect competition.
- *Existing products* and services in *new markets*—the desired standing of existing products in new markets, expressed in the local currency, and percentage points, and measured against direct and indirect competition.
- *Existing products* that should *be abandoned*—for technological reasons, because of market trends, to improve product mix, or as a result of management's decisions concerning what the business should be.
- *New products* needed in *existing markets*—the number of products, their properties, the dollar volume and the market share they should gain for themselves.
- *New markets* that *new products* should be developed for in terms of dollars and percentage points.
- *The distribution organization* needed to accomplish the marketing objectives and the pricing policy appropriate to them.
- *Service objectives* measuring how well the customer should be supplied with what he considers value by the company, its products, its sales and service organization.

Drucker now asks you, "Do you have marketing objectives in these key areas?"

Innovation Objectives   According to Drucker, there are three types of innovation. These are Product Innovation (innovation in products or services), Social Innovation (innovation in the marketplace and consumer behavior and values), and Managerial Innovation (innovation in the various skills and activities needed to make the products and services and to bring them to the market). The following are the areas where Drucker suggests Innovation Objectives are needed:[23]

- *New products or services* that are needed to attain marketing objectives.
- *New products or services* that will be needed because of technological changes that may make present products obsolete.
- *Product improvements* needed both to attain marketing objectives and to anticipate expected technological changes.
- *New processes and improvements* in old processes needed to satisfy marketing objectives: for instance, manufacturing improvements to make possible the attainment of pricing objectives.
- *Innovations and improvements* in all major areas of activity—in accounting or design, office management or labor relations—so as to keep up with advances in knowledge and skills.

Drucker now asks you, "Does your business have Innovation Objectives and in what areas?"

Putting Profit into Perspective

As you recall the first question Drucker asked in the morning meeting was, "What is the purpose of a business?" You replied, "To make a profit," and Drucker advised that you were wrong, "THE PURPOSE OF A BUSINESS IS TO CREATE A CUSTOMER." He now puts profit into perspective with the following comments:

- Profitability is not the purpose of, but a limiting factor on the business enterprise and business activity.
- Profit is not the explanation, cause, or rationale of business behavior and business decisions, but rather the test of their validity.

- Profit is needed to pay for the attainment of the objectives of the business.
- Profit is a condition of survival—it is the cost of the future, the cost of staying in business.
- It is the first duty of a business to survive. The guiding principle of business economics is not the maximization of profits—*it is the avoidance of loss.*
- A business that obtains enough profit to satisfy its objectives in the key areas is a business that has the means of survival.
- A business that falls short of the profitability demands made by its key objectives is a marginal and endangered business.
- Profit planning is necessary—but it is planning for a needed minimum profitability, rather than for the meaningless profit maximization.[24]

Profit vs. Cost Centers

Related to Drucker's views on profit was another recurring theme of his, in which he stated that "there are no profit centers within the business; there are only cost centers."[25]

On a somewhat humorous note, he added to this discussion several decades later when in *Managing in a Time of Great Change* (1995) he commented, "The only profit center is a customer whose check has not bounced."[26]

Drucker Concludes the Meeting

As Drucker concludes the meeting, he asks again, "Do you now understand the Purpose of a business?" He also asks, "Do you now know how to answer the three key questions?"

1. What is our business?
2. What will our business be?
3. What should our business be?

Chapter Summary

The key takeaways from this chapter should be your ability to ask the *key questions* Drucker posed during the interview and complete the Strategic Management Process as described in Figure 2.1 for your firm. Go back and review the questions, and make notes in terms of how your organization would answer him. There are also a number of Strategic Management Application Tools that are included in Appendix A to assist you in applying a number of Drucker's concepts on strategy covered during the interview.

This chapter included highlights of Drucker's views on strategy and marketing as he wrote over a span of nearly 50 years in a number of books starting with *The Practice of Management* (1954), *Managing for Results* (1964), *Management* (1973), "The Theory of the Business" in the *The Harvard Business Review* (September–October 1994), *Managing in a Time of Great Change* (1998), *Management Challenges for the 21ˢᵗ Century* (1999), and *The Essential Drucker* (2001). Many of his books published prior to his death were either highlight reels of his earlier works, such as *The Essential Drucker, The Daily Drucker* (2004) or his views as a social scientist in *Managing in the Next Society* (2002) where he commented on the Internet and e-commerce.

While his early thoughts on the subjects might have been considered to be on the cutting edge in the 1950s and early 1960s (considering that he wrote the first book on strategy), he appeared to be on the sidelines as other noted contributors to strategy and marketing passed him by in the 1980s. It is therefore necessary to supplement Drucker's thinking with additional concepts and tools from other contributors to strategic thinking, marketing, and marketing research in order to implement many of Drucker's concepts as he described in this chapter.

Endnotes

1. Peter F. Drucker, *The Practice of Management* (New York: Harper & Row, 1954), 34–38.
2. Robert W. Swaim, Ph.D., "The Drucker Files: Strategy and the Purpose of a Business—Part I & II." *Business Beijing* (October and November 2002).
3. This chapter is based on an article I originally wrote for *Business Beijing* magazine as part of the Drucker Files series. I have not edited it to reflect Drucker's death, and as such the chapter is written in the present tense as though he were still alive.
4. Peter F. Drucker, *The Practice of Management* (New York: Harper and Row, 1954), 37; and *Managing for Results* (London: William Heinemann Ltd., 1964), 110.
5. Peter F. Drucker, *Management: Tasks, Responsibilities, Practices* (New York: Harper & Row, 1973), 74–102.
6. Peter F. Drucker, *The Essential Drucker* (New York: HarperCollins, 2001), 25.
7. Peter F. Drucker, *Management: Tasks, Responsibilities, Practices,* (New York: Harper & Row, 1973), 83–86.

8. Peter F. Drucker, "The Theory of the Business." *Harvard Business Review* (September–October 1994).

9. Peter F. Drucker, *Management: Tasks, Responsibilities, Practices* (New York: Harper & Row, 1973), 86–88.

10. Describing the elements of the Mission Statement, adopted from Arthur A, Thompson, Jr. and A. J. Strickland III, *Strategic Management: Concepts and Cases,* 13th ed. (New York: McGraw Hill Irvin, 2003), 34.

11. Peter F. Drucker, *The Practice of Management* (New York: Harper & Row, 1954), 37.

12. Peter F. Drucker, *The Essential Drucker* (New York: HarperCollins, 2001), 21.

13. Peter F. Drucker, *Management: Tasks, Responsibilities, Practices* (New York: Harper & Row, 1973), 88–91.

14. Ibid., 89–91.

15. Ibid., 93–94.

16. Peter F. Drucker, *Management Challenges for the 21st Century* (New York: HarperCollins, 1999), 41–69.

17. Peter F. Drucker, *Management Challenges for the 21st Century* (New York: HarperCollins, 1999), 41–69; and *China Faces up to Aging Population* (Xinhua News Agency), January 2005.

18. Peter F. Drucker, *Management Challenges for the 21st Century* (New York: HarperCollins, 1999), 51.

19. Ibid., 41–69.

20. Peter F. Drucker, *The Practice of Management* (New York: Harper & Row, 1954), 62.

21. Peter F. Drucker, *Management: Tasks, Responsibilities, Practices* (New York: Harper & Row, 1973), 102.

22. Peter F. Drucker, *The Practice of Management* (New York: Harper & Row, 1954), 67–68.

23. Ibid., 69.

24. Peter F. Drucker, *The Essential Drucker* (New York: HarperCollins, 2001), 38.

25. Peter F. Drucker, *Managing for Results* (London: William Heinemann Ltd., 1964), 17.

26. Peter F. Drucker, *Management Changes for the 21st Century* (New York: HarperCollins, 1999), 123.

Dissecting the Interview and Drucker on Marketing

Part One: Dissecting the Interview
Post-Interview Observations and the Pundits

This chapter works much like a US presidential campaign. Typically, after one of the candidates has made a speech or been interviewed and has commented on a particular issue or hammered an opponent's weakness, a group of pundits will tell us what we think we heard, including their views where they might agree or differ with the candidate's remarks. This is the model this chapter and the others that follow will attempt to emulate. We will therefore review or dissect Drucker's views from the interview in Chapter 2 with the assistance of a number of strategic management and marketing pundits such as Michael Porter, Roger J. Best, Philip Kotler, Gary Hamel, Arthur A. Thompson, Jr., A. J. Strickland, and others.

Since Drucker stressed the need to ask questions, do the views expressed by Drucker in the previous chapter stand alone and contribute to strategy, or are they too weak and must be supplemented by other contributors? Has the subject of strategy moved "beyond Drucker"?

The Purpose of a Business

Drucker declared, "The purpose of a business is to create a customer." There is a huge Drucker gap here in his simple definition of a business that I had to fill by adding, ". . . and to *retain* a customer." Maybe a small detail, but huge when considering extensive marketing research has concluded that the cost of gaining a new customer is *five times more* than the cost to retain one.[1] Therefore, to fill this gap, I had to spend considerable more time on customer retention strategies that were a little more comprehensive than just "Going Outside." A contributor I added to fill this gap was Roger J. Best and his extensive treatment of customer retention in his book, *Market-Based Management: Strategies for Growing Customer Value and Profitability* (2004).[2] Best made the point that "customer satisfaction and retention are important linkages to a market-based strategy and profitability. The ultimate objective of any given market strategy should be to attract, satisfy, and *retain* target customers."[3] I felt this was a much better explanation than Drucker's "purpose of a business," and I added this to close the Drucker gap.

Best's discussion of customer retention strategies that I added to reinforce Drucker included a classification of types of customers. Best argued that "not all customers are the same. Some may be loyal and profitable, others profitable but not loyal, some loyal but not profitable, and others are neither loyal nor profitable."[4] He classified these customers as follows:

- *Core Customers* (Profitable and Loyal): These customers are the key source of a business's profits.
- *At-Risk Customers* (Profitable but Not Loyal): These are profitable customers who could leave the business due to declining customer satisfaction or weakening customer value.
- *Non-Profit Customers* (Not Profitable but Loyal): These customers are satisfied and retained but cannot be served profitably by the business.
- *Spinners* (Not Profitable and Not Loyal): These are price shoppers who are acquired and exit quickly.

Best went on to suggest various approaches and customer retention strategies with respect to these classifications of customers that I added to the Drucker Programs to close some of these Drucker gaps. Drucker continued over the years to cite his definition of the *purpose of a business* but still did not address the importance of customer retention. Still, he did get the attention of most pundits when he said the purpose of a business is *not* to make a profit— the typical answer we almost always received to that question as seen early in our interview. We see this view reinforced by the strategy pundits as witnessed by the comments of Thompson and Strickland who said, "Sometimes companies couch their business mission in terms of making a profit. This is misguided—profit is more correctly an objective and a result of what the company does. The desire to make a profit says nothing about the business arena in which profits are to be sought."[5] Other pundits, Peter Rea and Harold Kerzner were more to the point when they said, "The most basic objective of marketing strategy is to retain existing customers and to attract new ones."[6]

The Transaction vs. Lifetime Value of a Customer

Best also takes an opposite view from Drucker's in terms of how to view the business. Drucker, in *Managing for Results* spent considerable time on the cost structure of a business and on measuring transactions. He concluded, "Managers may never have thought of their business as a 'transaction system.' But once they grasp the idea they can usually apply it to the business they know."[7] Best, on the other hand, took a different point of view when he said, "Customers are a *marketing asset* that businesses have yet to quantify in their accounting systems. Yet, the business that can attract, satisfy and keep customers over their *lifetime* of purchases is in a powerful position to deliver superior levels of profitability." He went on to add, "Businesses that lack a market orientation look at customers as *individual purchase transactions*. A market-based business looks at customers as *lifetime partners*."[8] Philip Kotler shared a similar observation in *Marketing Management* (1991) where he said, "Companies normally focus on individual transactions with the aim of making a profit on each transaction. New economy companies add a focus on estimating individual customer *lifetime value* and designing their marketing offerings and prices to make a profit over the customer's lifetime."[9] Although Drucker spoke about the importance of understanding customer needs the concept of *lifetime value* was absent in his writing.

The "Theory of the Business"—Another View

Drucker's *Theory of the Business* was first published in the *Harvard Business Review* (September–October 1994). This was one of the more difficult concepts for our Chinese students to grasp, essentially because there is no "theory" in *The Theory of the Business*. I also found in presenting the Drucker Strategy Course that they did not like concepts and theories; they wanted practical application tools. To fill this Drucker gap it was necessary to substitute *strategy* for theory. Going along with Drucker that there has to be a "fit" between Mission, the External Environment and the organization's Core Competencies, only then can the appropriate strategy be determined. It was also necessary to describe the various strategies an organization can adopt, including business and competitive strategies. This was obviously contrary to Drucker's view in that if the strategy was not working, there was something wrong with the organization's Theory of the Business. Since we could not define "theory" and what might be wrong with it, instead of the strategy, we went back to assessing the external environment first, using Porter's Five Force Model of Competition, and then assessing the organization's core competencies.[10] Briefly, Porter proposed that the state of competition in an industry is composed of five competitive forces. These include:

- The rivalry among competing sellers in the industry and the intensity of the competition.
- The potential entry of new competitors.
- The attempts of companies in other industries to win customers over to their own *substitute* products.
- The competitive pressures stemming from supplier-seller collaboration and bargaining.
- The competitive pressures stemming from seller-buyer collaboration and bargaining.[11]

It was felt that by assessing the trends taking place with these forces, clues would be provided relative to possible problems with the business's strategy.

Specifications for a Valid Theory (Strategy) of the Business

Drucker outlined what he felt were the "specifications" for a valid theory of the business or what I would consider to be a test of a valid strategy. These include the following requirements:

- The assumptions about environment, mission and core competencies must fit reality.

- The assumptions in all three areas have to fit one another.
- The Theory of the Business must be known and understood.
- The Theory of the Business has to be tested constantly.[12]

Drucker did not really explain what he meant by "fitting reality" in his first specification; however, he did a much better job of this in his discussion of sources of innovation and assumptions about a market or industry. This will be covered in a later chapter on Innovation. His discussion of "fit" in the second specification should be clearer. As an example, one may have identified a great opportunity to pursue as a result of an assessment of the external environment; however, without having the necessary core competencies, it is difficult to get into the game to take advantage of them. This also holds true for having an all-encompassing mission of satisfying certain customer needs while lacking the internal capabilities to perform. The need for the theory (strategy) to be understood throughout the organization should be obvious in terms of how the organization plans to achieve its Vision. Jack Welch, the former chairman and CEO of General Electric continually stressed the importance of this as noted in his book, *Jack, Straight from the Gut* (2001).[13] The need for continuous testing should also be obvious as strategic planning and developing strategies should not be one-time events that can be filed away on the bookshelf when completed. Dramatic or even unnoticed changes in the firm's external environment create a need for senior management to rethink its strategy. This is also true of unexpected failures or successes (the business's or competitors') that may present opportunities for innovation. As Drucker stated, "Eventually every theory (strategy) of the business becomes obsolete and then invalid."[14] With respect to this assessment, Drucker also continued to stress the need for implementing his concept of Planned Abandonment and for obtaining feedback from non-customers. Drucker attempted to summarize how to diagnose when the firm's Theory of the Business was not working by looking for what he called several warning signs. These include the following:

- The organization attains its original objectives.
- The organization experiences rapid growth (doubles or triples its size in a relatively short period of time).
- Unexpected success or failure (own or a competitor's).[15]

It is interesting to contrast Drucker's warning signs of when the *Theory of the Business* is not working with Thompson and Strickland's factors to assess whether a company's *strategy* is working. These include:

- The firm's sales are growing faster, slower, or about the same pace as the market as a whole, thus resulting in a rising, eroding, or stable market share.
- The company is acquiring new customers at an attractive rate as well as retaining existing customers.
- The firm's profit margins are increasing or decreasing and how well its margins compare to rival firms' margins.
- Trends in the firm's net profits, return on investment, and economic value added, and how these compare to the same trends for other companies in the industry.
- The company's overall financial strength and credit rating are improving or on the decline.
- The company can demonstrate continuous improvements in such internal performance measures as unit cost, defect rate, scrap rate, employee motivation and morale, number of stock outs and customer back orders, fewer days of inventory, and so forth.
- How shareholders view the company based on trends in the company's stock price and shareholder value (relative to the market value added of other companies in the industry).
- The firm's image and reputation with its customers.
- Is the company regarded as a leader in technology, product innovations, e-commerce, product quality, short times from order to delivery, having the best prices, getting newly developed products to market quickly, or other relevant factors on which buyers base their choice of brands?[16]

Thompson and Strickland summarize these factors by stating, "The stronger the company's overall performance, the less likely the need for radical changes in strategy—the weaker the company's financial performance and market standing, the more its current strategy must be questioned. Weak performance is almost always a sign of weak strategy, weak execution, or both."[17] There are some factors where they agree with Drucker while they have also included a number that Drucker did not mention. The major difference is Drucker's focus on the Theory while Thompson and Strickland, and the direction we elected to go, focused on *strategy*.

Peter Rea and Harold Kerzner provided some additional insight on assessing the feasibility of a particular strategy in *Strategic Planning: A Practical Guide*. They proposed seven guidelines to use in this assessment of strategy, not "theory," as outlined below.[18]

Guidelines for Assessing the Feasibility of a Given Strategy

1. Does the Strategy Focus on the Environment? (According to Rea and Kerzner, the purpose of strategy is to help the organization respond to environmental opportunities and threats.)
2. Does the Strategy Create or Sustain a Competitive Advantage? (Does the company serve customers in ways that are difficult for competitors to match? This is similar to Porter's views.)
3. Does the Strategy Match Organizational Capabilities/Constraints? (There needs to be a "fit" between the strategy and the organization and its culture and talent.)
4. Does the Strategy Maintain Strategic Flexibility? (The strategy helps to manage some risks by remaining flexible—this deals with Drucker's "What will our business be?")
5. Does the Strategy Focus on the Fundamental Strategic Question (having the ability to resolve strategic issues that were raised during strategic thinking?)
6. Does the Strategy Allow for the Analysis of Financial Resources and Constraints? (Source and use of funds—pay dividends to shareholders or reinvest in R&D?)
7. Does the Strategy Allow Management to Think Systematically? (The need for interdisciplinary teams to be involved in planning process—to be discussed in a later chapter.)

Perhaps Drucker first came up with his Theory of the Business in *Managing for Results* when he spoke of the *Three Dimensions of Business Performance* as the Product, Market, and the Distributive Channel (now known as distribution) and the need for the three to be in balance.[19] This might also be viewed as his contribution to the concept of the four Ps where here he identified Product and Place. In any event, Drucker's Specifications for a Valid Theory might be changed to Specifications for a Valid Strategy.

Drucker on Mission

Drucker initially called this the "idea of the business" in his *Managing for Results* including the following criteria: "The idea of the business always defines a satisfaction to be supplied to the market or a knowledge to be made effective in economic performance," and "the idea of the business thereby also defines the area in which a company has to obtain and to hold a leadership position."[20] Drucker devoted considerable ink to the discussion of Mission in *Management* but omitted providing a precise example of what should be included in the definition of a Mission Statement and the elements it should include. The example provided in our interview was actually taken from Thompson's and Strickland's *Strategic Management: Concepts and Cases*, 13th edition.[21]

The other gap I had to fill was to provide examples of company mission statements for the students to assess and determine if they conformed to the model. The Johnson & Johnson (J&J) credo was added as an example of how an organization identified who was important to the company. In keeping with Drucker, J&J begins with the customer. Check out its website at www.jnj.com, when you have an opportunity to see who is listed next and in what order and you will find:

1. Customers
2. Employees
3. Community
4. Shareholders

The J&J list provides an interesting exercise, and when students are asked to rank these four in order of importance, typically Shareholders appear on the top of their list.

Drucker's early focus in his writings on the Mission laid the foundation for the others to build on. Philip Kotler reinforced Drucker's views when he wrote, "To define its mission, the company should address Peter Drucker's classic questions. What is our business? Who is the customer? What is of value to the customer? What will our business be? What should our business be? These simple sounding questions are among the most difficult (strategic) questions the company will ever have to answer. Successful companies continuously raise these questions and answer them thoughtfully and thoroughly."[22] Thompson and Strickland also helped to clarify the difference between Strategic Vision and the Mission Statement when they wrote, "Whereas the chief concern of a Strategic Vision is with 'Where are we going?' the term Mission Statement, as it is commonly used tends to deal with a company's present business scope—'Who are we and what do we do?'"[23]

Transforming Governance and the Challenge of Maintaining Balance

The following discussion deviates somewhat from Drucker's discussion on Mission but does relate to the previous discussion of shareholders. This also relates to the earlier issue that was described in Chapter 1 as the "Balancing act of the CEO."

> *But the worse mistake is trying to avoid the issue of governance. Many people I know try to duck the issue, hiding behind the misguided mantra of we are running this place for the short-term interest of the shareholder.*[24]

Drucker identified several challenges for the CEO. These included understanding the governance or ownership structure of today's public company, satisfying the short-term interests of shareholders with the long-term interests of the organization, maintaining a balance between continuity and change, and improving today and creating a tomorrow at the same time. Here I will only deal with the governance issue.

The key issue Drucker raised here deals with who essentially are the owners of today's public companies and what are their interests. The point he made, which should not be a surprise, is that the major shareholders of companies today are not what we used to know as the "little old lady from Pasadena" who inherited the several thousand shares of stock in her husband's portfolio when he passed away, but rather the institutions that now manage various retirement and pension plans. One only has to access the various stock market sites on the Internet to find that from 70 percent or higher of a company's shares are owned by institutional investors. And do these institutions have an interest in the company's strategy and long-term vision? Hardly. If they bought a block at $70 per share and their computer model says to sell at $80—so be it regardless of who the CEO is. If the company's quarterly earnings per share missed the "Street's" forecast by $0.02 per share, there is trouble in River City and maybe a new CEO is needed? Such is the CEO's balancing act Drucker cited here: how to satisfy the short-term interests of these constituencies with the long-term interests of the business? Unfortunately, Drucker did not suggest how to do this other than stating that some successful CEOs know how. Perhaps Drucker's gap with respect to the job of the CEO was best characterized by a statement contained in another book and attributed to Procter and Gamble's CEO, A.G. Lafley, a long-time client of Drucker's, that this was essentially "Drucker's unfinished chapter."[25]

What Will Our Business Be?

Drucker's second question, the one between "What is our business?"(Mission) and "What should our business be?" (Vision) was very confusing to the students. Did this mean the organization had to change its Mission, or should it change its Vision? This gap was closed by focusing more on offensive and defensive competitive strategies and how to react to competition. This did not mean the organization had to change its Mission, but rather to rethink the strategy to use to accomplish its Mission. This later point is reinforced by Philip Kotler when he wrote, "Mission statements should not be revised every few years in response to every new turn in the economy. However, a company must redefine its mission if that mission has lost creditability or no longer defines an optimal course for the company."[26]

A discussion of *Strategies for Competing in Turbulent, High-Velocity Markets* (Thompson & Strickland, *Strategic Management: Concepts and Cases*, was also added as another tool in dealing with Drucker's question "What Will Our Business Be?" This was selected as it closely reflected China's rapidly changing, growing, and dynamic business environment and how to deal with it. This included reviewing strategies for Reacting to Change, Anticipating Change, and Leading Change, and it outlined both the *what to do* and the *how to do it* relative to each of these strategies. This was another good example of adding the contributions of others to either reinforce a Drucker concept, close a Drucker gap, or move beyond Drucker.[27]

Still, Drucker's initial question of "What should our business be?" perhaps did lay the foundation for other strategic thinkers. As an example, Henry Mintzberg wrote in 1985, "The *hows* of a company's strategy are typically a blend of: (1) deliberate and purposeful actions, (2) as-needed reactions to unanticipated developments and fresh market conditions and competitive pressures, and (3) the collective learning of the organization over time."[28] Thompson and Strickland tended to echo Minztberg's position when they wrote, "It is normal for management's planned strategy to take on a different face as new strategy features are added and others are subtracted in response to shifting market conditions, altered customer needs and preferences, the strategic maneuvering of rival firms, the experience of what is working and what isn't, newly emerging opportunities and threats, unforeseen events, and fresh thinking about how to improve the strategy."[29] In both cases cited here, neither Mintzberg nor Thompson and Strickland advocated a change in mission but rather, a modification to the business's strategy. Therefore, Drucker's second question on "What will our business be?" continues to be relevant to a firm's strategy.[30]

Objectives vs. Strategy

Objectives are the fundamental strategy of a business.[31]

Drucker devoted considerable ink to the purpose of objectives in *Management* and perhaps is best summarized with the following quote. "Objectives must be derived from what our business is, what it will be, and what it should be. They are not abstractions. They are the action commitments through which the mission of a business is to be carried out, and the standards against which performance is to be measured. Objectives, in other words, are the *fundamental strategy of a business.*"[32] Here, most noted contributors on strategic management thinking would disagree with Drucker that objectives are the fundamental strategy of the business. To close this Drucker gap, it is necessary to refer to what can be considered the Five Tasks of Strategic Management as described in Thompson's and Strickland's *Strategic Management: Concepts and Cases.*[33] These are depicted in Figure 3.1.

Differentiating between objectives and strategy then, Thompson and Strickland provided the following definitions:

1. Developing a Strategic Vision and Business Mission
2. Setting Objectives
3. Crafting a Strategy to Achieve the Objectives
4. Implementing and Executing the Strategy
5. Evaluating Performance, Monitoring New Developments, and Initiating Corrective Action

Figure 3.1   Five Tasks of Strategic Management

- *Strategic Objectives* relate to outcomes that strengthen an organization's overall business position and competitive vitality.
- *A Company's Strategy* consists of the competitive efforts and business approaches that managers employ to please customers, compete successfully, and achieve organizational objectives.[34]

Strategic Objectives: Another Point of View

According to Thompson and Strickland, "strategic objectives aim at results that reflect increased competitiveness and a stronger business position—outcomes such as:

- Winning additional market share
- Overtaking competitors on product quality or customer service or product innovation
- Achieving lower overall costs than rivals
- Boosting the company's reputation with customers
- Winning a stronger foothold in international markets
- Exercising technological leadership
- Gaining a sustainable competitive advantage
- Capturing attractive growth opportunities"[35]

The obvious difference with Drucker here is that strategy is necessary to determine how these objectives will be achieved while Drucker stressed that objectives are the strategy. The following discussion reinforces this position that objectives are not strategy as Drucker suggested.

Crafting Strategy Thompson and Strickland explain: "A company's strategy represents management's answers to such fundamental business (strategic) questions as:

- Whether to concentrate on a single business or build a diversified group of businesses (one of Drucker's strategies)?
- Whether to cater to a broad range of customers or focus on a particular market niche (Drucker's concentration)?
- Whether to develop a wide or narrow product line (Drucker's specialization and diversification)?
- Whether to pursue a competitive advantage based on low cost or product superiority or unique organizational capabilities (Drucker's knowledge competencies)?
- How to respond to changing buyer preferences?
- How big a geographic market to try to cover?
- How to react to newly emerging market and competitive conditions?
- How to grow the enterprise over the long term?"[36]

In other words, to differentiate between objectives and strategy, strategy defines *how* to achieve results. Objectives are the "ends" and strategy is the "means" of achieving them and not the other way around.

Short-Term and Long-Term Objectives In the Drucker Strategy course it was necessary to differentiate between short-term and long-term objectives. Basically short-term objectives focus more on the near-term performance and results of the business while long-term objectives focus on what we have to do now to achieve our Vision in the future. Drucker did clarify this and we will cover it further in a later chapter on Strategic Planning. This also contributes to the CEO's balancing act—which objectives to concentrate on? Drucker's early focus on the importance of objectives and results led to the Management by Objectives (MBO) concept that is practiced by organizations throughout the world today.

What Should Our Business Be?

What should the business be? The first assumption must be that it will be different. "[37]

This third question of Drucker's was positioned as formulating a Vision for the future as outlined in the Strategic Management Process chart. I also added an Industry Attractiveness Assessment Tool (see Appendix A) to help the students deal with Drucker's third question and assist them in assessing what other businesses or industries their organizations should be in. This aided in answering another one of Drucker's (strategic) questions about the business the organization is in: "Knowing what we know today, would we do this?" Drucker stressed the importance of this question when in *Management* he said, "With respect to 'What *should* the business be?' the first assumption must be that it will be different."[38] The importance of Drucker's early views on Strategic Vision has been reinforced by nearly all of the strategy and marketing pundits mentioned at the beginning of this chapter. As such, this is still an extremely relevant concept in strategic management.

Drucker on "Going Outside"

Drucker continually stressed the importance of "Going Outside" and talking with customers and non-customers, a concept also known today as the "Voice of the Customer." As an example, in *Managing in a Time of Great Change* Drucker continued to stress this issue: "For strategy, we need organized information about the environment. Strategy has to be based on information about markets, customers, and non-customers, about technology in one's own industry and others; about worldwide finance; and about the changing world economy."[39] He emphasized throughout his many writings on strategy and marketing that "results are on the outside." Here, to close some Drucker gaps, it was necessary to add a considerable number of tools from marketing and marketing research. These included how to structure questionnaires and sampling methods, how to conduct a one-on-one interview, the use of focus groups, how to use such tools as conjoint analysis and value mapping to determine what attributes customers and non-customers value, and other concepts and tools from the marketing research discipline.

Some would also argue (such as Clayton Christensen) that focusing on the organization's large top-tier customers when Going Outside can mislead the organization in terms of its new product development efforts. This will be discussed in more detail in Chapter 5 on Innovation that includes a discussion of Christensen's concept of Disruptive Technologies.

The "Be Number One or Number Two" Myth (Planned Abandonment)

Drucker continued to push his concept of Planned Abandonment as one of the first things to be done in an assessment of the organization in the Strategic Management Process. One example of the implementation of Drucker's Concept of Planned Abandonment often cited is Jack Welch and GE. As the story is told, Drucker advised Welch when he took over as CEO of GE to assess each of GE's business units. If it were determined that the business unit could not be No.1 or No. 2 in its respective industry, and could not be restructured to achieve this, then the business unit should be abandoned (sold off or closed). Welch acknowledges this advice in his book, *Jack: Straight from the Gut* and discussed how he proceeded to implement the concept, mainly through a series of divestitures and acquisitions. "In the first two years, the No. 1 and No. 2 strategy generated a lot of action—most of it small. We sold 71 businesses and product lines, receiving a little over $500 million for them. We completed 118 other deals including acquisitions, joint ventures, and minority investments spending over $1 billion."[40]

He also clarified that Drucker's No.1 and No. 2 concept had certain limitations when he wrote, "Like most visions, the No. 1 and No. 2 strategy had limits. Obviously, some businesses have become so commoditized that leadership positions give you little or no competitive advantage. It made little difference if we were No. 1 in electric toasters or irons, for instance, where we had no pricing power and were facing low-cost imports."[41]

Finally, he added another caveat to the concept when he spoke about GE Capital, the financial services arm of GE that he built through acquisitions. "There are other multi-trillion dollar markets like financial services that cover the ocean. In those cases, not being No. 1 or No. 2 is less critical as long as you are strong in your niche—product or region."[42]

We find no argument here with the application of the concept of Planned Abandonment. Consider, however, what would happen if every CEO took the "be No.1 or No. 2 objective" seriously and applied it for his company and within his industry. Theoretically, then, consumers would have a choice of only two firms to do business with: as examples, two automobile companies (Toyota and GM), two airlines (take your pick), two oil companies (Exxon/Mobil and BP), two computer companies (HP and Dell), two hotel chains (Marriott and Hilton), and so forth. Not a very encouraging prospect? Planned Abandonment is okay—always being No.1 or No. 2 is obviously not realistic.

Other Drucker Contributions to Strategy and Marketing

The following are some additional contributions Drucker made to strategy and marketing dispersed throughout his many books.

Product Classifications   Drucker in *Managing for Results* came up with 11 categories to classify products, which are depicted in Figure 3.2.

He noted in coming up with these classifications: "Practically all products and distributive channels can be classified under a *small* number of major categories."[43] Drucker acknowledged that perhaps Repair Jobs, Unnecessary Specialties and Unjustified Specialties might be combined, still leaving us with nine classifications.

An Early SWOT Analysis?

Drucker devoted several chapters in *Managing for Results* to the need to build on one's strengths, minimize weaknesses, and pursue opportunities while assessing risk.[44] Although not quite presented in the same way, this may have laid the foundation for the more popular SWOT Analysis (Strengths, Weaknesses, Opportunities, and Threats) that is found in the current literature on strategy and marketing.

Products	Problem Children
1. Today's Breadwinners	6. Yesterday's Breadwinners
2. Tomorrow's Breadwinners	7. Repair Jobs
3. Productive Specialties	8. Unnecessary Specialties
4. Development Products	9. Unjustified Specialties
5. Failures	10. Investments in Managerial Ego
	11. Cinderellas (Sleepers)

Figure 3.2   Drucker's Product Classifications*
*Drucker, *Managing for Results*, p. 67–85.

Strengths and Weaknesses   As a forerunner to what would be called "strengths" in the more popular SWOT analysis, Drucker asked, "What is our excellence?"[45] He also described these strengths as knowledge excellence, which today would be considered core competencies in contemporary strategic management and marketing literature. Here, in *Managing for Results* (1964), he stated, "This is always knowledge excellence, a capacity of people to do something in such a manner as to give leadership to the enterprise. Identifying the excellence of a business therefore determines what its truly important efforts are and should be."[46] Drucker eventually clarified and expanded on this in *Managing in a Time of Great Change* (1995) when he discussed being able to match the opportunities identified in the external environment, as part of the Strategic Management Process, with the company's strengths and competence. There he commented, "It requires what I first (in my 1964 book *Managing for Results*) presented as 'strength analysis' and what now—thanks mainly to the work of Professors C.K. Prahalad and Gary Hamel—is coming to be known as the analysis of "core competence."[47] Drucker was referring to their article "The Core Competence of the Corporation," *Harvard Business Review* (May-June 1990) where they defined the three characteristics of core competency as follows: "(1) It is a source of competitive advantage in that it makes a significant contribution to perceived customer benefits, (2) it has a breath of applications to a wide variety of markets, and (3) it is difficult for competitors to imitate."[48]

With respect to Weaknesses, Drucker did not use the term but rather discussed the need for an analysis of knowledge needs and remarked that a "common gap is lack of adequate support to exploit opportunity and success." He asked, "What new knowledge of real importance is needed? Where does existing *core knowledge* (a possible prelude to "core competencies") need improvement, updating and advancement? Where does our knowledge need redefinition?"[49] Thus we have Drucker's initial views on the need for analysis, now commonly referred to as the SWOT Analysis.

Opportunities

Results are obtained by exploiting opportunities, not by solving problems.[50]

Drucker focused on what he called the analysis of the economic dimension of the business to identify what he classified as three kinds of opportunities. These included:

1. *Additive Opportunities:* He classified these as the extension of an existing product line into a new and growing market. Expanding geographically such as internationally might also be considered an additive opportunity under Drucker's classification. This should not be confused with product extensions, which are the most typical kinds of innovation. Drucker felt that these types of opportunities should "rarely be treated as high-priority efforts, the risks should be small and the returns are always limited."[51] He also commented that these opportunities should not be allowed to take resources away from the next classifications of opportunities: Complementary and Breakthrough. Furthermore, he did not feel this type of opportunity changed the character of the business.

    With today's focus on globalization and Drucker's comments on the need to be able to compete globally, it might be reasonable to assume that he would have placed a higher degree of importance on additive opportunities. On the other hand, since he originally came up with these classifications over 50 years ago, they tended to be replaced in his later writings, for example as Sources of Innovation in his book, *Innovation and Entrepreneurship.*

2. *Complementary Opportunities:* According to Drucker, "this type of opportunity will change the structure of the business as it offers something new which, when combined with the present business, results in a new total larger than the sum of its parts."[52] He also added that this type of opportunity will require at least one new knowledge area in which excellence has to be obtained. Drucker did not provide many examples of this type of opportunity and suggested that diversification through acquisitions might fit as an example of a complementary opportunity.

3. *Breakthrough Opportunities:* Drucker felt this is "typically the opportunity to make the future happen."[53] Here he cited Xerox and Xerography as an example of a breakthrough opportunity and of the fact that this type of opportunity

should always be capable of creating a new industry. This could also be considered as a "New to the world product," which represents less than 10 percent of all innovative products.

Drucker expanded on identifying opportunities in *Innovation and Entrepreneurship* and *Managing in a Time of Great Change* by suggesting that as part of the assessment in the Strategic Thinking Process "one should keep track of one's own and one's competitors' performances, looking especially for unexpected successes and unexpected poor performance in areas where one should have done well."[54] His rationale was that successes demonstrated what the market values and will pay for while nonsuccesses suggest either that the market is changing or that the company's competencies are weakening.

Drucker's Strategies

Drucker presented a few strategies for organizations to consider in *Managing for Results*; these included Specialization, Diversification and Integration. Within Integration he included mergers and acquisitions or the "buy" vs. "build" decision.[55] This was considered to be an oversimplification and as such, numerous other business and competitive strategies were presented in our programs to close this Drucker gap.

Also, Drucker's views changed over the years. As an example, in *Managing for Results* he advocated a combination of Specialization and Diversification when he said, "Every business needs a core—an area where it leads. Every business must therefore specialize. But every business must also try to obtain the most from its specialization. It must diversify." He went on to add, "A company should either be diversified in products, market, and end-uses and highly concentrated in its basic knowledge area; or it should be diversified in its knowledge areas and highly concentrated in its products, markets and end-uses. Anything in between is likely to be unsatisfactory."[56]

Approximately a decade later he wrote in reference to the multinational corporation, "The multinational has complexity built into its very structure. It is multi-cultural, it is multinational, it is multi-market, and also multi-management. Adding to this a diversity of business makes the company unmanageable." He then concluded, "The temptation to diversify, no matter how great in any given case, should be firmly resisted in a multinational corporation. The multinational conglomerate is an abomination."[57] Drucker left us hanging here when he discussed how the multinational should be structured in terms of management strategy. Here he voiced one opinion when he said, "A multinational strategy that takes into account only the overall company is condemned to futility." And then, out of the other side of his mouth, he said, "But the multinational strategy which is decentralized, that is, a strategy which considers each unit and each market as an autonomous business, is equally condemned to futility." Finally, and apparently throwing in the towel, he said, "It is impossible—theoretically as well as practically—to predict in advance whether the company-wide, overall approach to strategy or the market-by-market approach to strategy will be appropriate to a given situation."[58] Here is probably as good an example as any of a Drucker gap that required the addition of other contributors to apply Drucker's concepts relative to strategy such as Porter's Five Generic Competitive Strategies as well as global strategies.

Porter's Five Generic Competitive Strategies

Michael Porter in his discussion of competitive strategies suggested there are almost as many competitive strategies that could be described as there are competitors. He did attempt to narrow this down, however, by stating, "However, when one strips away the details to get at the real substance, the biggest and most important differences among competitive strategies boil down to (1) whether a company's target market is broad or narrow and (2) whether it is pursuing a competitive advantage linked to low cost or product differentiation."[59] Based on these criteria, he then put forth his now popular concept of the Five Generic Competitive Strategies.[60]

1. *A low-cost provider strategy* appeals to a broad spectrum of customers based on its being the overall low-cost provider of the product or service. Businesses employing this strategy are exceptionally good at finding ways to drive costs down (such as Southwest Airlines).
2. *A broad differentiation strategy* seeks to differentiate the company's product offering from rivals' in ways that will appeal to

a broad spectrum of buyers. The most appealing approaches to differentiation are those that are difficult or expensive for rivals to duplicate. Resourceful competitors (China for example) can, in time, clone almost any product or feature or attribute (such as Mercedes, BMW).

3. *A best-cost provider strategy* gives customers more value for money by incorporating good-to-excellent product attributes at a lower cost than rivals; the target is to have the lowest (best) costs and prices compared to rivals offering products with comparable attributes (such as Toyota's Lexus).

4. *A focused (or market niche) strategy* based on low cost concentrates on a narrow buyer segment and on outcompeting rivals by serving niche members at a lower cost than rivals (such as Motel 6).

5. *A focused (or market niche) strategy based on differentiation* concentrates on a narrow buyer segment and on outcompeting rivals by offering niche members customized attributes that meet their tastes and requirements better than rivals' products (such as Ritz-Carlton).

Drucker on Diversification and Drucker's Law

Drucker wrote extensively about diversification as a strategy in both *Managing for Results* and *Management*. In *Management*, he argued "The less diverse a business, the more manageable it is. Simplicity makes for clarity." He added, "The less complex a business is, the fewer things can go wrong." From this he developed Drucker's Law, in which he stated, "If one thing goes wrong, everything else will, and at the same time."[61]

After some lengthy discussions in *Management* on the pressures for and against diversification, he attempted a summary of what he considered the right and wrong diversification to be. "The right diversification produces businesses whose performance capacity almost equals that of the top performers among highly concentrated single-market or single-technology companies while the wrong diversification produces businesses performing poorly as a single-market or single-technology firm that is highly concentrated in the wrong business." The bottom line according to Drucker is this: "The difference is always that the performing diversified company has *a common core of unity* to its business or businesses."[62] Drucker's explanation as to a common core of unity could include anything from common technology, processes, customers, and so forth, and comes into play in our discussion later on when considering mergers and acquisitions as part of a growth strategy.

Strategy, Concentration, and Market-Standing Decision

Drucker in *Management* commented, "Whereas objectives are 'strategy,' the concentration decision is 'policy.'"[63] Here Drucker overcomplicates the issue of "What is our business?" Essentially, with a well-defined Mission, the organization can focus or *concentrate* its resources in the industry and market it desires, and is capable (core competencies) of pursuing.

With respect to the Market-Standing Decision, Drucker suggests, "One has to decide in which segment of the market, with what product, what services, what values, one should be the leader."[64] He expands on the problems of the marginal supplier and how vulnerable they are, particularly in a declining economy. This is also true of fragmented industries that we have seen being consolidated in both the United States and in China. Drucker went on to explain that obtaining the desired market-standing requires a market strategy without explaining what this strategy should be—another Drucker gap. This can be clarified by returning to Porter's Five Generic Competitive Strategies that describe market position vs. Drucker's market standing.

Structure Follows Strategy—Who said it First? James O'Toole wrote in an article for *New Management* about a number of Drucker's accomplishments: "He was the first to show that structure follows strategy."[65] However, Drucker was in fact influenced by others as he stated in *Managing for Results*, "Two recent books have documented the relationship between organizational structure and the ability of a company to produce results and grow. Structure, Professor Alfred Chandler demonstrates, follows strategy." Drucker went on to comment in a footnote on the same page, "I acknowledge here the stimulation and insight found in this work."[66] Chandler's work relative to strategy and structure[67] was also cited by Fremont E. Kast and James E. Rosenzweig in their book *Organization and Management: A Systems and Contingency Approach*, where they stated, "Chandler states that as firms develop new strategies in response to the changing social and economic environment, basic changes in structure are required."[68] Chandler first wrote about this concept in 1962, two years before Drucker's *Managing for Results*.[69] Drucker wrote again in *Management* that "Structure follows strategy," and also referenced Chandler's work.[70] He devoted a considerable discussion to structure in his classic *The Practice of Management* but did not discuss any relationship at that time between strategy and structure. His main point was this: "To improve organization structure—through the maximum of federal decentralization and through application of the principle of decentralization to functionally organized activities—will therefore always improve performance."[71]

Later in *Management* Drucker attempted to clarify this concept by stating, "Only a clear definition of the mission and purpose of the business makes possible clear and realistic business objectives. It is the foundation for priorities, strategies, plans and work assignments. It is the starting point for the design of managerial jobs and above all, for the design of managerial structures. Strategy determines what the key activities are in a given business."[72]

Why make a big deal of this? The point here is that it was necessary to close Drucker gaps in a number of cases to support or reinforce his views as illustrated here and 'to' clarify what Drucker's views were on strategy and structure.

Part Two: Drucker on Sales and Marketing

Drucker's earlier books such as *Managing for Results* and *Management* included numerous discussions relative to sales and marketing and a number of its concepts. I have assembled them here in the order of the "Four Ps of the Marketing Mix" (Product, Price, Place and Promotion) for discussion purposes wherever possible, although Drucker did not label them as such.

Drucker on Marketing

First, Drucker's earlier views on marketing such as those contained in *Managing for Results* suggested that not many people really understood the marketing concept. There he wrote, "'Marketing' has become a fashionable term. But a gravedigger remains a gravedigger even when called a 'mortician'—only the cost of the burial goes up. Many a sales manager has been renamed 'marketing vice president'—and all that happened was that costs and salaries went up." He continued his criticism by adding, "A good deal of what is called 'marketing' today is at best organized, systematic selling in which the major jobs—from sales forecasting to warehousing and advertising—are brought together and coordinated. But the starting point is still *our* products, *our* customers and *our* technology. The starting point is still the inside."[73]

Selling vs. Marketing

The difference between marketing and selling is more than semantic. Selling focuses on the needs of the seller, marketing on the needs of the buyer. Selling is preoccupied with the seller's need to convert his product into cash; marketing with the idea of satisfying the needs of the customer by means of the product and the whole cluster of things associated with creating, delivering, and finally consuming it.[74]

Theodore Levitt

The above quotation is from Theodore Levitt's classic 1960 *Harvard Business Review* article, "Marketing Myopia," which differentiated between the selling concept and the marketing concept. This is one of the more famous business articles and is frequently referenced in modern marketing literature. It was written four years prior to Drucker's *Managing for Results*.

Marketing Research and Marketing Analysis

It would appear that Levitt's views on marketing may have influenced Drucker's thinking: when referring to marketing research he wrote, "Marketing analysis is a good deal more than ordinary market research or customer research. It first tries to look at the entire business. And second, it tries to look not at *our* customer, *our* market, *our* products, but at the market, the customer, his purchases, his satisfaction, his values, his buying and spending patterns, his rationality."[75] The following are some other areas to be investigated or questions to be asked in the market analysis as suggested by Drucker.

Three Outside Dimensions and Other Market Analysis Questions[76]

1. Who buys?
2. Where is it bought?

3. What is it being bought for?
4. Who is the non-customer? Why does he not buy our products?
5. What does the customer buy altogether?
6. What share of the customer's total spending—his disposable income, his discretionary income, or his discretionary time—goes on their products, and whether the share is going up or down?
7. What do customers—and non-customers—buy from others? What satisfaction do they give that they cannot get from our products?
8. What product or service would fulfill the satisfaction areas of real importance—both those we now service and those we might serve?
9. What would enable the customer to do without our product or service? (*Note:* This is more closely associated with substitute products—gas prices forcing people to buy smaller cars vs. SUVs, using public transportation more, etc.)
10. Who are our non-competitors—and why? (*Note:* Who else might enter the industry and become our competitor?)
11. Whose non-competitor are we? (*Note:* Possibly identifying opportunities outside our industry.)

Once again we see Drucker focusing on the consumer market here. Many of these questions deal with what is important to the customer and non-customer, and they identify attributes that have importance.

The First P: The Product

With reference to Product and the previously mentioned Market Analysis, Drucker commented, "The analysis of the result areas has to start with products (or services) and in particular with a definition of 'product.'"[77] Classical marketing literature in discussing the Marketing Mix and the Product typically includes discussions of product variety, quality, design, features, brand name, packaging, sizes, services, warranties and returns.[78] The following are selected Drucker quotes on Product with a few brief observations from others.

"The customer rarely buys what the business thinks it sells him. One reason for this is, of course, that nobody pays for a 'product.' What is paid for is satisfaction. But nobody can make or supply satisfaction as such—at best, only the means to attaining them can be sold and delivered."[79] This might be somewhat of a generalization on the part of Drucker, which needs to be further investigated, as he suggested when he said, "What the people in the business think they know about customers and market is more likely to be wrong than right. Only by asking the customer, by watching him, by trying to understand his behavior can one find out who he is, what he does, how he buys, how he uses what he buys, what he expects, what he values and so on."[80] This ties into Drucker's focus on "Going Outside" but at the same time, he left many gaps in terms of what do we do when we do go outside. As an example, "Mr. Non-customer, I would like to ask you why you do not buy from us?"

Non-customer's response: "Your price is too high." Now what do we do? Is price really the issue here? What other attributes are important to the non-customer that our product does not provide? The gap has to be filled by providing a variety of tools from market research that are contained in numerous texts on the subject including such methods as secondary and exploratory research, descriptive research, causal research, sampling and other market research applications that Drucker never commented on. When marketers go outside (physically or via other methods), they should have an idea of what they are going to be asking and what methods they will be using to gather the marketing information needed for decision making.

Another comment made by Drucker that might possibly have been alluding to substitute products was this: "A corollary is that the goods or services which the manufacturer sees as direct competition rarely adequately define what and whom he is really competing with. They cover both too much and too little."[81] He expanded on this by writing, "Because the customer buys satisfaction, all goods and services compete intensively with goods and services that look quite different, seem to serve entirely different functions, are made, distributed, sold differently—but are alternative means for the customer to obtain the same satisfaction."[82] Once again this would appear to apply more to consumer products—should I join a country club, take a trip around the world, buy a timeshare in Hawaii? What is satisfaction to me? This will be examined in chapter 5.

The Second P: Price

We will discuss Price in more detail in Chapter 4, on the Five Deadly Business Sins, and so it will only briefly be commented on here. In *Management* Drucker wrote, "But price is only a part of value. There is a whole range of quality considerations which are not expressed in price: durability, freedom from breakdown, the maker's standing, service, etc."[83] Roger Best deals with this issue in his discussion of "Economic Benefits and Value Creation" where he identifies the total cost of purchases as consisting of disposal costs, ownership costs, maintenance costs, usage costs, acquisitions costs and the price paid for the product.[84] Drucker omitted discussions of the other elements that are typically covered under the discussion of Price such as list price, discounts, allowances, payment period, terms, and other concepts such as elasticity, bundling, and so forth.

The Third P: Place

This element of the Marketing Mix generally consists of channels, coverage, assortments, locations, inventory and transportation. Drucker did not cover all of these elements in any detail and focused on distribution channels. One interesting comments was this: "A business gets paid for its product is so obvious that it is never forgotten. But, though equally obvious, it is often overlooked that there has to be a market for the product. There also have to be distributive channels to get the product from the producer to the market. But many businessmen—especially makers of industrial products—are as unaware that they use distributive channels, let alone that they depend on them."[85]

I believe our pundits would question if businesses really overlook the market for their product since the Target Market is part of the firm's Marketing Mix and has been stressed for years. I worked for the largest Alcoa metals distributor in the United States in the 1970s, and there was no doubt on the company's part of how its products (aluminum extrusions, plate, and sheet) were sold to the end users, the aerospace companies in Los Angeles.

Drucker continued to stress in his early writings on marketing that marketing channels and, in particular, industrial distribution were not well understood as evidenced by the following quotes:

"The market and the distributive channel are often more crucial than the product." One could hardly disagree that if there is no market, it is difficult to sell a product whatever it is. He then went on to comment: "These two areas are much more difficult to control, precisely because they are outside. Management can order a product modification; it cannot order a market modification, or a modification of distributive channels."

In respect to distributive channels, there is one more complication which makes this a difficult as well as a crucial result area. There is no distributive channel which is not, at the same time, also a customer.

The customer of an industrial-goods product therefore plays a twofold role: he is genuine customer and genuine distributive channel. In either role he is crucial to the producer.

Finally, in a modern economy, distributive channels change rapidly—more rapidly, as a rule, than either technology or customer expectations and value. Indeed I have never seen a decision with respect to distributive channels that was not obsolescent five years later and badly in need of new thinking and fundamental change. Markets as well as distributive channels deserve a good deal of attention and study—much more than they usually receive."[86]

I believe most of our pundits would disagree with Drucker's views about distribution and marketing channels as expressed in these few quotes. Considerable literature exists on marketing channels and the work performed by these channels. Michael Marks, founder of the Florida-based Indian River Consulting Group, has specialized in the field of industrial distribution for over 30 years and is no doubt the foremost authority on distribution in the United States. His book *Working at Cross-Purposes: How Distributors and Manufacturers Can Manage Conflict Successfully* provides a great deal of insight on how these channels can be designed, managed and changed if necessary.[87] Drucker also added in 1962 that, "We know little more about distribution today than Napoleon's contemporaries knew about the interior of Africa. We know it is there, and we know it is big; and that's about all."[88]

The Fourth P: Promotion

The promotional element of the Marketing Mix generally consists of sales promotion, advertising, the sales force, public relations, direct mail, telemarketing, and the Internet. Drucker commented on some of these elements over the years.

Drucker on Advertising With respect to advertising, Drucker wrote in *Managing for Results,* "There is a good deal of evidence that national advertising, though ostensibly directed at the consumer, is most effective with the retailer, is indeed the best way to move him to promote a brand. But there is also plenty of evidence—contrary to all that is said about 'hidden persuaders'—that distributors, no matter how powerfully supported by advertising, cannot sell a product that the consumer for whatever reason does not accept."[89] Drucker in commenting on the "hidden persuaders" was alluding to a popular 1950s book *The Hidden Persuaders* by Vance Packard that discussed various advertising techniques based on motivational research that Packard felt were manipulative.[90] What Drucker was describing in this quote, however, might be considered today as "Push vs. Pull" marketing communications strategies. Roger Best described these two strategies when he wrote, "The objectives of *pull-through* marketing communications are to build awareness, attraction and loyalty and to reduce search costs. When *pull* marketing communications are successful, customers seek out certain products or services and, in essence, by the interest they create, pull the product through the channel. A *pull* strategy requires channel intermediaries to carry certain products or brands in order to attract and satisfy target customers." He then went on to describe a *push* strategy as, "Push communications are directed at channel intermediaries. The objective in this case is to motivate channel intermediaries to carry a particular product brand and, in this way, make it more available to customers."[91] The pull strategy here would refer to Drucker's observation of advertising directed at the consumer to create the demand, while the push strategy is directed at the channel to stock the product and make it available. Essentially, Drucker was ahead of his time in describing these marketing communications strategies, but unfortunately, he did not expand on the concept in his later years.

An added note from *The Hidden Persuaders* mentioned the results of a management consulting firm study that concluded that accepting the word of a customer as to what he wants is "the least reliable" index the manufacturer can have on what he ought to do to win customers. Packard went on to say, "First they (marketers) decided, you can't assume that people know that they want."[92] This obviously presents somewhat of a dilemma for marketers, as Drucker concluded: "The customers have to be assumed to be rational. It is the manufacturer's job or supplier's job to find out why the customer behaves in what seems to be an irrational manner."[93]

Drucker on Selling and Marketing Another element under Promotion is Personal Selling. Perhaps Drucker was somewhat idealistic when he wrote about marketing eliminating the need for selling if the function was performed well. In *Management,* he wrote, "There will always, one can assume, be a need for some selling. But the aim of marketing is to make selling superfluous. The aim of marketing is to know and understand the customer so well that the product or service fits him and sells itself." He expanded on this by saying, "Ideally, marketing should result in a customer who is ready to buy. All that should be needed then is to make the product or service available, i.e., logistics rather than salesmanship, and statistical distribution rather than promotion."[94]

Figure 3.3 depicts the cost-effectiveness of the various promotional tools available to the marketer, including Personal Selling. As can be seen, Personal Selling is still the most cost-effective tool in gaining the order along with Sales Promotion.[95]

Our marketing pundits differentiate how the various promotional tools are used, based on whether the marketer is addressing the consumer or the business market. With respect to the consumer market, marketers spend in order of priority on sales promotion, advertising, personal selling and public relations,

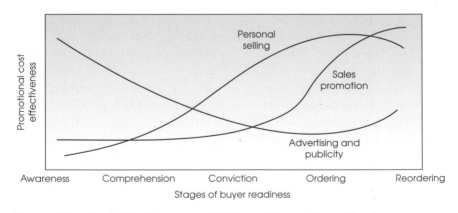

Figure 3.3   Cost-Effectiveness of Different Promotional Tools
Adopted from Philip Kotler, *Marketing Management,* 11th ed. (Upper Saddle River, NJ: Pearson Education, Inc., 2003), p. 581.

while for the business market they spend on personal selling, sales promotion, advertising and public relations. They also noted that personal selling is used more with complex, expensive, and risky goods and in markets with fewer and larger sellers, therefore, business markets.[96] Returning to Drucker's initial quote then, it is doubtful that regardless of how effective a marketing function performs, it will not eliminate the need for Personal Selling, particularly in the business or industrial market.

The Purchasing Decision   Drucker observed that there may be a number of people involved in the purchasing decision, particularly in the business market. As an example, he wrote in *Managing for Results*, "All statements so far imply that we know who the customer is. However, a marketing analysis has to be based on the assumption that a business normally does not know but needs to find out. Not 'who' pays but 'who determines the buying decision.'" Drucker expanded on this when he said, "The minimum number of customers with decisive impact on the buying decision is always two: the ultimate buyer and the distributive channel."[97]

However, Drucker later, in *Management*, allowed that "there are usually at least two—sometimes more."[98] Philip Kotler expanded on Drucker's observations by identifying the participants in the business buying process. These he identified as follows:

1. *Initiators:* Those who request that something be purchased. They may be users or others in the organization.
2. *Users:* Those who will use the product or service. In many cases, the users initiate the buying proposal and help define the product requirements.
3. *Influencers:* People who influence the buying decision. They often help define specifications and also provide information for evaluation alternatives. Technical personnel are particularly important influencers.
4. *Deciders:* People who decide on product requirements and suppliers.
5. *Approvers:* People who authorize the proposed actions of deciders or buyers.
6. *Buyers:* People who have formal authority to select the supplier and arrange the purchase terms. Buyers may help

shape product specifications, but they play their major role in selecting vendors and negotiating. In more complex purchases, the buyers might include high-level managers.

7. *Gatekeepers:* People who have the power to prevent sellers or information from reaching members of the buying circle. For example, purchasing agents, receptionists, and telephone operators may prevent salespersons from contacting users or deciders.[99]

Although he did not refer to Drucker's estimation of the number of people involved in the buying decision, Kotler commented, "The average number of people involved in a buying decision ranges from about three (for services and items used in day-to-day operations) to almost five (for such high-ticket purchases as construction work and machinery)." Reinforcing Drucker's views however, he said, "To target their efforts properly, business marketers have to figure out:

- Who are the major decision participants?
- What decisions do they influence?
- What is their level of influence?
- What evaluation criteria do they use?"[100]

Summary

Overall, much of Drucker's work on strategy and marketing is relevant, based on the time that he put forth these thoughts. However, while he might have been on the cutting edge with respect to many of his views, he neglected to build on his earlier works and eventually was bypassed by others as they moved beyond Drucker.

Endnotes

1. Roger J. Best, *Market-Based Management: Strategies for Growing Customer Value and Profitability,* 3rd ed. (Upper Saddle River, NJ: Pearson Education, Inc., 2004), 17.
2. Ibid.,?
3. Ibid., 15.
4. Ibid., 19.
5. A.J. Strickland III and Arthur A. Thompson, Jr., *Strategic Management: Concepts & Cases,* 13th ed. (New York: McGraw-Hill Companies, Inc., 2003), 33.
6. Peter Rea, Ph.D. and Harold Kerzner, Ph.D., *Strategic Planning: A Practical Guide* (New York: John Wiley & Sons, Inc., 1997), 35.

7. Peter F. Drucker, *Managing for Results* (London: William Heinemann Ltd., 1964), 47–53.
8. Roger J. Best, *Market-Based Management: Strategies for Growing Customer Value and Profitability*, 3rd ed. (Upper Saddle River, NJ: Pearson Education, Inc., 2004), 15.
9. Philip Kotler, *Marketing Management*, 11th ed. (Upper Saddle River, NJ: Prentice Hall, 2003), 38.
10. Michael E. Porter, "What Is Strategy?" *Harvard Business Review* (November–December 1996).
11. Michael E. Porter, *Competitive Strategy: Techniques for Analyzing Industries and Competitors* (New York: Free Press, 1980), Chapter 3–33.
12. Peter F. Drucker, *Managing in a Time of Great Change*, (New York: Truman Talley Books, 1998), 30–31.
13. Jack Welch, *Jack, Straight From the Gut* (New York: Warner Books, Inc., 2001).
14. Peter F. Drucker, *Managing in a Time of Great Change*, (New York: Truman Talley Books, 1998), 32.
15. Ibid., 34–35.
16. A.J. Strickland III and Arthur A. Thompson, Jr., *Strategic Management: Concepts & Cases*, 13th ed. (New York: McGraw-Hill Companies, Inc., 2003), 117.
17. Ibid. *Strategic Management*, 116–117.
18. Peter Rea, Ph.D. and Harold Kerzner, Ph.D., *Strategic Planning: A Practical Guide* (New York: John Wiley & Sons, Inc., 1997), 59–60.
19. Peter F. Drucker, *Managing for Results* (London: William Heinemann Ltd., 1964), 34–39.
20. Ibid., 224–227.
21. A.J. Strickland III and Arthur A. Thompson, Jr., *Strategic Management: Concepts & Cases*, 13th ed. (New York: McGraw-Hill Companies, Inc., 2003), 34.
22. Philip Kotler, *Marketing Management*, 11th ed. (Upper Saddle River, NJ: Prentice Hall, 2003), 90.
23. A.J. Strickland III and Arthur A. Thompson, Jr., *Strategic Management: Concepts & Cases*, 13th ed. (New York: McGraw-Hill Companies, Inc., 2003), 6.
24. Peter F. Drucker, *Managing in the Next Society* (New York: Truman Talley Books, 2002), 81.
25. Elizabeth, Haas Edersheim, *The Definitive Drucker* (New York: McGraw-Hill, 2007), 209.
26. Philip Kotler, *Marketing Management*, 11th ed. (Upper Saddle River, NJ: Prentice Hall, 2003), 92.
27. A.J. Strickland III and Arthur A. Thompson, Jr., *Strategic Management: Concepts & Cases*, 13th ed. (New York: McGraw-Hill Companies, Inc., 2003), 265.
28. Henry Mintzberg and J.A. Waters, "Of Strategies, Deliberate and Emergent," *Strategic Management Journal* (1985) 6(3): 257–272.
29. A.J. Strickland III and Arthur A. Thompson, Jr., *Strategic Management: Concepts & Cases*, 13th ed. (New York: McGraw-Hill Companies, Inc., 2003), 10–11.
30. Peter F. Drucker, *Management: Tasks, Responsibilities, Practices* (New York: Harper & Row, 1973), 88–91.
31. Ibid., 99.
32. Ibid., 99.

33. A.J. Strickland III and Arthur A. Thompson, Jr., *Strategic Management: Concepts & Cases*, 13th ed. (New York: McGraw-Hill Companies, Inc., 2003), 6–20.
34. Ibid., 10.
35. Ibid., 10.
36. Ibid., 10.
37. Peter F. Drucker, *Management: Tasks, Responsibilities, Practices* (New York: Harper & Row, 1973), 137.
38. Ibid., 122.
39. Peter F. Drucker, *Managing in a Time of Great Change*, (New York: Truman Talley Books, 1998), 137.
40. Jack Welch, *Jock, Straight from the Gut* (New York: Warner Books, Inc., 2001) 109.
41. Ibid., 109.
42. Ibid., 109.
43. Peter F. Drucker, *Managing for Results* (London: William Heinemann Ltd., 1964), 67–85.
44. Peter F. Drucker, *Managing for Results*, 153–198.
45. Peter F. Drucker, *Managing for Results* (London: William Heinemann Ltd., 1964), 227–229.
46. Ibid., 228–229.
47. Peter F. Drucker, *Managing in a Time of Great Change* (New York: Truman Talley Books, 1998), 43.
48. C. K. Prahalad and Gary Hamel, "The Core Competence of the Corporation," *Harvard Business Review*, 68.
49. Peter F. Drucker, *Managing for Results* (London: William Heinemann Ltd., 1964), 148–149.
50. Ibid., 18.
51. Ibid., 232.
52. Ibid., 232.
53. Ibid., 233.
54. Peter F. Drucker, *Managing in a Time of Great Change*, (New York: Truman Talley Books, 1998), 133.
55. Peter F. Drucker, *Managing for Results* (London: William Heinemann Ltd., 1964), 241.
56. Ibid., 238.
57. Peter F. Drucker, *Management: Tasks, Responsibilities, Practices* (New York: Harper & Row, 1973), 743.
58. Ibid., 742.
59. Michael E. Porter, *Competitive Strategy: Techniques for Analyzing Industries and Competitors*, (New York: Free Press, 1980) 35–39, 44–46.
60. Ibid., 35–40.
61. Peter F. Drucker, *Management: Tasks, Responsibilities, Practices* (New York: Harper & Row, 1973), 681.
62. Ibid., 692–693.
63. Ibid., 104–105.
64. Ibid., 105–107.
65. James O. O'Toole, "Peter Drucker: Father of the New Management," *New Management*, 2 (Winter 1985): 4.

66. Peter F. Drucker, *Managing for Results* (London: William Heinemann Ltd., 1964), 245.
67. Alfred D. Chandler Jr., *Strategy and Structure: Chapters in the History of the American Industrial Enterprise* (Cambridge, MA: M.I.T. Press, 1962).
68. Fremont E. Kast and James E. Rosenzweig, *Organization and Management: A Systems and Contingency Approach* (New York: McGraw-Hill, Inc., 1979), 217.
69. Alfred D. Chandler Jr., *Strategy and Structure: Chapters in the History of the American Industrial Enterprise* (Cambridge, MA: M.I.T. Press, 1962).
70. Peter F. Drucker, *Management: Tasks, Responsibilities, Practices* (New York: Harper & Row, 1973), 523.
71. Peter F. Drucker, *The Practice of Management* (New York: Harper & Row, Publishers, Inc., 1951), 226.
72. Peter F. Drucker, *Management: Tasks, Responsibilities, Practices* (New York: Harper & Row, 1973), 75.
73. Peter F. Drucker, *Managing for Results* (London: William Heinemann Ltd., 1964), 112–113.
74. Theodore Levitt, "Marketing Myopia," *Harvard Business Review* (1960).
75. Peter F. Drucker, *Managing for Results* (London: William Heinemann Ltd., 1964), 131.
76. Ibid., 120–131.
77. Ibid., 31.
78. Philip Kotler, *Marketing Management*, 11th ed. (Upper Saddle River, NJ: Prentice Hall, 2003), 16.
79. Peter F. Drucker, *Managing for Results* (London: William Heinemann Ltd., 1964), 113.
80. Ibid., 113.
81. Ibid., 114–115.
82. Ibid., 114–115.
83. Peter F. Drucker, *Management: Tasks, Responsibilities, Practices* (New York: Harper & Row, 1973), 85–86.
84. Roger J. Best, *Market-Based Management: Strategies for Growing Customer Value and Profitability*, 3rd ed. (Upper Saddle River, NJ: Pearson Education, Inc., 2004), 88–91.
85. Peter F. Drucker, *Managing for Results* (London: William Heinemann Ltd., 1964), 34.
86. Ibid., 35–38.
87. Michael Marks, *Working at Cross-Purposes: How Distributors and Manufacturers Can Manage Conflict Successfully* (Washington, DC: National Association of Wholesale-Distributors, Distribution Research and Education Foundation, 2006).
88. Ibid., 11.
89. Peter F. Drucker, *Managing for Results* (London: William Heinemann Ltd., 1964), 118.
90. Vance Packard, *The Hidden Persuaders* (New York: David McKay Company, 1957).
91. Roger J. Best, *Market-Based Management: Strategies for Growing Customer Value and Profitability*, 3rd ed. (Upper Saddle River, NJ: Pearson Education, Inc., 2004), 255–257.
92. Packard, *Hidden Persuaders*, (New York: David McKay Company, 1957), 8–9.

93. Peter F. Drucker, *Managing for Results* (London: William Heinemann Ltd., 1964), 116.
94. Peter F. Drucker, *Management: Tasks, Responsibilities, Practices* (New York: Harper & Row, 1973), 65–65.
95. Philip Kotler, *Marketing Management*, 11ᵗʰ ed. (Upper Saddle River, NJ: Prentice Hall, 2003), 581–582.
96. Ibid., 581.
97. Peter F. Drucker, *Managing for Results* (London: William Heinemann Ltd., 1964), 117–118.
98. Peter F. Drucker, *Management: Tasks, Responsibilities, Practices* (New York: Harper & Row, 1973), 80–81.
99. Philip Kotler, Marketing Management, 11ᵗʰ ed. (Upper Saddle River, NJ: Prentice Hall, 2003), 221.
100. Peter F. Drucker, *Managing for Results* (London: William Heinemann Ltd., 1964), 220–221.

The Five Deadly Business Sins

There is no excuse for management to indulge in the five deadly business sins.[1]

Introduction

The "Five Deadly Business Sins" first appeared in *The Wall Street Journal* in August 1993. After that article, Drucker did not devote much ink to the concept, and it was mentioned only briefly, with no expansion, in one of his last books, *The Daily Drucker*. A training company did take up the concept and under a license developed an interactive video program with a workbook, which simply reformatted Drucker's original article. In his 1985 book *Innovation and Entrepreneurship* Drucker wrote about the Five Bad Habits of organizations, which closely match his Five Sins, particularly with respect to his views on the pricing of new products. The Five Sins might well be considered an additional Drucker contribution to Pricing, one of the four P's of the Marketing Mix.[2]

The Five Deadly Business Sins

Drucker commented that there is no one formula for business success since each business and industry is different. Each business needs policies and strategies that are appropriate for that business but there are Five Deadly Business Sins that need to be avoided (see Table 4.1). If any of these sins are committed, it can have disastrous effects on the business.

Table 4.1 The Five Deadly Business Sins

Sin One: Worship of High Profit Margins and Premium Prices

Sin Two: Charging for New Products What the Market Will Bear

Sin Three: Cost-Driven Pricing vs. Price-Driven Costing

Sin Four: Killing Tomorrow's Opportunities on the Altar of Yesterday

Sin Five: Feeding Problems and Starving Opportunities[3]

Sin 1: Worship of High Profit Margins and Premium Prices

The worship of the high profit margin is thus not only a dangerous fallacy—it is worshipping a false god.[4]

According to Drucker, "Profit is not the same as a profit margin. Profit is margin multiplied by the turnover of capital. Therefore, maximum profitability and maximum profit flow are obtained by the profit margin that produces the optimum market standing with the optimum turnover of capital."[5] (Note that Drucker did not define "optimum.") Drucker also noted that one of the reasons for this problem is that a high profit margin is an accounting delusion. His view was that such thinking looks at the cost of making a product, but does not take into consideration the cost of selling or servicing it, even though these costs are typically much higher for high-margin products than for low-margin products. Roger Best's concept of Net Marketing Contribution tends to support Drucker's views here.

According to Drucker, the worship of high profit margins presents an opportunity for competition to take over the market. The following are two examples of this.

Case One: Xerox

Xerox invented the first copier that was able to make copies on plain paper (based on the innovation of Xerography by Chester Carlson). Few business innovations have been as successful as the first Xerox 813 and 914 copiers. In the early 1960s, Xerox commanded over 80 percent market share (over 85 percent as late as 1980), and even to this day, making a copy is called "Xeroxing" no matter what copying machine is used. I happened to be a Regional Marketing Manager for Xerox in the late 1960s and watched Xerox continue to focus on the high end of the market that produced high profit margins and premium prices, as well as continuing to add more and expensive features to its high-speed and high-volume copiers, which smaller customers did not want. This also made the machines more difficult and expensive to service. In addition, the sales compensation system drove sales of higher-volume copiers at the expense of the smaller, desk-top copier. Sales people will gravitate to the point of least resistance when it comes to making money, and Xerox was successful—at least in getting the results it wanted from the sales force.

By ignoring the low end of the market, however (the smaller customer that Xerox initially built its base on), and with the patents to Xerography having eventually expired, the Japanese company Canon was able to quickly produce low-quality, but inexpensive versions of the original Xerox low-end copiers, and it captured the US copier market within a few years (Xerox's market share fell to less than 15 percent by 1985). It is interesting to note that in 2006 Xerox acquired Global Imaging Systems which makes printers and copiers for small- and mid-size businesses for $1.5 billion in order to return to the small copier market segment they had previously surrendered to Canon. In doing so, Xerox acquired 200,000 customers and access to the $44 billion market for small and mid-sized businesses.[6]

On the other hand, Canon's entry into this market may not have been the result of Xerox's complete focus on high profit margins but may be a better example of disruptive technologies.

Case Two: Kodak

Kodak allowed Fuji to take over the world film market because of Kodak's focus on high profit margins. As an added note, Kodak also missed the shift in the marketplace from film to digital. Its brand has helped to regain significant market share in digital but at the expense of profits.

Drucker's Incomplete Examples   One could argue that Xerox lost market share to Canon for numerous other reasons in addition to the one cited by Drucker. This included its ill-fated venture into PCs that was going to challenge Apple in the late 1970s coupled with its poorly timed acquisition of a mainframe scientific computer company (Scientific Data Systems (SDS)), which folded several years later at a cost of several hundred millions of dollars when the company's largest customer, the government, had no money to spend on these expensive toys. Another foray into the insurance business via another acquisition proved just as disastrous.

The problems of the Big Three auto companies, along with those of Xerox, could also be attributed to the lack of understanding of changing customer needs in certain market segments.

There may also be some other exceptions to Drucker's views on pricing. As an example, a Rolex watch can cost anywhere from $5,000 to well over $10,000. The company is still able to attract a market segment willing to pay a premium price not for telling time, but for what the wearing of the watch implies to others (status, prestige, wealth). Rolls-Royce is another example of charging a premium price (although now manufactured by BMW) as well as some of the more expensive Italian sports cars. Could this not be a better example of niche marketing and finding target segments that are willing to pay premium prices and therefore do not hold an umbrella for competition? Therefore, maybe charging premium prices is not always a sin as Drucker suggests.

Sin 2: Charging for New Products What the Market Will Bear

> *The right way of pricing a new product or service is to price it right away at the price it will have to be sold three years hence when its costs have fallen. Of course, this means not reaping huge profits the first few years. It may even mean an actual loss for the first year or so.*[7]

This sin is closely related to the first one—attempting to price a new product at what the market will bear. According to Drucker, the right policy to price a new product is based on the learning curve. Essentially, the learning curve concept is that the cost of manufacturing a new product will decrease as the business gains more experience in manufacturing it. According to Drucker, it is not unusual for these costs to decrease by over 40 percent within three years.[8] Therefore, within three years after a new product is introduced, the costs of manufacturing the product will be almost half of what they were when it was first introduced. Strategy consultants, Peter Rea and Harold Kerzner, attribute this reduction in costs to the following factors:

- Labor efficiency (most important)
- Work specialization and methods improvement (task specialization: Taylor's Scientific Management)
- New production processes
- Getting better performance from production equipment (increased output: for instance, the capacity of a fluid catalytic cracking unit typically grows about 50 percent over a 10-year period)
- Changes in the resource mix (less-expensive resources used over time: low skilled labor replaces expensive labor, automation, etc.)
- Product standardization
- Product redesign
- Incentives and disincentives (compensation)[9]

Drucker advocated that the new product should be *initially priced* at what it would have to be sold for within three years as a likely result of new competitive, or substitute, products being sold at lower prices. This initial pricing strategy, he felt, makes it difficult for competitors and substitute products to enter the market.

Figure 4.1 is an example of how Texas Instruments (TI) utilized the learning curve in its electronic calculator pricing strategies. As can be seen, TI's cost to produce the calculators decreases with volume to $8 while competitor A's cost is $9 and competitor B's cost is $10. If TI priced according to Drucker's suggestion, they would price at $9 driving A from the market since it would be losing $1 on each sale and B most likely would also have to eventually exit the market since it is only breaking even if it tried to match TI's price. TI has been successful in implementing this strategy with respect to semiconductors and preventing competition from entering the market.

The following example demonstrates what can happen to industries that typically charge what the market will bear.

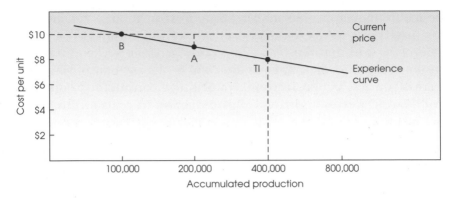

Figure 4.1[*] **TI Learning/Experience Curve**
[*]Adopted from Philip Kotler, *Marketing Management*, 11th ed. (Upper Saddle River, NJ: Pearson Education, Inc., 2003), p. 447.

Case Four: The Pharmaceutical Industry

An industry that typically prices products at what the market will bear is the pharmaceutical industry. Premium prices are charged for new drugs with the argument that companies have to recapture their research and development costs. When the patents expire and generic drugs are introduced to the market at dramatically lower prices, the strategy of pricing what the market will bear no longer works. This results in lower company profitability, which creates concern in the financial markets about the company's performance, particularly with its decreasing stock price. This, according to Drucker, motivated many "mergers of despair" between these companies in the 1980s and 1990s.

These problems will continue to plague the pharmaceutical industry in the next few years. By the end of 2006, the patents on 16 drugs had expired, and by 2010, up to a quarter of the drug sales booked in 2006 will be eroded by generics—an estimated $25 billion. Fourteen drugs faced patent expiration in 2007 alone, with a total of $11 billion in sales at stake. Industry experts predict that the percentage of prescriptions that are generic is expected to increase to 75 percent in 2011 from 56 percent now.[10] The pharmaceutical companies are attempting to counter this by introducing their own generics as line extensions, and the days of charging what the market will bear seem to be quickly coming to an end. The industry's sin of charging what the market will bear opened the door for generic competition.

Drucker's Incomplete Examples It is important to note that new products that are "new to the world," such as the original video cassette recorder (VCR), constitute only 10 percent of all the new products that are introduced to the marketplace. Most new products are improvements ("new and improved," as typically advertised) and product-line extensions. This suggests that Drucker's views about this sin have only limited application to the marketing or product managers in their new product pricing decisions.

Drucker also contradicts himself in *Innovation and Entrepreneurship*, where he discussed various strategies to introduce an innovation. In his discussion of the First With the Most Strategy, which aims at market leadership (a strategy that works only for "major" innovations), he stated, "The entrepreneur who has attained leadership by being First With the Most has to be the one who systematically cuts the price of his own product or process."[11] This raises a question—cut prices from what level? This suggests that the entrepreneur had charged a price that was not necessarily the learning curve price three years after introduction of the product—was it perhaps a premium price? This is another Drucker gap.

Other Pundits' Views Peter Rea and Harold Kerzner feel that Drucker overlooked a number of limitations associated with the Learning Curve Pricing:

- The learning curve does not continue forever. The percentage decline in hours/dollars required to make the product diminishes over time.
- The learning-curve knowledge gained on one product may not be extended to other products unless there exist shared experiences.
- Cost data may not be available in order to construct a meaningful learning curve. Other problems can occur if overhead costs are included with the direct labor costs, or if the accounting codes cannot separate work packages sufficiently in order to identify those elements that truly demonstrate experience effects.
- Quantity discounts can distort the costs and the perceived benefits of learning curves.

- Inflation must be expressed in constant dollars. Otherwise, the gains realized from experience may be neutralized.
- Learning curves are most useful on long-term horizons (years). On short-term horizons, benefits perceived may not be the result of learning curves.
- External influences such as limitations on materials, patents, or even government regulations, can restrict the benefits of learning curves.
- Constant annual production (i.e., no growth) may have a limiting experience effect after a few years."[12]

Sin 3: Cost-Driven Pricing vs. Price-Driven Costing

Customers do not see it as their job to ensure that manufacturers make a profit.[13]

Companies commit the cost-driven pricing sin by totaling costs and then adding a profit to arrive at the price to be charged the customer. In contrast, price-driven costing designs the product or service. The following examples illustrate each approach.

Case Five: Cost-Driven Pricing Example: Control Data vs. IBM

When computers became popular in the early 1960s, Control Data had what was considered the world's most advanced computer. The price it arrived at for the computer at the time was the manufacturing costs plus a profit. The result was that the computer was too expensive for most customers, and although potential customers conceded it was the best computer available—sales did not materialize.

IBM on the other hand, asked the question *What is the business customer willing to pay for a computer?*[14] It then designed a computer that was technically inferior to Control Data's, but it was priced using the Price-Driven Costing Approach, and the rest is history in terms of where both companies are today.

Case Six: Price-Driven Costing Example: Henry Ford

Many historians credit Henry Ford for inventing the assembly line to manufacture the Model T Ford that sold for $500. Actually, Henry Ford was one of the first to use the Price-Driven Costing Approach. He asked, "What is the price the average customer is willing to pay for a very basic automobile that came in one color, black?" His marketing research concluded that $500 was the right price, still high in those days, and he therefore instructed his engineers to determine how they could manufacture the auto and make a profit selling it for $500.[15]

Sin 4: Killing Tomorrow's Opportunities on the Altar of Yesterday

By 2020 or so, it's reasonably certain that the surviving businesses will be those that did not commit the sin of slaughtering on the altar of yesterday the new opportunity—that is e-commerce, whether business-to-business or business-to-consumer.[16]

Businesses often attempt to keep and shore up present products when they feel they have a few good years left, even though sales are declining and customer preferences and the market are changing. Drucker spoke about this in his concept of Planned Abandonment—when to abandon a product and introduce new products. As a result of attempting to preserve yesterday, opportunities for tomorrow are lost. Drucker also argued that often times the best performing people in the organization are assigned to such problems instead of focusing on opportunities.

Case Seven: General Motors and the Saturn

The Saturn, a Japanese-designed auto, but manufactured in a hi-tech plant in the United States with innovative employee compensation incentives and no auto workers union, became an immediate success in the US auto market. At the same time, sales of the older General Motors' models, the Buick and Oldsmobile were declining as a result of changing consumer preferences.

(continued)

Instead of continuing to invest in the Saturn, GM's strategy was to attempt to save these two dying yesterday's models. As a result, the Saturn is no longer competitive in the US market, Buick is an also ran, although it has had exceptional success in China, becoming the number two selling auto in 2006, and the Oldsmobile has eventually been discontinued from the GM product line. GM continues to struggle—losing over $10 billion in 2005, and the same huge losses from 2006–2008—and is focused on the problems, plant closings and significant reductions in force, and so forth but has yet to define the opportunities it should pursue.

Case Eight: IBM and Dell Computer

IBM took over the PC market from Apple Computer (the company that invented the PC industry) when it was able to include an operating system (DOS) in a computer that was inferior to Apple's. Despite this success, IBM was concerned that by concentrating on PCs it would lose its mainframe business for larger customers (Yesterday's product). By diverting its resources to preserving Yesterday, IBM allowed Dell Computer to become the largest PC company in the world in terms of revenues in a little over 12 years. IBM finally abandoned the PC business by selling that division to the Chinese computer company Lenovo in 2004.

Sin 5: Feeding Problems and Starving Opportunities

The fourth and fifth sins are very closely related. Basically Sin 5 deals with attempting to preserve Yesterday and ignoring Tomorrow, but from a slighty different perspective. This issue is compounded by the organization's reporting system that focuses on problems and on where objectives are not being met, usually on the first page of the weekly or monthly management report. Opportunities for the organization to pursue are not listed here and, if listed at all, are buried somewhere in the report.

Drucker commented that better-performing organizations assign their best people to pursuing opportunities for growth. They also have two pages to their management reports, the typical problems and status page, and an Opportunity page. Drucker had continued to stress over the years that organizations that do not innovate will not survive. Therefore, the identification of opportunities and assigning resources (innovation budget and top-performing people) are critical to the organization's survival.

Summary

Peter Drucker advised that these Five Deadly Business Sins need to be avoided if a business is to survive and grow. The key take-aways from this chapter deal essentially with two issues:

1. *Pricing Strategies*: What is the most appropriate strategy for the introduction of a new product? Drucker suggests Price-Based Costing and Learning Curve Pricing.
2. *Innovation*: The need for innovation that will be covered in more detail in Chapter 5.

With respect to pricing, Drucker's Learning Curve Pricing is but one strategy an organization can consider, depending on a number of variables. Kotler expanded on Drucker's deadly sins by suggesting there are other mistakes made in pricing decisions. He outlined these as follows:

1. Pricing is too cost-oriented.
2. Price is not revised often enough to capitalize on market changes.
3. Price is set independent of the marketing mix rather than as an intrinsic element of market-positioning strategy.
4. Price is not varied enough for different product items, market segments, distribution channels and purchase occasions.[17]

Kotler also detailed the steps that are necessary in establishing a price. These steps include:

1. Selecting the pricing objective
2. Determining demand
3. Estimating costs
4. Analyzing competitors' costs, prices, and offers
5. Selecting a pricing method
6. Selecting the final price[18]

According to Kotler, pricing objectives can vary from simply being able to survive as a business all the way to gaining product-quality leadership. He classified five pricing objectives:[19]

1. *Survival*: Applies to the firm that is faced with overcapacity, intense competition, or changing customer wants. If the price can cover variable and fixed costs, the company can stay in business. This he considered as a short-term strategy, and if the firm cannot eventually add value, it will face extinction.

2. *Maximize Current Profits*: Maximize current profit, cash flow, or rate of return on investment. This strategy assumes the firm can determine demand and cost functions. By emphasizing current performance, it may sacrifice long-run performance by ignoring effects of other marketing-mix variables, such as competitors' reactions, or legal restraints on price.

3. *Maximize Market Share*: Some believe a higher sales volume equates to lower unit costs and thus higher long-run profits. The strategy is to set the lowest price assuming the market is price sensitive (elastic). Texas Instruments (TI) practices Market-Penetration Pricing: it builds a large plant, sets a low price to gain market share, and lowers the price again (learning curve effects). This strategy discourages competition from entering the market as was described by Drucker.

4. *Market Skimming*: Applies to companies introducing new technology. One example is Sony and the first high-definition television: the price was $43,000 in 1990 when first introduced, in 1993 price declined dramatically to $6,000, and in 2001 the price plunged to $2,000. A personal example was my purchasing a HP calculator for $500 to use for my Pepperdine University MBA courses in the mid–1970s. Nearly 40 years later a calculator that can perform the same and even more functions can be purchased for less than $5. Kotler suggests that Market Skimming works when there are sufficient buyers and high current demand, unit cost of producing small volume is not too high, high initial price does not attract more competitors to the market, and the high price communicates an image of a superior product. This strategy is related to Drucker's sin of Charging What the Market Will Bear.

5. *Product-Quality Leadership*: This strategy attempts to sell value and other features to convince customers that the product is worth the extra price. As an example, Xerox's pricing, as compared to the competition when it was first introduced in the late 1950s, focused on the use of plain versus coated paper and the combination of copy quality and ease of use compared to

existing coated paper copies. Also the initial strategy of charging by the copy versus having to buy the copier (which Xerox would not initially do) was a unique approach that allowed the company to initially achieve this objective.

According to Roger Best, there are numerous Cost-Based and Market-Based pricing strategies depending on where the product is in its lifecycle.[20] Cost-Based pricing strategies range from Floor Pricing to Harvest Pricing while Market-Based strategies range from Skim Pricing to Plus One Pricing.

The concept of "elasticity" also needs to be considered in determining price (Kotler's second step). The use of "bundling" and "unbundling" as pricing strategies as well as the impact of cannibalization caused by the introduction of new products were neglected in Drucker's discussions here and creates further Gaps that need to be closed. A detailed discussion of these strategies and other pricing considerations is not included here, but there are many marketing books that can close these Gaps.

Endnotes

1. Peter F. Drucker, "The Five Deadly Business Sins." *Corpedia Education, Corpedia 8108 On-line Program* (2001).
2. Robert W. Swaim, Ph.D., "The Drucker Files: The Five Deadly Business Sins," *Business Beijing* (December 2002).
3. Peter F. Drucker, "Five Deadly Business Sins." MTS Video No. 3, Ahead of Change Series. London: *MTS Publishers, Ltd.* (1999).
4. Peter F. Drucker, "The Five Deadly Business Sins." *Corpedia Education, Corpedia 8108 On-line Program* (2001).
5. Ibid.
6. R.M. Schneiderman, "Xerox Turns to Burns for Growth," *Forbes.com* (April 4, 2006).
7. Peter F. Drucker, "The Five Deadly Business Sins." *Corpedia Education, Corpedia 8108 On-line Program* (2001).
8. Ibid.
9. Peter Rea, Ph.D. and Harold Kerzner, Ph.D., *Strategic Planning: A Practical Guide* (New York: John Wiley & Sons, Inc., 1997), 133–135.
10. Matthew Herper, "The Generic Onslaught," *Forbes.com* (June 23, 2006), and "Threat of Substitute Products Real," *Forbes.com* (July 7, 2006).
11. Peter F. Drucker, *Innovation and Entrepreneurship* (New York: Harper & Row, 1985), 217.
12. Peter Rea, Ph.D. and Harold Kerzner, Ph.D., *Strategic Planning: A Practical Guide* (New York: John Wiley & Sons, Inc., 1997), 141–142.

13. Peter F. Drucker, "The Five Deadly Business Sins." *Corpedia Education, Corpedia 8108 On-line Program* (2001).

14. Ibid.

15. Theodore Levitt, "Marketing Myopia: What Ford Put First," *Harvard Business Review* (September–October 1960): 187–188.

16. Peter F. Drucker, "The Five Deadly Business Sins." *Corpedia Education, Corpedia 8108 On-line Program* (2001).

17. Philip Kotler, *Marketing Management,* 11th ed. (Upper Saddle River, NJ: Pearson Education, 2003), 471.

18. Ibid., 473.

19. Ibid., 474–475.

20. Roger J. Best, *Market-Based Management* 3rd ed. (Upper Saddle River, NJ: Prentice Hall, 2004).

Innovation and Entrepreneurship

The entrepreneur always searches for change, responds to it, and exploits it as an opportunity.[1]

Part One: Continuing Organic Growth Strategies

Introduction

While working on my Ph.D. at Claremont, I had the opportunity to take a number of classes from Drucker. I can recall one evening when he asked the class, "What invention revolutionized warfare?" Drucker almost always took delight in putting a student down who attempted to answer one of his questions, and I can recall only one individual over a period of almost two years who ever answered a question to his satisfaction. Such was the case when the class volunteered answers from gunpowder, to the howitzer, to the atomic bomb, and, of course, all to his dissatisfaction. Finally, the class gave up and waited for his answer. "The stirrup," he said. He then went on to explain that until the stirrup was invented, the soldier on horseback had no real advantage over the foot soldier who could knock him off the horse with a lance or spear. With the stirrup, the soldier on horseback could dig in his feet and could not be as easily unseated. This then led to the expansion of the cavalry and mounted soldiers that according to Drucker, revolutionized warfare.[2] I seriously doubt you can find this in any of his writings, including *Innovation and Entrepreneurship*, which he wrote in 1985 and expands on how organizations can grow organically. This chapter highlights some of his key points about innovation and entrepreneurship.

Defining Entrepreneurs and Entrepreneurship

The entrepreneur has often been defined as one who starts his or her own, new, small business. But as Drucker pointed out, "Not every new small business is entrepreneurial or represents entrepreneurship." The husband and wife who open a restaurant in the Beijing suburbs surely take a risk. But are they entrepreneurs? What they have done has been done many times before. They gamble on the increasing popularity of eating out in their area, but they have not created new consumer satisfaction or new consumer demand. In this perspective, according to Drucker, they are surely not entrepreneurs, even though theirs is a new venture. They may also have been buying a job as many owners of very small businesses do. That is, the revenues and the net profits of a very small business may be no more than the individual could earn as a salary working for a company. In effect, these business people have purchased their own jobs. On the other hand, Drucker cited McDonald's as an example of entrepreneurship through the application of management concepts and processes such as standardizing the "product."[3]

According to Drucker, entrepreneurs and entrepreneurship are distinct features of an individual or an organization. Also, the organization does not need to be small and new to be an entrepreneur since entrepreneurship is being practiced by large and often old enterprises as in the case of 3M, which Drucker cited as one of the most innovative companies around, having developed over 60,000 new products. Entrepreneurship therefore, according to Drucker, "Is a 'behavior' rather than a personality 'trait' whose foundation lies in concept and theory rather than intuition. Entrepreneurs see change as the norm, and as healthy. Usually they do not bring about change themselves. But—and this distinguishes the entrepreneur from entrepreneurship—the entrepreneur always searches for change, responds to it, and exploits it as an opportunity."[4]

Definition of Innovation

Drucker had continually stressed that the purpose of a business is to create a customer. Therefore, in his view, the business enterprise had two—and only two—basic functions: *marketing* and *innovation.* The second function of a business is innovation, the provision of different economic satisfaction.

Drucker defined innovation, "As the task of endowing human and material resources with new and greater wealth-producing capacity." He expanded on this: "Managers must convert society's needs into opportunities for profitable business. That, too, is a definition of innovation."[5] This is consistent with the steps cited in the *Strategic Management Process* as described in Chapter 2 and the assessment of the organization's external environment to identify opportunities for innovation and growth.

One example he cited was the *Penicillium* mold. It was a pest, not a resource. Bacteriologists went to great lengths to protect their bacterial cultures against contamination by mold until, in the 1920s, a London doctor realized that this pest was precisely the bacterial killer that had long been sought. The mold became a valuable resource.[6] Finally Drucker suggested, "Innovation is not invention. Innovation is a term of economics rather than technology."[7]

Types and Requirements of Innovation

Drucker said: "It is not enough for the business to provide just any economic goods and services; it must provide better and more economic ones." He pointed out, "The most productive innovation is a different product or service creating a new potential satisfaction, rather than an improvement."[8] A study by the consulting firm Booz, Allen and Hamilton, in the 1980s, identified types of innovation as consisting of new product lines, additions to existing product lines, improvements or revisions of existing product lines (which is where most innovative activity takes place according to the study), repositioning of products, cost reductions, and new-to-the-world products, which was identified as consisting of less than 10 percent of all innovations.[9] Much of Drucker's focus was on new-to-the-world products although he did mention several other innovative opportunities.

Innovation may also be the finding of new uses for old products, such as the use of Arm & Hammer Baking Soda to remove food odors from refrigerators and as a toothpaste. Drucker's Requirements for Innovation are summarized in Table 5.1.

Table 5.1   Requirements for Innovation

Better and more economical products and services

A different product (new-to-the-world)—not an improvement of existing ones

New uses for old products[10]

Identifying Sources of Innovation: Drucker's First Principle

Drucker suggested that purposeful, systematic innovation begins with analysis of the opportunities, and classifies Seven Sources of Innovative Opportunity as shown in Table 5.2.[11] He classified these as Sources Within the Business or Industry and those that deal with Changes Outside the Enterprise or Industry.

According to Drucker, "The first four lie within the business or industry. They are basically 'symptoms' but are reliable indicators of changes that have already taken place or which can be made to occur with little effort." The following is a brief discussion of these sources.

Table 5.2   Sources of Innovation

Sources Within the Business or Industry	Changes Outside the Enterprise or Industry
1. Unexpected Successes and Unexpected Failures	1. Changes in Demographics
	2. Changes in Meaning and Perception
2. Incongruities	3. New Knowledge
3. Process Needs	
4. Changes in Industry and Market Structure	

Unexpected Successes and Unexpected Failures[12] Drucker suggested the best potential source for successful innovation is from an Unexpected Success or Failure. Exploitation of this requires analysis simply because an unexpected success is a symptom. Suppose that one particular product in the business's product line is outperforming all other products beyond management's expectations. Why is that occurring? A competitor is having unexpected success in a particular market segment. Management must find out why this is happening, asking themselves what it would mean if they exploited it. A classic example dates back to the early days when Marriott was still a restaurant chain before it expanded into hotels. Management observed that one of its restaurants in Washington, DC, was outperforming all others in the chain in terms of monthly revenues. Upon investigation, it found that the restaurant was located across from Hoover Field, the city's first airport. This was before airlines served meals on planes, and Marriott discovered that airline passengers would stop by the restaurant and purchase sandwiches and snacks to take on the plane with them. Marriott met with the old Eastern Airlines and proposed to provide food to be served on the plane—thus the beginning of the airline catering business.

Unexpected Failures can also lead to other opportunities for innovation as suggested by the following quotation by a former CEO of Johnson and Johnson, another firm Drucker identified as being innovative.

Failure is our most important product.
　　　　　R. W. Johnson, Jr., former CEO, Johnson & Johnson

In another example, the Ford Motor Company developed a new automobile, the Edsel, in 1957. The auto's design supposedly stemmed from extensive market research about customer preferences in appearance and styling, yet the Edsel became a total failure immediately after it was introduced—one of the greatest failures in the history of the automotive industry.

Instead of blaming the "irrational consumer," Ford's management decided there was something happening that was not in line with general auto-industry assumptions about consumer behavior. After reinvestigating the market, the company discovered a new "lifestyle segment" to which it quickly responded by producing the superbly designed and produced Thunderbird model—one of the greatest successes in US auto history. Ford should perhaps revisit this experience today, along with the other two US automakers, as they attempt to survive the growing challenge of Japanese auto makers.

You can learn from success, but you have to work at it; it's a lot easier to learn from failure.

Lewis Lehr, former CEO, 3M Corporation

A classic example is 3M's Post-It notes, the little yellow stick-ons that are used in offices throughout the world. They were originally to be used in an industrial application but failed. Later, a 3M scientist who took some of the material home discovered his daughter had cut up some of these sheets and was using them to post notes on the refrigerator, reminding her mother of what to buy at the supermarket. From this failure evolved a product that 3M has been selling for decades. Has your business had any successes or failures that perhaps should be investigated further?

Incongruities   Drucker described an incongruity as a discrepancy, a dissonance, between what is and what "ought" to be, or between what is and what everybody assumes it to be. Like the unexpected event, whether success or failure, an incongruity is a symptom of change that has already occurred, or change that can be made to happen.[13]

According to Drucker, there are several kinds of incongruities:

- An incongruity between the economic realities of an industry
- An incongruity between the reality of an industry and the assumptions about it
- An incongruity between the efforts of an industry and the values and expectations of its customers[14]
- An incongruity within the rhythm or logic of a process

Incongruity Between the Economic Realities of an Industry   Drucker pointed out that if demand for a product or service is growing steadily, its economic performance should steadily improve, too. It should easily be profitable in an industry with steadily rising demand because it is carried by the tide. A lack of profitability in such an industry suggests an incongruity between economic realities.

This type of incongruity typically occurs within a whole industry or a whole service sector, and presents a major opportunity for innovation for a small and highly focused new enterprise, new process, or new service. Also, the innovator who exploits this incongruity can count on few competitors for a long time before they wake up to the fact that they have new and dangerous competition. The inception of the "mini" steel mill is an example of successfully exploiting an incongruity before the management of the larger integrated steel mills in the United States realized what was occurring in the industry. What incongruities can be exploited in the various industries that you have observed?

Incongruity Between the Reality of an Industry and the Assumptions About It   This type of incongruity occurs when management in an industry has a misconception about the real state of affairs in its industry and therefore makes erroneous assumptions about it, resulting in misdirected efforts. According to Drucker, they concentrate on the area where results do not exist, and offer an opportunity for an innovator who can perceive and exploit it.

Drucker cited an example of this incongruity in the ocean-going freighter industry that was believed to be dying in the 1950s. The major assumption about the industry was that the main expense of the ship was while it was traveling from point A to point B. Considerable efforts were directed at getting faster and more efficient ships, fewer crew members, and so forth, in order to reduce costs. An innovator concluded that these assumptions about the industry were wrong and that the major costs were while the ship was idle in port, waiting for cargo unloading and new cargo to be loaded.

The result was the innovation of the cargo container, the roll-on, roll-off ship and the container vessel. Overall costs were reduced by 60 percent, and the industry has grown dramatically ever since. Actually the shipping container was developed by Malcolm McLean in the late 1950s and saw its original application by the government in shipping supplies for the Vietnam War.

Incongruity Between the Efforts of an Industry and the Values and Expectations of its Customers   Of all incongruities, this one may be the most common. Producers and suppliers typically misconceive what it is the customer actually buys. They assume that what is "value" to them is equally of "value" to the customer, whose expectations and values are usually different. The customer seldom perceives what he or she is buying as what the producer or supplier delivers.

While producers and suppliers may complain about "irrational" customer behavior, there are potential opportunities for an innovation that is highly specific and focused. Numerous examples exist of people taking advantage of this incongruity, with a successful innovation such as by the Edward Jones Company, a financial service firm, exploiting the misperceptions of larger Wall Street firms relative to customer values. Jones identified a market segment, farmers and people about to retire, as having a desire for a secure investment before their retirement in contrast to the frequent trader of stocks that Wall Street firms focused on. As a result, it has become one of the largest financial services firms in the United States.[15]

Incongruity Within the Rhythm or Logic of a Process   This incongruity looks for something that is missing in a particular process, specifically how a consumer may use a product. The innovation of the Scotts Spreader to allow homeowners to spread fertilizer evenly is an example of taking advantage of this incongruity.

Process Needs   Innovations in Process Needs essentially look for a weak or missing link in an existing process. Opportunities for innovation exist if there is a recognized need to complete the process. It must be felt that there is a "better way" to do something that will be enthusiastically received by users. Here Drucker pointed out that innovation in this area starts out with the job to be done and perfects a process that already exists.[16]

According to Drucker, successful innovations based on process needs require five basic criteria, as depicted in Table 5.3.

Drucker added that the need for a better way must be understood. A classic example of this source of innovation is the little-known inventor who made his name a part of our vocabulary, Elijah McCoy. In 1870 he earned a degree in engineering but as a black man in the 1870s, the only job he could find was that of an oiler on the Michigan Central Railroad. Trains had to stop frequently then and had to be oiled by hand. McCoy figured out there must

Table 5.3 Criteria for Process Need Innovations

1. A self-contained process.
2. One weak or missing link.
3. A clear definition of the objective.
4. Specifications for the solution can be clearly defined.
5. Widespread realization that "there ought to be a better way."[17]

be a better way and designed a lubricating cup that automatically dripped oil onto the moving parts. His innovation became a hit and soon, no piece of heavy machinery was considered complete unless it had a McCoy lubricator. And people looking at a machine's lubricator begin to ask a question we're still asking . . . is it the real McCoy?

Changes in Industry and Market Structures[18] Changes in industry and market structure usually take place as a result of changing customer preferences, tastes and values. Also, the rapid growth of a particular industry is a reliable indicator of changing industry structures. Japanese penetration of the US auto market with smaller and more fuel-efficient cars in the 1970s allowed them to take advantage of changing consumer preferences for autos, motivated largely by dramatic increases in gasoline prices (the price of *used* Japanese fuel-efficient autos such as Hondas and Toyotas had increased considerably in mid-2008 as a result of gasoline selling for over $4 per gallon).

Drucker classified the second set of sources for innovative opportunity as involving changes outside the business or industry.

Changes in Demographics[19] Drucker felt that changes in demographics (age, education, disposable income, geographic shift and so forth) are one of the most reliable predictors of the future and offer opportunities for innovation. Those doing business in China should explore what opportunities an aging population, the one-child family, or increased disposable income in China offer for innovation.

Changes in Meaning and Perception[20]   The earlier discussion of Unexpected Successes and Unexpected Failures demonstrated that they are often an indication of a change in perception and meaning. The success of Ford's Thunderbird and the failure of its Edsel were attributed to changes in perception. The automobile market that had always been segmented by income group was seen by customers as segmented by lifestyles. Identifying opportunities for innovation in this category requires timing and judgment; are there actual changes taking place in perception, or just fads that will be short-lived?

New Knowledge (Scientific and Nonscientific)[21]   New knowledge can be a source of innovative opportunities, but according to Drucker, it has the longest lead time of all sources of innovations. There is a long time span between the emergence of new knowledge and when it becomes applicable to technology—plus more time before the new technology turns into products in the marketplace. Another characteristic of knowledge-based innovations is that they are almost never based on one factor but on the convergence of several different kinds of knowledge. A classic example of the length of time from knowledge to a commercial application is the jet engine, which was originally patented in 1930. Its first military test was in 1941, and the first commercial jet plane was the Comet in 1952. Boeing eventually developed the 707 and by 1958, it became operational, 28 years after the patent. Development of the new plane required the convergence of the technologies of aerodynamics, new materials, and fuels.

Finally, it is important that knowledge-based innovation be clear in establishing a strategic (leadership) position before others and that it has a clear focus on the market—in short, creating a market for its products. Drucker cited DuPont that did not sell Nylon immediately after developing it. The firm first created a consumer market for women's hosiery and underwear made from Nylon as well as a market for automobile tires also using Nylon. DuPont then sold the Nylon to manufacturers to make the articles for which it had already created a demand.

Drucker also commented on the Bright Idea as one of the major sources of patents, but few reach product development and introduction to the marketplace. He concluded that Bright Ideas are the most risky and least successful source of innovative opportunities.[22]

The Principles of Innovation

Drucker formulated his Principles of Innovation:

1. Analyze the sources of innovation for opportunities.
2. Determine customer needs, wants and expectations.
3. Innovation should be simple and focused.
4. Innovation should start small.
5. Innovation should aim at leadership.[23]

According to Drucker, innovations that are simple and focused should be directed toward a specific, clear and designed application, and should be focused on a specific need that it satisfies and the specific end result that it produces. This is a reasonable requirement. If the consumer does not understand what the product does, the innovative product will not sell.

In addition to the principles, he also cited a number of things that should not be done relative to innovation.

1. *Do not try to be clever:* Drucker suggested that innovation not be too sophisticated as "incompetence, after all, is the only thing in an abundant and never-failing supply."[24]
2. *Do not diversify or splinter efforts:* Essentially, focus on the innovative effort and do not chase too many opportunities at the same time.
3. *Do not innovate for the future:* The innovation should have immediate application. However, he added, "Innovative opportunities sometimes have long lead times. In pharmaceutical research, 10 years of research and development work are by no means uncommon or particularly long. And yet no pharmaceutical company would dream of starting a research project for something which does not, if successful, have immediate application as a drug for healthcare needs that already exist."[25]

While not all of these ideas left Drucker gaps, it is helpful to expand on these points by offering an abstract from the views of Philip Kotler.

Characteristics of Innovation Adoption: Another Perspective[26]

Some products catch on immediately, whereas others take a long time to gain acceptance. Five characteristics influence the rate of adoption of an innovation.

The first is *relative advantage*—the degree to which the innovation appears superior to existing products.

The second is *compatibility*—the degree to which the innovation matches the values and experiences of the individuals.

Third is *complexity*—the degree to which the innovation is relatively difficult to understand or use.

The fourth is *divisibility*—the degree to which the innovation can be tried on a limited basis.

The fifth is *communicability*—the degree to which the beneficial results of use are observable or describable to others.

Other characteristics that influence the rate of adoption are cost, risk and uncertainty, scientific credibility, and social approval. The new-product marketer has to research all of these factors and give the key ones maximum attention in designing the new product and its marketing program.

With respect to Drucker's view that innovation should start small, once again 3M probably illustrates this principle best with its saying, "Make a little, sell a little."[27]

Drucker expanded on his principle that innovation should aim at leadership: "If an innovation does not aim at leadership from the beginning, it is unlikely to be innovative enough, and therefore unlikely to be capable of establishing itself."[28] He then clarified this by indicating that leadership could be in a particular market or a market niche, which is more realistic than attempting to conquer the world with a new product.

Part Two: Innovation and Entrepreneurship

Entrepreneurial Strategies

Part Two discusses the various *strategies* Drucker suggested to introduce an innovation into the marketplace. Table 5.4 outlines his strategies in terms of each of their objectives and the elements that comprise each strategy. This table identifies the two objectives

Table 5.4   Strategies to Introduce Innovation

Objective	Strategy	Elements of Strategy
Market Leadership and Dominance	First with the Most	Creative Imitation
	Hit Them Where They Are Not	Entrepreneurial Judo Toll Gate Strategy
Market Control and Monopoly	High-Profit Niche Strategies	Specialty Skill Strategy Specialty Market Strategy

Drucker suggested for an innovation, the strategies to achieve these objectives and the elements or subsets of these strategies.

Market Leadership and Dominance Objective

One set of strategies deals with the objective of gaining market leadership and dominance with the introduction of the new innovation:

First with the Most: This strategy looks to attain market leadership, if not outright dominance. In order to achieve this, the new product (innovation) being introduced must be more than an improvement. It must have major product differentiation and be both new to the market and new to the customer. Examples of companies who have successfully implemented this strategy and quickly gained market leadership were Wang Laboratories and the introduction of the first word processor, and Apple Computer with the introduction of the first personal computer.[29] Sony is perhaps one of the better examples of using this strategy considering the innovations it introduced that made it the market leader such as the first magnetic tape recorder in 1950, the first all-transistor radio in 1955, the first pocket-sized radio in 1964, and the Sony Walkman in 1979.

Hit Them Where They are Not (Creative Imitation): This strategy aims at market or industry leadership but without the risk of creating the market. It is designed to outflank the leader by creative imitation by improving on something that someone else created. For this strategy to work, the original product must be a success. Examples of successful implementation of this strategy were IBM, introducing its own PC after Apple created the market, and the Japanese company Seiko introducing digital watches to replace the more traditional Swiss watch movements. Both companies, through creative imitation, quickly gained market leadership.[30]

Entrepreneurial Judo: Judo is the fighting technique that uses the other person's strength and weight against him with the various moves to throw him down. Entrepreneurial Judo looks for what the current market leaders consider their strengths to be. It then bases its innovative strategy on this. Typically, these leaders have a fixation on the high-end of the market and the most profitable one. They attempt to offer everything in a single package and they believe that quality is defined by them rather than by the customer—good examples of Drucker's Business Sins. Entrepreneurial Judo assumes that the leaders will continue their behavior as they settle into patterns of predictable behavior and refuse to change even if they are being repeatedly defeated. Canon, the Japanese copier manufacturer, using Entrepreneurial Judo and assessing the behavior of Xerox, which was then the leader, was able to successfully take a large share of the copier market away from Xerox, starting with the low end of the market and then eventually also taking a large share of the high end. Another example of this strategy was MCI and Sprint using AT&T's own pricing system to take away a large percentage of the long distance telephone market in the United States.[31]

Market Control and Monopoly Objective (High-Profit Niche Strategies)

The objective of these strategies is to obtain market control and become a monopoly in a particular highly profitable market niche. The goal is to be so discreet that, despite making the product or service indispensable, no one is likely to move into the niche and try to compete.

Toll-Gate Strategy: This strategy entails developing a product or service that is an indispensable part of a larger process. The strategy only works where some existing step in a process is out of line with all the other steps and requires drastically different actions, making the cost of using the product eventually irrelevant. The innovation of the blow-out preventer for offshore oil wells is a classic example of this strategy. The cost of the preventer is irrelevant versus the cost of cleaning up a large oil spill in the ocean, obviously a huge concern as more offshore drilling is being recommended to deal with rising oil prices. Another requirement of this strategy is the market must be so limited that whoever occupies the niche first is able to bar anyone else from entering it. On the other hand, the risk of this strategy is that it offers limited growth potential since future growth is dependent on the expansion of the overall process. If oil companies are not drilling offshore oil wells, the growth potential for the sale of blow-out preventers is limited.[32]

Specialty Skill Strategy: This strategy involves assessing opportunities in a new or upcoming market or industry trend and developing a high-skill product or service to serve the market. Once the market begins to grow, the innovator has a significant head start over potential competitors and has already become a standard industry supplier. A classic example of this strategy is companies who make brake pads, electrical circuits, or headlamps that go into the manufacture and assembly of automobiles. These companies have been major suppliers to the auto industry for decades, getting in early with the Specialty Skills Strategy, and few people even know who these companies are. Once again, a potential risk of this strategy is that one must rely on someone else to make a market for the industry's foundation product.[33]

Specialty Market Niche Strategy: According to Drucker, this is the most profitable of the Market Niche strategies. The goal is to establish a specialty market niche big enough to be profitable, but small enough not to make it worthwhile for potential competitors to invade.

An example of this strategy was the innovation of the American Express Travelers Checks for business people and vacationers, eliminating the risk of carrying cash on their travels. American Express dominated this market niche for decades until banks added these services for their customers, with no service fees. A more *recent* example was the Big Bertha golf driver developed by Callaway Golf targeted at the amateur, weekend golfer that was extremely successful for years until others such as TaylorMade entered the market with its driver.[34]

Pundits' Views and Closing Drucker Gaps

In our discussion of potential Drucker gaps relative to innovation, we asked whether Creative Imitation, Entrepreneurial Judo, Market Niche, and so forth are really "strategies" or whether they are questions to ask during product development as to positioning of the product—a marketing decision. For instance, once an innovative opportunity has been identified (Drucker's Sources of Innovation), what type of product should be developed, and where should it be positioned in the marketplace? The "how" it gets introduced into the marketplace is actually the "strategy" that includes pricing, branding, channel and other decisions not mentioned by Drucker.

Other Contributors

While Drucker discussed various strategies to introduce an innovation, his strategies did not deal with the many issues that need to be considered when launching a new product that typically falls under the Four Ps of marketing. Decisions relative to branding, pricing, selecting the appropriate channels, and so forth are missing from Drucker's discussion, even though he stressed the importance of marketing as one of the "only" two functions of an organization along with innovation. It was therefore necessary to include a more comprehensive discussion of marketing and its related tools in our programs. Here we relied on the contributions of Philip Kotler and Roger Best to supplement Drucker's views on the marketing element, as alluded to in Chapter 3.

I also added some other elements of innovation that Drucker did not cover, such as a discussion of the rate of adoption of innovation, the growing concept of Disruptive Technologies by Clayton Christensen as other sources of innovation.

The Roles of Management and the "Big E"

In order to reinforce the importance of innovation and entrepreneurship in our programs, I relied on the excellent work of Ichak Adizes in his Roles of Management theory.[35]

In *Managing Corporate Lifecycles* (1999), Adizes describes the four roles that are necessary to be performed in an organization as the P (Purposeful Performance), A (Administrative), I (Integrative), and E (Entrepreneurial) roles. These roles and their focus are depicted in Figure 5.1.

Adizes also describes which role or roles should predominate in the organization over its lifecycle (see Figure 5.2).[36]

As the organization is growing, the E Role is prevalent in "Infant" and "Go-Go" Phases of the organization's lifecycle. A critical

MANAGEMENT ROLES	FOCUS
"P" ROLE **P**urposeful **P**erformance	**P**rovide desired needs of clients. **P**roduce the results to which you are committed. **P**erform as expected.
"A" ROLE **A**dministration	**A**dminister – systemize, program, and organize.
"E" ROLE **E**ntrepreneurial	**E**ntrepreneur – visualizing future changing needs, and *proactively* positioning the organization for that future.
"I" ROLE **I**ntegrating	**I**ntegrating develops a culture of interdependency and affinity, nurturing a unique corporate culture.

Figure 5.1   The Four Management Roles
Source: Ichak Adizes, *Managing Corporate Lifecycles* (Paramus, NJ: Prentice Hall, 1999), 193–204.

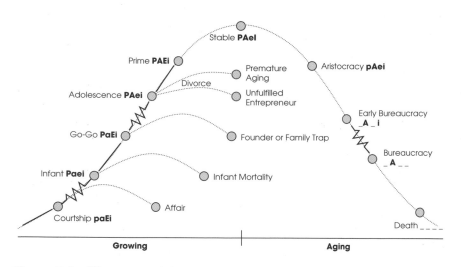

Figure 5.2   Lifecycles of Organizations and Management Roles
Adopted with permission from Ichak Adizes, *How to Solve the Mismanagement Crisis*, (Los Angles: Adizes Institute Publications, 1980), p. 93.

phase in the lifecycle is in "Adolescence" when the organization needs to stop chasing all of the opportunities it has identified and become more organized and systematic in its approach to business. This often entails hiring a CFO or other administrative head (the

A Role) who establishes more controls, policies and procedures, and so forth, much to the disdain of the E. Where the E sees only opportunities, the A sees only problems, and they are in conflict with each other. If the A prevails too long in a position of power (PAei) the E may eventually be driven from the organization. The importance of the E Role is depicted in Figure 5.2.

When the E becomes weak, or leaves the organization, the organization loses its creative element and innovation. Without new products as shown in Figure 5.2, the organization begins to age in a negative sense and, unless this trend is reversed, will eventually die.

New Product Adoption Process

Figure 5.3 depicts the traditional view of the Adoption Process of innovation and the categories of those who adopt the new innovation over time, from Innovators, the first to accept the product, to Laggards, the last to accept the new product.

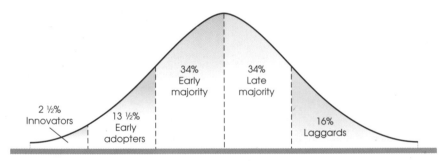

Figure 5.3   Time of Adoption of Innovations*

*Source: From Philip Kotler, *Marketing Management,* 11th ed. (Upper Saddle River, NJ: Pearson Education, Inc., 2003), p. 377, as redrawn from Everett M. Rogers, *Diffusion of Innovation* (New York: The Free Press, 1983). Permission granted by Pearson Education, Inc. (27 August 2008).

The Product and Innovation

To supplement Drucker's views on innovation and close some gaps, it is necessary to become more specific relative to the product itself and what the customer desires in terms of an innovation, drawing on the work of Clayton Christensen. This includes a brief discussion of the product's functionality, reliability and convenience.[37]

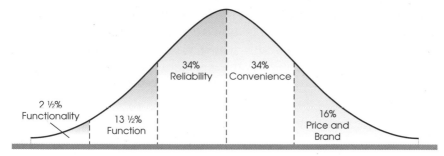

Figure 5.4   Adoption of Innovations, A Needs Satisfaction Perspective
Source: Chart derived and adapted from Clayton Christensen, Innovation and the General Manager (New York: McGraw–Hill Companies, Inc. 1999), p. 135–136.

1. *Functionality:* Product does what it is supposed to do.
2. *Reliability:* Product always does what it is supposed to do.
3. *Convenience:* Product is easy to find (buy) and use.
4. *Price:* Product creates Value vs. Cost.

Based on these new product requirements or customer needs then, the Adoption of Innovation Process can be viewed from a customer needs perspective as depicted in Figure 5.4.

The following is a brief review of the needs satisfied for the various adopters of innovation, from the Early Adopters to the Laggards.

Innovators and Early Adopters

- Need the new product's *functionality*
- Willing to put up with some unreliability and inconvenience
- Better performing products will command a price premium

Early Majority

- Demand for *functionality* has been met
- Need for *reliability*

Late Majority

- Demand for *functionality* and *reliability* have been met
- Need for *convenience*

Laggards

- All other demands satisfied, need for *price*

Table 5.5   Sustaining and Disruptive Technologies[38]

Sustaining Technologies	Disruptive Technologies
Innovations maintain a trajectory of performance improvements that has been established in the market.	Disruptive innovations have different attributes from mainstream customer's value.
Give customers more and better attributes they already value.	Products perform worse in several dimensions of performance that are important to these customers—unable to use.
Example: Help integrated circuits process more information at higher speeds.	Only valued in new low-end markets or applications. Example: Sony and transistor pocket radios.

Sustaining and Disruptive Technologies: Another Source of Innovation

Table 5.5 outlines Christensen's distinction between two classes of innovation, Sustaining and Disruptive Technologies.

The key to identifying Disruptive Technologies is generally their initial poor performance compared to Sustaining Technologies and as such do not appeal to customers who need certain functionality.

Characteristics of Disruptive Technologies   According to Christensen, Disruptive Technologies exhibit the following characteristics:

- *Underperform:* Disruptive Technologies underperform along traditional metrics of functionality compared to products of Sustaining Technologies.
- *Cheaper:* They are less expensive than products of Sustaining Technologies.
- *Simpler and More Convenient to Use:* Generally, Disruptive Technology products are less complicated compared to those of Sustaining Technology products and are more convenient to use.
- *Secure Foothold in Low-End or Emerging Market:* The Disruptive Technology product will enter at the low-end of the market or an emerging market. As an example, Canon's entry into the desk-top copier segment that was ignored by Xerox.
- *Rapid Technological Improvement:* Disruptive Technology products are rapidly improved and eventually made good enough to attack the mainstream market from the underside. Once again, Canon is a good example of moving up into the higher volume copiers to take the market away from Xerox.

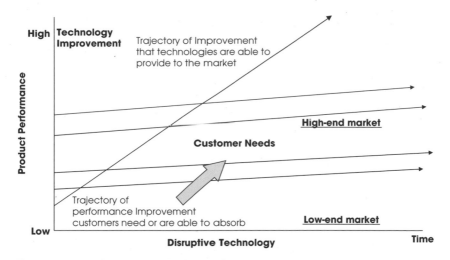

Figure 5.5   Intersecting Trajectories

Source: Chart derived and adapted from Clayton Christensen, *Innovation and the General Manager* (New York: McGraw-Hill Companies, Inc. 1999). p. 7.

Technological Improvement and Customer Needs   How much better does a product have to be to continue to attract customers with the new and improved so and so? Figure 5.5 depicts the Intersecting Trajectories of Technology Improvement, Customer Needs and Disruptive Technology. Typical innovations (product improvements and the largest category of innovative products) follow the Technology Improvement Line over time. This is typically directed at the company's best customers and the high-end market where profit margins are higher: therefore, they are the focus of the organization's innovative efforts and resources.

With respect to customer needs, as can be seen, technological development can eventually exceed what the customer needs or can absorb unless product functionality is missing. For example, Xerox continued to make faster high-volume duplicators with various accessories such as collating, binding, stapling and so forth. As a result, we typically see the trajectory of technological improvement is greater than the trajectory of customer needs as managers push products into higher tiers and higher margins.

Disruptive Technologies address a lower market or a market that is not fully developed as can be seen on Figure 5.5. These are markets that do not need the functionality of products that the high-end market requires. On the other hand, they will have a trajectory to move up. Japanese auto manufacturers also utilized this approach, delivering less expensive, but more fuel efficient autos to the low end of the market and eventually taking the US car market away from the Big Three.

Why We Don't See Impending Threats   Clayton Christensen's views about why companies such as Xerox or the Big Three typically do not see impending threats from Disruptive Technologies (products) supplements Drucker's views of why Entrepreneurial Judo often succeeds as a strategy:

- *Complacency:* Good performance results in complacency—we are doing okay, don't worry.
- *Product Differentiation:* We have superior products—no one can touch us (Xerox and GM).
- *Patent Protection:* We are protected by patents—but competition can get around this (China and intellectual property rights), and they do run out (Xerox and patented drugs).
- *Customer Satisfaction:* Our customers are satisfied. But have we asked recently (surveys), and how about non-customers and those on the other end of the Rate of Adoption Curve?
- *Disruptive Technologies Ignored:* The PC has no memory; it is just a toy (IBM).

Why Disruptive Technologies Are Ignored   Christensen expands on the last reason why Disruptive Technologies (products) are ignored and attributed it to the current business model and processes of companies. Essentially, companies focus on market size and customer needs and therefore invest in the development of higher value-added products to sell at higher profit margins. This leads to the shift in the weighted average of product sales into progressively higher tiers of the market—higher gross margins in higher market tiers versus lower market tiers. This model influences what innovation proposals will be adopted and given resources and which ones will be ignored.

Christensen also attributes the ignoring of Disruptive Technologies to the Voice of the Customer Dilemma. The instinct of good management, as Drucker had stressed, is to listen to and respond to customer needs. As a result, important customers are asked about new ideas and are asked to assess the value of innovative products (focus groups).

Since the company's customers also attempt to stay ahead of their competitors in terms of improving the performance of their products, they continue to demand the highest performance from their suppliers. Christensen concludes that lead customers are reliably accurate in assessing the potential for Sustaining Technologies but are reliably inaccurate for assessing the potential for Disruptive Technologies. In his view, "They are the wrong people to ask."[39]

Nintendo and the Wii   According to Christensen, Nintendo's Wii is an example of a disruptive technology. While Sony and Microsoft focused on the hard-core gamers or, as some have described them, teenage boys with fast thumbs, Nintendo's Wii targeted the non-gamer who found existing video game systems too complicated and time consuming (convenience buyers). Nintendo's strategy was to develop a system that was so easy to use that even video game novices can enjoy game play within minutes. Selling for $250 (also appealing to the Brand and Price buyers) Nintendo cannot make the Wii fast enough to meet demand and is dramatically outperforming the PS3 and Xbox 360.[40]

Innovation and the Drucker Gap   Drucker briefly mentioned Federal Express in *Innovation and Entrepreneurship*. This was in his discussion of sources of innovation attributed to changes in Industry Structure and the slow response of an industry leader to respond to a challenge from an innovator. He commented, "The United States Postal Service did not react for many years to innovators who took away larger and larger chunks of the most profitable service. First, United Parcel Service took away the ordinary parcel post; then Emery Air Freight and Federal Express took away the even more profitable delivery of urgent or high-value merchandise and letters. What made the Postal Service so vulnerable was its rapid growth. Volume grew so fast that it neglected what seemed to be minor categories, and thus practically delivered an invitation to the innovators."[41]

Summary

According to Drucker, there are many strategies to consider when introducing an innovation to the marketplace. Drucker strongly suggested that the innovation should aim at market leadership. The strategies discussed here are targeted to achieve market leadership and dominance or to become a monopoly in a high-profit niche market. The strategy of being the First with the Most potentially offers the highest rewards, but is also the one with the highest risk. According to Drucker, the innovator must be right the first time because there will be no second opportunities, although he failed to provide any examples of this occurring.

Drucker also suggested that one of the best strategies to consider when introducing an innovation is to attack a market that has already been created by someone else with Creative Imitation. Here, however, there is always a risk that the original innovator will develop its own creative imitation and beat the newcomer at its own game.

Many difficult decisions must be made relative to what strategy to select in order to introduce an innovation, but it is critical that the organization continue to innovate.

The key takeaway is Sources of Innovation and in particular, Unexpected Failures. There has to be a tolerance for mistakes and failures in the organization in order to create an entrepreneurial environment where people can take risks.

Drucker's Strategies should be considered when deciding how to position a new product in the marketplace once the opportunity has been identified. Considerably more background from marketing, particularly in the areas of branding, pricing and channel decisions are required to close the Drucker gaps relative to innovation.

Application Tool

The following is one Application Tool that was developed to enable the students to identify potential sources of innovation for their organizations.

Potential Sources of Innovation Matrix

Instructions
1. Review the Potential Sources of Innovation listed in Column One in Table 5.6.
2. Indicate what you have observed relative to each of the Potential Sources of Innovation in Column Two. Is there an opportunity for innovation?
3. Briefly describe what you feel the potential product or service might be to take advantage of this opportunity and source of innovation in Column Three.

Table 5.6 Innovation Matrix

Potential Source of Innovation	What Observed Relative to Source	Potential Product/ Service
Unexpected Success (Own or Competitor)		
Unexpected Failure (Own or Competitor)		
Incongruity: (List Type)		
Process Need		
Changes in Industry & Market Structures		
Demographic Changes		
Changes in Meaning & Perception		
New Knowledge		
"Bright Idea"		

Our company has, indeed, stumbled *onto some of its new products. But never forget that you can only stumble if you're moving.*
                      Richard P. Carlton, former CEO, 3M Corporation

Endnotes

1. Peter F. Drucker, *Innovation & Entrepreneurship* (New York: Harper & Row, 1985), 28.
2. During class at the Claremont Graduate School, Fall 1977.
3. Peter F. Drucker, *Innovation & Entrepreneurship* (New York: Harper & Row, 1985), 21.
4. Ibid., 28.
5. Peter F. Drucker, *The Essential Drucker* (New York: HarperCollins, 2001), 22–23.
6. Reg Jennings, Charles Cox, and Cary L. Cooper, *Business Elites: the Psychology of Entrepreneurs and Intrapreneurs* (London: Routledge, 2004), 37.
7. Peter F. Drucker, *The Essential Drucker* (New York: HarperCollins, 2001), 22.
8. Ibid., 22.
9. Booz, Allen & Hamilton, *New Products Management for the 1980s.* (New York: Booz, Allen & Hamilton, 1982).
10. Peter F. Drucker, *The Essential Drucker* (New York: HarperCollins, 2001), 22.

11. Peter F. Drucker, *Innovation & Entrepreneurship* (New York: Harper & Row, 1985), 35

12. Ibid., 37–56.

13. Ibid., 57–68.

14. Ibid., 57–68.

15. "Edward Jones." Boston: *Harvard Business School* 9-700-009, Rev. June 15, 2000.

16. Peter F. Drucker, *Innovation & Entrepreneurship* (New York: Harper & Row, 1985), 69.

17. Ibid., 73.

18. Ibid., 76.

19. Ibid., 88.

20. Ibid., 99.

21. Ibid., 107.

22. Ibid., 130–132.

23. Ibid., 134–136.

24. Ibid., 136.

25. Ibid., 137–138.

26. Philip Kotler, *Marketing Management*. 11th ed. (Upper Saddle River, NJ: Pearson Education, Inc., 2003), 378.

27. Earnets Gundling, *The 3m Way to Innovation*, (Tokyo: Kondansha International Ltd., 2000), 46.

28. Peter F. Drucker, *Innovation & Entrepreneurship* (New York: Harper & Row, 1985), 136.

29. Ibid., 209–219.

30. Ibid., 220–225.

31. Ibid., 225–232.

32. Ibid., 233–236.

33. Ibid., 236–240.

34. Ibid., 240–242.

35. Ichak Adizes, Ph.D., *Managing Corporate Lifecycles* (Paramus, NJ: Prentice Hall, 1999), 193–217.

36. Ibid., 237–260.

37. Clayton M. Christensen, *Innovation and the General Manager* (New York: McGraw-Hill, 1999), 135–136.

38. Ibid., 8–9.

39. Ibid., 19.

40. Clayton M. Christensen and Scott D. Anthony, "What Should Sony Do Next?" *Forbes.com*, (August 1, 2007).

41. Peter F. Drucker, *Innovation & Entrepreneurship* (New York: Harper & Row, 1985), 86.

Getting Rid of Yesterday

Part One: Peter Drucker's Concept of Planned Abandonment

Introduction

This chapter expands on Drucker's Concept of Planned Abandonment by introducing an additional contributor and a how-to tool in order to apply the concept.

Getting Rid of Yesterday: The First Step in Strategic Thinking and Planning

Peter Drucker had stressed in many of his books that the first step in strategic thinking and planning and developing a vision for the future of the organization must start with "getting rid of yesterday."[1] Too many organizations, Drucker had observed, continue to devote organizational resources in terms of money and people to "preserving the past" when they should be allocated to "creating tomorrow." The first part of this chapter describes Drucker's Concept of Planned Abandonment and how to apply this concept to your organization. The second part of the chapter will present a tool that is useful in applying his concept. Both Drucker's concept and its application will also be illustrated in a two-part case study, "Shanghai Industrial Lubricants."

The Concept of Planned Abandonment [2]

In addition to having a vision for the future, Drucker stressed "that management needs to make a systematic analysis of its present businesses and products. The old that no longer fits the Purpose and Mission of the business, no longer conveys satisfaction to the customer or customers, and no longer makes a superior contribution." He argued that these dying products, services, or processes always demand the greatest care and the greatest efforts and tie down the most productive and ablest people. Drucker recommended that all existing products, services, processes, markets, end users and distribution channels need to be assessed on a regular basis. He also observed that by keeping a declining product, service, market, or process, the new and growing product or market is stunted or neglected. This was illustrated by the case of General Motors which although it had a bright star in the Saturn automobile, continued to commit resources to dying product lines, such as the Oldsmobile, at the expense of really growing the Saturn. This Concept of Planned Abandonment needs to be implemented, Drucker argued, even if the existing but aging product is still making money, as shown in Figure 6.1. Drucker would suggest that in assessing a product in the Decline stage, one should not wait until it is no longer making a profit, but rather consider abandoning it before it reaches that point. The arrow on Figure 6.1 suggests the point in this product's lifecycle where consideration should be given to abandoning it.

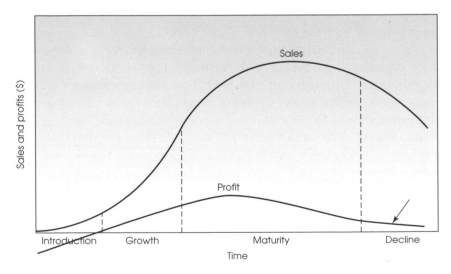

Figure 6.1   Product Life Cycles and Profitability

Source: Chart adopted and modified by R.W. Swaim from philip Kotter *Marketing management*, llthed. (upper Saddle River, N.J: Pearson education, inc,.2003), Figure 11.3, P.328.

Application to Your Organization

Drucker stressed the key questions that need to be asked about the abandonment of old products or services:

1. Are they still viable?
2. Are they likely to remain viable?
3. Do they still give value to the customer?
4. Are they likely to do so tomorrow?
5. Do they still fit the realities of population and markets, of technology and economy?
6. If not, how can we best abandon them—or at least stop pouring in further resources and efforts?[3]

Finally, another important question Drucker suggested management ask is, "If we did not do this already, would we go into it now?" This question pertains more to assessing an industry or a market the organization is presently in and whether this should be abandoned as well. This could also lead to the divesture of a subsidiary. An Industry Attractiveness Assessment Tool is provided in Appendix A to deal with this question.

Planned Abandonment Case Study: Shanghai Industrial Lubricants

The following is a short case study that illustrates both the wrong and righr ways to use Drucker's Concept of Planned Abandonment.

Situation

Shanghai Industrial Lubricants has sales of US$125 million built around five product lines. The company is profitable overall, but two of the product lines have not performed well. In response, the senior management team of the company met to review its product line performance. In preparation for the senior management review, the chief financial officer prepared the profitability summary presented in Table 6.1.

Using this information, the CFO argued:

We are wasting our resources on the Synthetic Oils and Metal Working Coolants product lines. One product line does not make any money (Metal Working Coolants) and the other loses money

(Synthetic Oils). I recommend we drop both product lines and refocus our marketing efforts on the profitable lines. These are dying products and dropping them is in line with Drucker's Concept of Planned Abandonment.

Table 6.1   Shanghai Industrial Lubricants Product Line Profitability

Performance (US$ millions)	Hydr. Oils	Ind. Greases	Comp. Gear Oils	Synth. Oils	Metal Working Coolants	Company Total
Sales Revenues	$60.0	$25.0	$15.0	$10.0	$15.0	$125
Cost of Goods Sold	$37.5	$16.0	$7.5	$8.0	$11.0	$80
Gross Profit	$22.5	$9.0	$7.5	$2.0	$4.0	$45
Operating Expenses	$17.0	$7.0	$4.0	$3.0	$4.0	$35
Net Profit (Before Taxes)	$5.5	$2.0	$3.5	($1.0)	$0.0	$10

Source: Case adopted and modified from Roger Best, *Marketing-Based Management,* 3rd ed. (Upper Saddle River, NJ: Pearson Education, Inc., 2004), pp. 35–39.

Questions

1. Would the CFO's recommendation be a good decision? Why or why not?
2. If the two product lines were dropped, what would the impact be on future net profit? Would it increase or decrease and why?

Conclusions

If you agreed with the CFO in this case, on the surface he appears to be applying Drucker's Concept of Planned Abandonment, and consideration should be given to dropping these two product lines. Theoretically then, net profit before taxes should improve to $11.0 million (dropping a line that breaks even and the other losing $1.0 million).

Both conclusions are *wrong!* Another tool is needed to effectively apply Drucker's concept, which will be presented in Part Two of this chapter.

Part Two: Applying the Concept of Planned Abandonment

Part One of "Getting Rid of Yesterday" reviewed Peter Drucker's Concept of Planned Abandonment. Essentially, Drucker stressed that too often organizations commit resources in the way of money and people to dying or declining products or even businesses. There is a time Drucker suggested, when all products, services, markets and processes of the organization need to be assessed, and if they are no longer viable or contributing to results, they should be abandoned. He also stressed that this should be done even if the product may still be making money: the resources being used to keep it alive should be allocated to tomorrow's opportunities and new products.

The Drucker Gap

As illustrated in the case study, just randomly applying Drucker's concept is not sufficient and may lead to poor business decisions. Additional tools are needed to determine if planned abandonment of a product should be pursued. An excellent tool from marketing can be applied here to support Drucker's concept: the concept of Net Marketing Contribution.

Net Marketing Contribution: A Drucker Planned Abandonment Assessment Tool

Table 6.2 depicts how the company in our case traditionally reports its revenues, expenses and profits. The company's chief financial officer (CFO) recommended implementing Drucker's Concept of Planned Abandonment and abandoning the Synthetic Oils and Metal Working Coolants product lines. We have concluded that this would not be a good decision. We will now explain why another tool, called Net Marketing Contribution (NMC), would be useful in further assessing if these product lines should be abandoned and how we reached that conclusion. The NMC concept was put forth by Roger Best in *Market-Based Management* and helps to apply Drucker's concept.[4]

Table 6.2   Shanghai Industrial Lubricants Product Line Profitability

Performance (US$ millions)	Hydr. Oils	Ind. Greases	Comp. Gear Oils	Synth. Oils	Metal Working Coolants	Company Total
Sales Revenues	$60.0	$25.0	$15.0	$10.0	$15.0	$125
Cost of Goods Sold	$37.5	$16.0	$7.5	$8.0	$11.0	$80
Gross Profit	$22.5	$9.0	$7.5	$2.0	$4.0	$45
Operating Expenses	$17.0	$7.0	$4.0	$3.0	$4.0	$35
Net Profit (Before Taxes)	$5.5	$2.0	$3.5	($1.0)	$0.0	$10

Source: Case adopted and modified from Roger Best, *Marketing-Based Management*, 3rd ed. (Upper Saddle River, NJ: Pearson Education, Inc., 2004), pp. 35–39.

Another Look at Expenses

Column One in Table 6.3 below classifies a business's expenses into three major categories: *Cost of Goods Sold, Marketing and Sales Expenses,* and *Operating Expenses.* Column Two describes what type of expenses are included under these categories.

Table 6.3   Cost of Goods Sold, Marketing Expense and Operating Expenses

Cost of Goods Sold	**The total cost of producing a product varies with the volume sold**
Variable Cost	Includes purchase materials, direct labor, packaging, transportation costs, and any other costs associated with making and shipping a product.
Manufacturing Overhead	This is an allocated cost based on use of the fixed manufacturing plant, equipment and other fixed expenses needed to run the production operation.
Marketing & Sales Expense*	**A direct expense that varies with marketing strategy.**
Marketing Management	Expenses associated with marketing management and resources needed to support this function.

Sales, Service, & Support	Expenses associated with the sales force, customer service and technical and administrative support services.
Advertising & Promotion	All expenses associated with the marketing communications budget.
Operating Expenses	**Indirect expenses that do not vary with the marketing strategy**
Research & Development	Expenses for developing new products and/or improving old products.
Corporate Overhead	Overhead expenses for corporate staff, legal counsel, professional services, corporate advertising, and the salaries of senior management and their staff.

* Marketing & Sales Expenses are traditionally part of Sales, General & Administrative (SG&A) in most income statements.

Source: Roger Best, *Marketing-Based Management*, 3rd ed. (Upper Saddle River, NJ: Pearson Education, Inc., 2004), p. 36.

Net Marketing Contribution (NMC)

Net Marketing Contribution allows us to measure more closely the elements of profitability and marketing profitability of a product line or business unit and assists us in determining whether Drucker's Concept of Planned Abandonment should be applied to a possible declining product or business unit. To illustrate how this is applied, let's return to the Shanghai Industrial Lubricants Case and review the Synthetic Oils product line from the traditional approach and then from the NMC approach. Using the traditional approach that the CFO used, we see that this product line lost $1 million before taxes as shown in Figure 6.2.

Figure 6.2   Traditional Approach

Net Profits before Taxes = Sales — Cost of — Operating
(Synthetic Oils)   Revenues   Goods Sold   Expenses

= $10 million — $8 million — $3 million

= $1 million

To understand marketing profitability and how it contributes to a business's profits, we need to isolate marketing and sales expense. Assume that of the total operating expenses for Synthetic Oils of $3 million, the marketing and sales expenses were $1 million. Using the

NMC approach and breaking out marketing and sales expenses from the operating expenses, we can calculate the NMC as shown in Figure 6.3.

Figure 6.3   NMC Approach

Net Profits before Taxes (Synthetic Oils)	= Sales Revenues	—	Cost of Goods Sold	—	Marketing & Sales Expenses	—	Other Operating Expenses

−$1 million = | $10 million − $8 million − $1 million | − $2 million

−$1 million = $1 million   − $2 million
                Net Marketing   Other Operating
                Contribution   Expenses

NMC is determined by deducting marketing and sales expenses from gross profit (sales revenues minus cost of goods sold) as shown in Figure 6.3. Here we see that the NMC for Synthetic Oils is a positive $1 million. By breaking out marketing and sales expenses for each product line, we can then calculate NMC for each of Shanghai Industrial Lubricants' products as depicted in Table 6.4.

Table 6.4   Product Line: Net Marketing Contribution

Performance (US$ millions)	Hydr. Oils	Ind. Greases	Comp. Gear Oils	Synth. Oils	Metal Working Coolants	Company Total
Sales Revenues	$60.0	$25.0	$15.0	$10.0	$15.0	$125
Cost of Goods Sold	$37.5	$16.0	$7.5	$8.0	$11.0	$80
Gross Profit	$22.5	$9.0	$7.5	$2.0	$4.0	$45
Marketing & Sales Expense	$7.0	$3.0	$2.0	$1.0	$2.0	$15

Table 6.4 (*Continued*)

Performance (US$ millions)	Hydr. Oils	Ind. Greases	Comp. Gear Oils	Synth. Oils	Metal Working Coolants	Company Total
Net Marketing Contribution	$15.5	$6.0	$5.5	$1.0	$2.0	$30
Operating Expenses	$10.0	$4.0	$2.0	$2.0	$2.0	$20
Net Profit (Before Taxes)	$5.5	$2.0	$3.5	($1.0)	$0.0	$10

Should We Abandon Synthetic Oils and Metal Working Lubricants?

Using the Net Marketing Contribution concept, we can then calculate the impact on Shanghai Industrial Lubricant's net profits if the two product lines were abandoned as shown in Table 6.5.

Table 6.5   Product Line: Net Marketing Contribution Excluding Synthetic Oils and Metal Working Coolants

Performance (US$ millions)	Hydr. Oils	Ind. Greases	Comp. Gear Oils	Synth. Oils	Metal Working Coolants	Company Total
Sales Revenues	$60.0	$25.0	$15.0			$100
Cost of Goods Sold	$37.5	$16.0	$7.5			$61
Gross Profit	$22.5	$9.0	$7.5			$39
Marketing & Sales Expense	$7.0	$3.0	$2.0			$12
Net Marketing Contribution	$15.5	$6.0	$5.5			$27
Operating Expenses	$11.4	$5.3	$3.3	< $2.0	< $2.0	$20
Net Profit (Before Taxes)	$4.1	$0.7	$2.2			$7

Note: $4 million of operating expenses from Synthetic Oils and Metal Working Coolants were allocated one-third each to the remaining product lines: Hydraulic Oils—$1.4 million; Industrial Greases—$1.3 million; and Compounded Gear Oils—$1.3 million.

Case Study Conclusions

1. Each product line is making a positive Net Marketing Contribution (see Table 6.4.)
2. Operating expenses will not change with the elimination of the Synthetic Oils and Metal Working Coolants product lines. The CEO and his staff still need to be paid as well as other operating expenses (see Table 6.5.)
3. There could possibly be some reduction in operating expenses if these two lines were produced in separate facilities and were closed and sold off, but not all Shanghai Industrial Lubricants' operating expenses will go away. They need to be allocated somewhere.
4. Elimination of the two product lines would reduce sales by $25 million, but would reduce the Net Profits of the company from $10 million to $7 million by the elimination of their Net Marketing Contribution (see Tables 6.4 and 6.5.)
5. Drucker's Concept of Planned Abandonment should *not* be applied to these two products.

Summary

In Part One, we learned about Drucker's Concept of Planned Abandonment (*what* to do) and the importance of applying this concept in assessing existing products, services, markets, processes and business units. The objective is to stop, or reduce, committing resources *to yesterday* and channel them into future opportunities for *tomorrow's* growth. Part Two presented a tool, Net Marketing Contribution, to help apply Drucker's concept to determine if abandonment of a particular product or business unit would be a good business decision (the *how* to do it.)

Application

To apply the Concept of Planned Abandonment in your organization:

1. Schedule a special time with your key management staff, and develop a list of potential products, services, markets, processes, business units, etc., that may be in the declining stages of their lifecycle.

2. Answer the key questions Drucker suggested as outlined in Part One of this chapter.
3. For the products under review, do a further analysis by using the NMC tool. If you come up with a negative NMC, you know what you have to do—*get rid of yesterday.*

Endnotes

1. Peter F. Drucker, *Management: Tasks, Responsibilities, Practices* (New York: Harper & Row, 1973), 93–94.
2. Peter F. Drucker, *Managing for Results* (London: William Heinemann Ltd., 1964), 166–167.
3. Peter F. Drucker, *Management: Tasks, Responsibilities, Practices* (New York: Harper & Row, 1973), 93–94.
4. Roger J. Best, *Market-Based Management*, 3rd ed. (Upper Saddle River, NJ: Pearson Education, Inc., 2004), 39–41.

External Growth Strategies

DRUCKER'S RULES FOR MERGERS AND ACQUISITIONS AND STRATEGIC ALLIANCES

The proportion of acquisitions that turn out to be expensive mistakes or at least disappointments, is substantial. I would put it close to 50 percent.[1]

Introduction

Earlier chapters addressed Drucker's and others' views on how to grow organically through sales, marketing and innovation. This chapter will deal with growing externally through mergers and acquisitions and other strategic alliances, both formal and informal. As a personal note, I spent over 20 years in the mergers and acquisitions field, including running my own M&A firm, mostly as an intermediary on the sell side, either assisting private business owners in selling their businesses, selling to management and employees through Employee Stock Ownership Plans (ESOPs), or raising capital for growth. My firm also provided M&A integration planning services, an often overlooked critical step in the acquisition process several decades prior to its becoming a more popular topic among human resources professionals. I was first introduced to mergers and acquisitions in the early 1980s when, as the director of organizational development for Occidental Petroleum Corporation's E&P Company (Oxy), I was charged with the responsibility of planning and overseeing the integration of Oxy's E&P Group with the Cities Service Company's E&P Group. This was the second-largest acquisition in US history at the time and the largest leveraged buyout (LBO) at $4.0 billion. I retained Peter Drucker as a consultant to assist me on this task; however, in planning the integration we did not have the benefit of Drucker's Rules for Mergers and Acquisitions, which will be covered in this chapter.

The first part of this chapter is also based on an article I wrote for *Business Beijing* magazine a number of years ago that presents a review of Drucker's Rules[2] and provides some background information on mergers and acquisitions, and why they generally are not successful (in fact, research suggests that between 50 and 80 percent are financial failures). Although there are considerable references to China again, the concepts presented here are applicable to deals being done anywhere.

The second part of this chapter deals with both informal and formal strategic alliances in what I have entitled the Spectrum of Alliances and also includes Drucker's Rules for Strategic Alliances. In both parts of this chapter I have included considerable background information on mergers and acquisitions to supplement Drucker's Rules. This chapter therefore deviates from earlier chapters, in that it establishes a foundation relative to the topic of mergers and acquisitions prior to reviewing Drucker's insight.

This foundation briefly covers how to classify various M&A deals in terms of their growth strategies and some of the mechanics and process of doing deals.

Part One: Mergers and Acquisitions

Mergers versus Acquisitions Defined

As a point of clarification, there are actually very few mergers. Most are acquisitions. As an example, let's imagine that a company with $1 billion in revenues acquires another company with revenues of $100 million. For the wealthier company, the deal is an acquisition. For the less wealthy firm, it's a merger. How so? Simply, it's more of a psychological issue in terms of describing the transaction, since few managers and employees in the smaller company want to admit that they have been acquired—that is, taken over as though they were performing poorly or in trouble. Hence their perception of the deal was a merger. This attitude also creates negative reactions in the smaller company, and more times than not contributes to the eventual failure of the new business combination, as I will attempt to explain. The term *M&A* then generally refers to acquisitions, not mergers although the term tends to be used interchangeably.

Classification of Types of Mergers and Acquisitions

If we can classify mergers and acquisitions by type, we can identify why the deal is being done, what is motivating the transaction, and how it contributes to a growth strategy. Table 7.1 depicts the major M&A classifications and their motivation.

Vertical M&A: There are two types of Vertical M&As, Backward and Forward. Backward is acquiring a firm that the business had a supplier relationship with. This is essentially motivated by the need to guarantee a source of supply such as raw materials used in the manufacturing process as well as lower materials costs. As an example, a Chinese steel company acquiring an Australian iron ore mining company. The obvious disadvantage is selling the excess capacity in the event market conditions change and the demand for the manufacturer's product (for instance, steel) declines. A Forward M&A is acquiring a firm that the business had a distribution relationship with, motivated by the need to lower marketing and channel costs as well as get closer to customers to better understand their needs.

Horizontal M&A: The two most common horizontal acquisitions are acquiring a firm that has a comparable product, or a product extension. The second is expanding geographically into a new market. Both acquisitions add to the business's growth strategy. These

Table 7.1   M&A Classification

Classification	Motivation & Growth Strategy
Vertical	Backward (relationship with supplier)
	Forward (closer to customer)
Horizontal	Product Extension
	Market Extension
	Diversification
Conglomerate	Financial Strategy
Hostile Takeover	Dominate Industry or Capture a Customer
	Eliminate a Competitor

are the types of acquisitions that relate to Drucker's saying, "It is cheaper to buy than to build." These types of acquisitions could also be part of a diversification strategy, acquiring a business in a related or different industry. Several examples of horizontal deals that were completed in China include a number of multinational beer companies (SABMiller, InBev, Anheuser Busch) acquiring local Chinese brewers to gain access to the Chinese market. In the home appliance industry, Best Buy, one of the larger big box firms in the United States also entered China through an acquisition of a Chinese appliance firm, China Paradise in 2006.

Conglomerate: These are acquisitions made essentially for financial reasons with no relationship to the other companies in the business's portfolio. Each business is run as a separate entity with the requirement that a strong management team be in place, since the executives of the holding company cannot be experts or have experience in all aspects of the business. GE is one example, being involved in financial services, jet engines, medical diagnostic equipment, and a host of other businesses.

Hostile Takeovers: These are generally rare and can only occur if the target is a publicly traded company—it is impossible to take over a privately owned firm. Hostile takeovers are motivated by growth strategies that seek to dominate an industry, capture a large customer, or eliminate a major competitor.

M&A Failure Rate

History shows that between 50 and 80 percent of all mergers and acquisitions will be financial disappointments.[3] Studies by leading academic and business research institutions that have analyzed M&A performance over several decades have concluded that there will be:

- Lower productivity in the acquired company due to reduced management and employee commitment.
- Increased conflict arising from insensitivity to differing cultures and management and leadership styles.
- Loss of key management and staff, usually within six to 12 months after the transaction has been completed.
- An erosion of customer base and market share.
- It is also a fact that one-third of all acquired companies are sold off within five years, and that as many as 90 percent of all mergers fail to live up to expectations.

Failures: The Reasons

Many factors contribute to the high failure rate:

1. Inadequate evaluation of the compatibility of the acquired company in terms of style, structure and business practices.
2. The fact that top management does not have adequate time to plan in the period after the transaction is closed.
3. Managers (in the acquiring company) underestimate the negative reactions to being acquired because these are usually not openly expressed.
4. In an effort to reassure employees of the acquired company, the new management often says, "Nothing will change" or "There will be no changes in management." Statements of this nature immediately undermine the credibility of the acquiring company's management.
5. Management does not appreciate how much effort is needed to gain credibility with the people in the acquired company.
6. Commitments are made that subsequently are not honored, thus undermining confidence in the new management.
7. The transition period is too lengthy, and because decisions are not made quickly, the negative reactions in the acquired firm become the dominant force. Typically, this is caused by the failure to define a "Mission" and "Vision" for the new business combination, thus not providing a direction for managers and employees to follow.
8. The transition manager or transition team cannot gain access to objective information and are thus forced to make decisions based on misleading or inadequate information.
9. Management in the acquiring firm is inclined to try to assimilate the new subsidiary into the established way of working, rather than adapting to and recognizing the merits and values of the acquired firm's culture.
10. The assessment of people chosen to hold key positions in the new combined organization is biased toward managers and employees of the acquiring company rather than based on objective analysis of position requirements and the talents available in both companies. An all-too-common attitude is: "My people are smarter than your people—otherwise, your company would have bought us."

Many of these issues can be prevented through proper merger integration planning and important questions need to be asked before making the acquisition. Drucker provided some excellent insight in this area.

Drucker's Rules for Mergers and Acquisitions

The merger boom of the last few years (1980s) is not based on business reasons. It is financial manipulation, pure and simple. But an acquisition must make business sense, or it does not work even as a financial move. It leads to both business and financial failure.[4]

Drucker said this in 1986 and it is just as applicable today. He listed the rules that should be followed and the key questions to be asked before an organization makes an acquisition. Initially, he had listed five rules in *The Frontiers of Management* and then added a sixth to an online program for Corpedia a training company that had an agreement with Drucker to convert some of his works into on-line training programs.

Rule One: Acquisitions Should be Based on Business, Not Financial, Strategy

According to Drucker, "acquisitions based on financial strategies are more or less doomed to failure."[5] Without a business strategy, the acquiring firm does not know what to do with the company it bought. Successful acquisitions are based upon business plans, not financial analysis. Drucker cited GE Capital as one of the more successful companies that expanded through acquisitions that were mainly based on business strategy. It should be noted, however, that although companies that are considering an acquisition as part of their growth strategy should base this decision on business strategy; private equity groups, which represent a significant number of the acquisitions taking place, are usually based on financial strategy. They will acquire or invest in a company that meets their investment criteria, is synergistic with their other portfolio companies, attempt to increase value perhaps through add-on acquisitions, and use an IPO or sale to another buyer as their exit strategy. This typically takes place over a period of five to seven years as they are not in it for the long haul as strategic buyers would be.

Rule Two: What the Acquirer Should Contribute

Because we are not competent to manage our own business, we better go into another one of which we know even less.[6]

This quote was specifically directed at making an acquisition to diversify, which according to Drucker would fail if the objective was to cure a weakness on the part of the acquiring company. He commented, "The successful acquisition is based on what the acquirer contributes to the acquisition, not the reverse. It has to be more than money, something that gives the acquired business a new potential of performance. This contribution needs to be thought through, and planned for, before the actual acquisition takes place. It has to become fact fairly quickly."[7] Drucker cited the acquisition of Citibank by Travelers as a good example of this rule, with Travelers adding more services than Citi had as a traditional bank. He also cited the acquisition of Chrysler by Daimler-Benz as another good example of applying this rule with what he considered to be Daimler-Benz's contribution of a "tremendous distribution capacity in the world's only growth markets for motor cars: Asia, especially South Asia, and Latin America."[8] Somehow this contribution fell through the cracks for other reasons as Daimler-Benz sold off Chrysler to a private equity group in 2007 and actually helped finance the transaction when credit for big deals dried up.

Rule Three: Common Core of Unity

Drucker's Third Rule states that the successful acquisition requires a common core of unity between the acquiring and acquired company. They have to have something in common, and it has to be an area in which both parties have high competence. It must also be truly important to the business of each, and a core competence. Drucker cited having common technologies, markets and customers, research and development, and so forth. He felt this was important to create a common language in order to understand each other and communicate. Drucker added, "We talk a good deal these days of a company's culture. A core of unity is a common culture."[9]

Rule Four: Respect the Business, Products, Customers, and Values

The acquiring company must respect the business of its acquired counterpart. No acquisition is likely to work unless people in the acquiring company believe in the business they take over. They must believe that it makes a contribution and, equally, have respect for its products, markets and its customers. The acquisition must be a "temperamental fit." Drucker cited pharmaceutical companies' acquisitions of cosmetic companies as a strategy to diversify that proved to be largely unsuccessful because it violates this rule. According to Drucker, "Pharmacologists and biochemists are 'serious' people concerned about health and disease. Lipsticks and lipstick users are frivolous to them."[10]

Rule Five: Provide Top Management

Drucker felt that an acquisition is unlikely to do well unless the acquiring company is able and prepared to provide the acquired company with new top management within one year at most. In many acquisitions, the acquirer is attracted to the purchase because the acquisition has such good management. The acquirer believes this management will be there and will continue to run the company, only to quickly discover that these highly regarded people are quitting—even if the reward for staying on is made very profitable for them. One reason why top management of the acquired business quits is that they were used to being the boss; now they find themselves to be mere "division managers" or the like. Drucker added, "If they were owners or part-owners, the merger has made them so wealthy they don't have to stay if they don't enjoy it."[11]

He went on to say in his updated version of the Rules: "Actually, the management of the acquired business should not stay as a rule, no matter how competent they are. This applies particularly to a CEO who originally built the company."[12] To this person, the business is still very much his child. The moment it becomes owned by someone else invariably makes him protective and will see him defending the child against one of those unfeeling interlopers who now own the company. Inevitably, a good many acquirers have learned that it is cheaper to pay these people to leave the company, no matter how good they are, rather than to have to fight with them for control.

On the other hand, if this is a company in which a private equity group has made an investment and taken a large equity stake in the company, they will want a good management team to remain in place and generally will provide employment contracts and other incentives to retain them. Drucker's Rules did not take into account the various types of buyers and investors that comprise today's M&A transaction environment. Once again, this will vary depending on the type of buyer or investor and their objectives. Also, how much integration and consolidation will take place will have an impact on the requirements for management continuity or redundancies.

Rule Six: Promote Across Lines

Drucker suggested that within the first few months following the acquisition, a number of people on both sides should be promoted to better jobs across lines—from one of the former companies to the other.[13] The rationale here according to Drucker is to demonstrate that there are opportunities for advancement, regardless of what company the employee is in, and to avoid the "my people are smarter than your people" syndrome. Without seeing the new business combination as an opportunity, key and the best performing people will soon exit the organization, usually to join your competitors. This is essentially the policy we adopted in the integration of Oxy and Cities with Cities management given responsibility for Domestic Operations and Research and Development even though Oxy was the acquiring company. It is important to point out that it was necessary to develop a common evaluation system across both companies and then select the most qualified people for key positions from either company.

Additional Drucker Insight

Drucker also suggested that an acquirer asks some probing questions prior to making an acquisition:

- Why are we doing this?
- Does the acquisition fit with our Mission, Vision, and Strategy?
- What do we contribute to the business combination?
- Do we know anything about the business?
- Is this an industry we should be in? Is it growing, stable or declining?
- What would we do with our resources if we did not acquire this company?

Additional Views from the Pundits and the Drucker Gap

Drucker did not devote much ink to the topic of mergers and acquisitions. Since M&A activity has been increasing in the Asia-Pacific region and China, it was necessary to add more content in our Drucker Programs to better prepare our students, particularly those in state-owned enterprises and fragmented industries that are undergoing consolidation in China. This included a more comprehensive review of how to buy and sell businesses and other aspects of doing transactions. Table 7.2 depicts the key questions organizations need to answer when considering making an acquisition. These topics were then addressed in a Drucker MBA course on M&A.

Acquisition Motivation Factors

Why Buy and the Strategy   Drucker's first rule of making the acquisition based on business strategy and his follow-up question, "Why are we doing this?" need to be expanded on. The key here is this: Does an acquisition fit a company's growth strategy?

Who and Where to Buy?   Once it is determined how an acquisition fits with the business's strategy, target criteria need to be developed in terms of the ideal acquisition candidate. Where should they be located if this is a market expansion what size should they be in terms of revenues, profits, employees and other criteria? The next step involves developing a list of target companies that meet the criteria by performing an acquisition search. The targets then have to be

Table 7.2   Buying a Business: Key Questions

Key Questions	Topics Covered in Programs
Why Buy?	Acquisition Motivation Factors
Who and Where to Buy?	Establish Target Criteria
What to Buy?	Asset or Stock Purchase
How Much to Pay?	Business Valuation Approaches
How to Pay?	Cash, Stock, Combination, Other
When to Pay?	Now, Installments, Earn-out
What Approvals Are Required?	Government and Province M&A Laws
What to Do With It?	M&A Integration

screened to determine which ones are willing to sell, particularly if they are privately held firms.

What to Buy? Assets versus Stock   What to buy? This may sound like a redundant question but differs from "who" we are going to buy in terms of how the deal is to be structured. Generally, the seller prefers to sell stock while the buyer prefers to buy assets. The advantage to the seller in selling stock is that the buyer acquires the entire business including all assets and liabilities. The buyer on the other hand may only desire to acquire certain assets and assume a limited amount of liabilities. A major reason for only acquiring assets and certain liabilities is to avoid "contingent liabilities," or liabilities or events that are unknown now but could occur in the future. The classic example of this was Occidental Petroleum's acquisition of Niagara Falls, New York-based Hooker Chemical which had been discharging hazardous chemical waste into the Love Canal for decades prior to Oxy's acquisition until the Environmental Protection Agency (EPA) mandated it stop. The canal was eventually filled in with dirt, burying the hazardous chemicals and the land was later donated by Hooker to the City of Niagara Falls. The city subsequently sold the land to a developer who built a housing tract on the property. Several decades later the families and residents of these homes became seriously ill, miscarriages were higher than normal, children were born with birth defects, cancer rates increased compared to other areas, and so on. An investigation concluded that the illnesses were being caused by the seepage of the hazardous chemical waste into the basements of the homes. After years of litigation the home owners were awarded extensive damages that Oxy had to pay, including the provision of new homes, even though the problem had been created by Hooker decades prior to Oxy's acquisition. The total damages Oxy had to pay for this contingent liability exceeded the original cost to acquire Hooker.

How Much to Pay, How to Pay, and When to Pay?   How much to pay involves determining the fair market value of the business or using other financial criteria the firm may use in assessing investments. How to pay involves determining if cash, company stock, notes, and so on, or a combination, will be used to pay for the acquisition. When to pay involves paying for the entire acquisition at closing, paying over time in installments, or structuring an "earn-out." The earn-out involves paying the seller a certain amount of the purchase price now and then paying a bonus based on the achievement of mutually agreed-to performance objectives. This is a good technique to keep the owner active in the business for a period of time, generally one to two years versus leaving with all of his money the day the deal closes. All of these issues obviously have to be negotiated with the seller.

M&A Integration Planning

In addition to following Drucker's Rules in asking the key questions outlined before an acquisition is made, it is necessary to have a well-thought-out merger integration plan in advance of the deal's closing. This is extremely important and can help to greatly reduce the 50 to 80 percent failure rate that has haunted past mergers and acquisitions.

The Objectives of the Integration Plan are to:

1. Develop an effective communications strategy announcing the formation of the new entity to the company's management and employees as well as important constituencies in the company's external environment (customers, suppliers, trade associations, the financial community and other important relationships). This should include the development of a Mission and Vision Statement for the new business combination.
2. Allow for an orderly integration of the companies that is least disruptive and ensures continuity of operations. Allows people to focus on new performance objectives.
3. Reduce uncertainty, maintain employee morale and prevent the loss of key management and staff. Timely and accurate communications can reduce rumours and build confidence and trust in new management.
4. Allow the new entity to quickly take advantage of identified "*Synergistic Opportunities*" which will reduce costs, improve operating efficiency, increase market share, and increase profitability and share value.
5. Identify external resources that may be required to implement various elements of the Plan (inventory management and logistics specialist, computer systems specialist, employee benefits specialists, etc.).

The plan should be jointly developed by senior management and key staff from both the acquiring and selling companies and address the following key areas:

1. *Acquisition/Merger Motivation Factors* – What factors are motivating this merger? It is important for everyone to understand why the deal is being done.
2. *Expectations* – What are the short term, intermediate, and long term expectations for the new business combination? Factors assessed should include the organization's mission and goals, management, human resources, structure, technology and the performance of work as well as key functional areas such sales and marketing and the external environment.
3. *Opportunity Analysis* – What are the opportunities in order of their relative importance to capitalize on as a result of the new business combination?
4. *Preliminary Mission Statement* – A statement of the purpose, philosophy, values, and beliefs of the new business combination.
5. *Goals/Milestones and Obstacles* – Establish preliminary performance goals for the new business combination and how they will be measured. Identifies obstacles that may hinder goal attainment.
6. *Management and Key Staff Assessment* – Assessment of each company's management and key staff and their potential roles in the new business combination. Complies with Drucker's Rule of selecting the most qualified people form either company for key positions.
7. *Comparative Team Analysis* – A comparison of the new business combination relative to competition. Once again, how to take advantage of the combined strengths (core competencies) of the new business combination versus major competitors.
8. *Redundancies* – How redundancies will be handled in terms of assessment, compensation, support in securing other employment, such as interviewing skills training, resume preparation, mailing and phone services, and "staying bonuses" for those that may be required to stay for a specified period of time to assist in the integration of their function.

Selling a Business or Divesting a Subsidiary

Selling a business or divesting a subsidiary that might be a part of implementing Drucker's Concept of Planned Abandonment, such as the strategy Jack Welch used at GE, is a classic example of Drucker advocating *what* to do, but requiring us to go beyond Drucker in learning *how* to do this. Since state–owned enterprises in China are also attempting to privatize or sell off various businesses and assets it was therefore important to address the process of selling a business or business unit in the Drucker MBA course. Table 7.3 depicts the key questions that organizations or private business owners need to ask when contemplating the sale of their business.

The following is a brief discussion of some of the "key questions" that are outlined in Table 7.3 and were addressed in the Drucker M&A Course. Selling a small privately owned business differs somewhat from selling a subsidiary of a larger public company. As such, this chapter will treat the discussion of the Selling Process from the latter perspective and as a component of implementing Drucker's Planned Abandonment.

Why Sell? "The business no longer fits our strategy," is a quote often seen in the business pages when a company reports it is spinning off a subsidiary or a piece of its business. This can be attributed to the company possibly implementing Drucker's Planned

Table 7.3   Selling a Business: Key Questions

Key Questions	Topics Covered in Programs
1. Why Sell?	Seller's Motivation Factors
2. Is This a Good Time to Sell?	Deal Activity (Buyers & Sellers) Macro and Micro Economy
3. Whom to Sell to?	Establish Buyer/Investor Criteria
4. What to Sell?	Assets vs. Stock Sale
5. Selling Price?	Business Valuation Approaches
6. How to Get Paid?	Cash, Stock, Combination, Other
7. When to Get Paid?	Now, Installment, Earn-Out
8. What Approvals Are Required?	Government and Province M&A Laws
9. What to Do Next?	Willing to Stay With Business or Leave

Abandonment Concept. On the other hand, if this was an acquisition the company made in the last five years, it also suggests it did a poor job of integrating the acquisition, it has been a financial disappointment, and as such, is being sold off. In fact, research has shown that approximately one-third of acquisitions will be sold off again within five years.

Is This a Good Time to Sell? Micro and macro economic factors obviously must be considered, particularly with respect to the availability of debt and equity financing. Are there more buyers than sellers, and what is the deal environment like?

Whom to Sell to in Order to Maximize Value (Selling Price)? How would the subsidiary fit with the strategy of possible buyers? As an example, would this be a synergistic fit and comply with Drucker's Rules from the buyer's perspective? If this is part of a Planned Abandonment strategy, the possibility of maximizing the selling price would not be good. Most likely, there might have been too much "harvesting" taking place before deciding to sell, creating an aging organization with questionable value.

First Rule of M&A

With respect to maximizing value, the first rule of M&A is that the first person to mention a number loses. As an example, I once read an article that said, "the company has retained Goldman Sachs as its investment banker and hopes to receive $2 billion for the subsidiary." Having now established a ceiling on the selling price why would a prospective buyer offer any more for the business?

China and Global Mergers and Acquisitions

A more comprehensive discussion was added to our programs that dealt with the increasing trend of Chinese companies buying foreign companies. Starting in 2004, there were a number of high-profile deals including Lenovo's successful acquisition of IBM's PC business and the unsuccessful attempt of the Chinese National Offshore Oil Company's (CNOOC) to acquire the Union Oil Company of California (Unocal). This was added to allow the participants to analyze why the deal was so strongly opposed in the US Congress and how it might have been completed by better pre-acquisition planning and anticipating these objections as well as possibly using a different deal structure (asset versus stock deal).

Part One Summary

The key takeaway for this part should be to think through Drucker's Rules prior to making your next acquisition and also answer the key question: Why are we doing this—is it for business or financial reasons?

Don't make acquisitions because they are there; make them because they are right.[14]

A Deal Isn't a Deal Until You Get the Money

While Drucker and I worked on the Oxy-Cities integration project, he shared a story with me about one of his first M&A assignments.

One of Drucker's first jobs after he left Germany in 1933 was with an investment bank in London. He was given an assignment to go to Argentina and negotiate the sale of a railroad that the British owned and sell it to the Argentina government. After he got there, Drucker inspected the railroad and found it to be in terrible condition and in need of considerable repair. "It was mostly rust," he commented. He then added that he negotiated with the government for several days and finally arrived at a price for the railroad. "I got back to the hotel and really felt bad."

"Why was that?" I asked.

"Because the price I negotiated was outrageously high considering what the railroad was actually worth," he replied. "But then, when I got back on the boat to London, half way to London I felt much better," he added.

"Why was that, Peter?" I asked.

"Because I realized the Argentina government was never going to pay the British anyway," and he smiled.

I happened to meet with a friend from Argentina several years ago and he confirmed that the British was not paid for the railroad.[15]

Part Two: The Strategic Alliance Spectrum and Drucker's Rules for Alliances

Introduction

Companies throughout the world including those in or attempting to enter China have been forming strategic alliances with other companies and organizations, such as universities, for a number of reasons. This Part will briefly review the types of alliances that are formed or the "Spectrum of Alliances," from informal-non-equity alliances, to the more formal-equity alliances, and the reasons for these alliances. The most formal of alliances, mergers and acquisitions, was covered in Part One. There, I commented, however, that between 50 to 80 percent of all mergers and acquisitions fail, and the potential for failure is also the case with other forms of alliances. Therefore, just as the Part One reviewed Drucker's Rules for Mergers and Acquisitions, Part Two will also address Drucker's Rules for Alliances and how to make them more successful. First, it will be helpful to briefly review the types of alliances Drucker suggested organizations can enter into.[16]

Non-Equity (Partnership) and Equity Alliances (Ownership)

Alliances fall into two major categories: *non-equity* and *equity* alliances. "Non-equity" means that little or no money is contributed by either partner when forming the alliance. It is a form of a partnership where there are no ownership rights to the alliance. "Equity" means that the parties to the alliance have contributed some resources in the form of capital, technology, or management expertise, and there are ownership rights to the alliance.

The Spectrum of Alliances and Time, Cost and Risk

Alliances can also be described as comprising a Spectrum of Alliances from a three-dimensional perspective; of *time, cost* and *risk*. Time deals with the length of the alliance, from a short marketing agreement to the hopefully long-term merger or acquisition. Cost deals with what it costs to enter into the relationship—as well as what it costs to get out of it if things do not work out. Risk deals with the type of alliance, from informal non-equity to formal equity alliances, and the risk of their not achieving each or one of the party's objectives

The following is a brief discussion of each of these alliances and the reasons or objectives of the partners who enter into them. We might also substitute "agreements" for these alliances so as to better understand the relationship.

Informal Non-Equity Alliances (Partnership Agreements)

These alliances include: *marketing and distribution agreements, original equipment manufacturing (OEM), agreements* and *private label agreements* (see Figure 7.1.) The Spectrum of Alliances positions these alliances on the spectrum of time, cost and risk.

Distribution and Marketing Agreements   Assume that a manufacturer in Shanghai desires to sell its products in Xi'an. One alternative is that the manufacturer can open up a sales office there, hire and train sales people, and start developing customers for its products—a long and expensive process. The other alternative is to find a local distributor who will stock and sell its products with its own sales force and enter into a distribution agreement. No equity or money is

Spectrum of Alliances

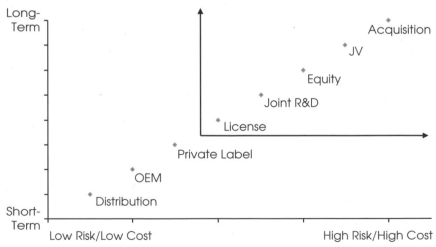

Figure 7.1 The Spectrum of Alliances

involved. The distributor agrees to buy the manufacturer's products, carry a local inventory and sell them to customers in the Xi'an area. In return, the manufacturer may give the distributor an exclusive right (no other distributors will be used by the manufacturer) to sell its products in Xi'an. The length of time for this type of agreement usually has a termination date that can be extended depending on the desire of either party. The manufacturer may also cancel the distribution agreement if the distributor is not meeting sales performance objectives or the distributor may cancel if it is not happy with the terms of the agreement such as prices charged by the manufacturer or the manufacturer's performance in terms of poor delivery, product quality, lack of technical support, and so forth. In either case, the risk and cost of entering into and getting out of this type of agreement is very low.

An example of a case I advised on in China was a marketing and distribution agreement between a Chinese wood flooring manufacturer and a Texas distributor of wood flooring. The Texas distributor wanted special wood flooring manufactured to its specifications by the Chinese company. The Chinese company wanted to expand its market for its products in the United States. Both entered into a marketing and distribution agreement, and the only time that money changed hands was when the Texas Company ordered flooring from the Chinese company. The Texas Company could cancel the agreement if the Chinese company failed to meet its product quality standards, and the Chinese company could cancel if the Texas Company did not mutually agree to sales objectives.

Original Equipment Manufacturer (OEM) Agreements I have a client in the Shanghai area that manufactures industrial products for a company in Europe that then sells these products under its own brand name. Once again, there was no contribution of money to the agreement and no ownership rights to the agreement.

Private Label Agreements This is somewhat similar to the OEM agreement. A well-known company is famous for its brand. If one shops at a popular retailer, you may typically have a choice of purchasing a famous brand product or the retailer's own brand. Since the retailer does not have a plant that produces this product, it is highly likely the retailer's own brand was also made by the well-known company under a private label agreement. Many such agreements can be found in almost any consumer product from food to clothing. Once again, these agreements do not involve any contribution of capital or ownership rights.

License Agreements This type of agreement typically involves the licensing of technology for a fee. As an example, Sony licensed the use of the transistor that was developed by the Bell Laboratories in the United States for use in the manufacture of smaller portable radios in the 1950s. This license agreement actually put Sony on the map. Within a few years, it had captured the entire worldwide portable radio market. PC companies typically may pay software or other component manufacturer a license fee when included in their products. As an example, Lenovo, the Chinese PC maker licenses the use of lithium ion batteries used in its laptops from the 3M Corporation. These are still non-equity agreements (no ownership), although in this case there is some compensation from one party for the license to the other.

Joint R&D Agreements   As we move across the spectrum of alliances, many firms have found it is more economical to outsource their research and development efforts to another party, such as a university. Pharmaceutical companies typically have formed alliances with universities for the development of new drugs. These alliances or agreements still mainly comprise a non-equity relationship, however, there may be some revenue sharing in the way of royalties once a new product has been developed and brought to the marketplace. Microsoft has entered into a considerable number of these R&D agreements with small- to medium-sized software development firms in China.

Formal Equity Alliances

At the far end of the spectrum of alliances is the more formal equity alliances such as joint ventures and mergers and acquisitions. We covered mergers and acquisitions earlier and one can see that they entail a long time commitment. There is a higher risk of their being unsuccessful, and a higher cost to get into (acquisition costs) and get out if things do not work out (divestiture).

The Joint Venture (JV)   This was the most common alliance foreign companies used in order to enter the Chinese market in the early 1980s. One of the oldest joint ventures that continues to exist today is the JV between the First Automobile Works of China (FAW) and Volkswagen (VW) of Germany for the manufacture of VWs and Audis. Another interesting JV in China is between Sony (Japan) and Ericsson (Sweden) for the manufacture of mobile telephones in China, the majority of which are then exported. Most recently, Chery (China) entered into a 50–50 joint venture with Fiat (Italy) for the production of up to 175,000 Chery, Fiat and Alfa Romeo automobiles for both China and for export. In all of these examples, each party may have contributed capital, technology, or other resources to the joint venture and has an equity (ownership) percentage in the alliance. It is important to note that the joint venture is a separate entity with its own management while the partners to the alliance continue as their own corporate entities. These are the formal alliances that are high on the spectrum in terms of time, cost and risk that Drucker addressed in his *Rules for Alliances.*

Drucker's Rules for Alliances

Many of Drucker's *Rules for Alliances* (joint ventures) could also apply to mergers and acquisitions in the "strategic thinking" phase of answering the question, "Why do we want to do this?" Here then, is a brief summary of his rules.

> *Strategy Formulation and Objectives:* Determine how a joint venture would fit into the overall business strategy of the organization and what objectives it would hope to achieve: expand into other markets, complement the product line, obtain needed technology, and so forth.
>
> *Partner Criteria and Solicitation:* Develop potential partner criteria particularly with respect to the capabilities you are looking for. This is very similar to establishing the criteria for the target you are looking to acquire if acquisitions are part of the strategy. Once potential partners have been identified, the next step would be to contact them and explore their interests in an alliance.
>
> *Due Diligence:* Prior to entering into any formal alliance, it is essential to perform due diligence relative to all aspects of potential partners. Do they have the capabilities you are looking for? What is their reputation in the marketplace,

and would you want to be associated with them? Are they financially healthy? What can be said about their management, business practices, leadership style, and culture? Would there be potential conflicts in these areas if an alliance were formed? I once had a consulting assignment with a joint venture in Saudi Arabia where there were three partners, the Saudis, an Italian firm, and one from Finland. Needless to say, there were many cultural differences resulting in the creation of three corporate ghettos within the organization making communications difficult.

Valuation of Assets Contributed: What is each party going to contribute to the new JV other than cash? If it is technology or equipment, what is the value of the technology and equipment that is being contributed to the JV? An initial valuation of these assets is important when it comes time to dissolve the venture to determine each partner's equity in the alliance.

Structure and Governance: How the alliance should be structured from an organizational perspective needs to be determined before the alliance is formed. Also, how will the alliance be governed in terms of policies, procedures and reporting relationships?

Management: The alliance must have its own management and be held accountable and responsible for results. It cannot be managed by a committee of representatives from both parties. Alliance management must also know who they go to for "important" not day-to-day operational decisions.

Objectives for the Alliance: What objectives does it plan to achieve (units produced, revenues, and so forth) and over what period of time? How will results be measured and when? These need to be established and mutually agreed to in advance of formalizing the alliance.

Future Capital Contributions: How will future capital contributions that may be required by the alliance be handled by the partners? Will they share equally in contributing future capital? These issues also need to be clarified prior to forming the alliance.

Conflict Resolution and Disagreements: How will potential disagreements and conflict be handled between the partners? Will serious disputes be handled through arbitration (recommended) or litigation (costly)?

Profit Sharing: How will profits be allocated? Will they remain in the alliance to fund future growth and expansion or be distributed to the partners?

Patents and Technology Transfer: Who will own patents and licenses that are developed in the alliance? How will existing patents and technology of the partners be protected?

Length of Alliance: For what period of time will the alliance be formed? Will there be opportunities to extend or cancel the alliance earlier and under what conditions? How will proceeds and assets be valued and distributed upon termination of the alliance?

Documentation: Just as in the case of a merger and acquisition agreement, all the above terms and conditions plus other aspects of the alliance need to be formalized in a Joint Venture Agreement.

Reasons for Not Forming an Alliance

Although alliances can be part of the business's growth strategy, Rudy A. Champa in *Strategic Thinking and Boardroom Debate* [17] provided some different guidelines or reasons for not forming a partnership.

1. Do not try to correct a weakness by forming an alliance.
   - The party that brings a weakness to the alliance will be, from that day forward, the inferior party to the alliance.
2. Do not form an alliance with a partner that is trying to correct one of its own weaknesses.
   - Your company will inherit the weakness.
3. The Worst Alliance.
   - Both partners are trying to correct their own weaknesses through the alliance.
   - This alliance is doomed from the start.

Part Two: Summary

Alliances form a middle ground between outsourcing (service agreements) and the more formal merger or acquisition. Alliances are an alternative to consider when the firm has strategic gaps in critical differential capabilities that may take too long to develop internally as well as be expensive. Alliances can be viewed on a spectrum of time, cost, and risk, and fall into two major categories of the informal non-equity alliance and the more formal equity alliance. Just as mergers and acquisitions have a high failure rate, the more formal equity alliances can also run into difficulty. Drucker has suggested some rules with respect to joint ventures and the work that should be done before forming the alliance to ensure a higher probability of success.

Endnotes

1. Peter F. Drucker, *Management: Tasks, Responsibilities, Practices* (New York: Harper & Row, 1973), 715.
2. Robert W. Swaim, Ph.D., "The Drucker Files: Mergers & Acquisitions," *Business Beijing* (March 2002).
3. Price Pritchett, *After the Merger: Managing the Shockwaves* (New York: Dow Jones-Irwin, 1985), 7–9.
4. Peter F. Drucker, *The Frontiers of Management* (New York: Truman Talley Books. 1986), 257–260.
5. Peter F. Drucker, "The Successful Acquisition." *Corpedia On-Line Program 8106* (2001).
6. Peter F. Drucker, *Management: Tasks, Responsibilities, Practices* (New York: Harper & Row, 1973), 708.
7. Peter F. Drucker, "The Successful Acquisition." *Corpedia On-Line Program 8106* (2001).
8. Ibid.
9. Ibid.
10. Peter F. Drucker, *The Frontiers of Management* (New York: Truman Talley Books. 1986), 258.
11. Ibid., 259
12. Peter F. Drucker, "The Successful Acquisition." *Corpedia On-Line Program 8106* (2001).
13. Peter F. Drucker, *The Frontiers of Management*, 259; and Drucker, "The Successful Acquisition."
14. Peter F. Drucker, "The Successful Acquisition." *Corpedia On-Line Program 8106* (2001).
15. A conversation with Peter Drucker during our integration planning assignment, April 1982.
16. Peter F. Drucker, "Rules for Strategic Alliances." *Corpedia On-Line Program 8106* (2001).
17. Rudy A. Champa, *Strategic Thinking and Boardroom Debate* (Mission Viejo, CA, Critical Thinker Press, 2001), 170.

Family Business Management

Both the business and the family will only survive and do well if the family serves the business. Neither will do well if the business is run to serve the family. The controlling word in "family managed business" is not family. It has to be "business."[1]

Part One: Drucker's Rules for Family Business Management

Introduction

The previous chapters have dealt with Drucker's views on organic and external growth strategies as well as the contributions of various pundits when it was necessary to reinforce his concepts or to go beyond Drucker. Generally speaking, the various strategies discussed are applicable in various degrees to all types of businesses, from the Fortune 500 multinational corporation to the privately owned firm. While all of these forms of businesses must be concerned with growth, one type, the family business, has other strategic issues that need to be addressed as well—survival and ownership succession.

Part One of this chapter therefore deals with the topic of the family business and Drucker's Rules for Family Business Management. Part Two of this chapter will deal with the important issues of Exit Strategies and Management Succession in the Family Business. Once again, as in the case of some of the previous chapters, reference will be made to China; however, the concepts will generally apply to many family businesses.

The Family Business in Perspective

Of the 25.2 million businesses in the United States, more than 80 percent are family-owned and managed. These companies employ more than 77 million people, or approximately six out of every 10 workers in the United States, pay 65 percent of all wages, and generate 55 percent of the nation's gross domestic product. In the 1990s, family businesses created eight out of every 10 new jobs in the United States.[2]

Not All Family Businesses Are Small

Contrary to popular belief, not all family businesses are small such as the husband-and-wife team running the local restaurant. Approximately 200 of the Fortune 500 companies (largest companies in the United States ranked by annual revenues) are family-owned. Even publicly traded companies, such as Ford, are still controlled by family members as a result of the preferential treatment of family-owned stock, even though the number of shares owned would appear to be a minority of all outstanding shares. There are also large Chinese family-owned businesses. For example, 40 percent of Hong Kong's market capitalization is controlled by 15 Chinese family groups, in Taiwan 16 of the top 20 companies in terms of total assets are family-owned and family-controlled, in Indonesia nine out of the top 10 businesses are owned by Chinese families, and in Thailand Chinese families own four of the country's largest banks.[3]

The Family Business and Size

According to Drucker, "there is little doubt that beyond a certain size a business can no longer reserve management to family members and remain viable. Beyond a certain size—and that usually means beyond being fair-sized—the management burden increasingly has to be borne by professional managers."[4] This chapter presents Drucker's Rules for Family Business Management and the role of the family and nonfamily professional managers in the family business. The Chinese family business may differ considerably from family businesses found in the West, and the Chinese family business owner will have to determine which, if any, of Drucker's Rules apply. In fact, how the older owner of the Chinese family business converts his equity in the business into personal wealth is essentially a non-issue. He basically gives the business to the eldest son and can rely on the younger generation to take care of him in his later years. Such is obviously not the case in the West, and as a result, there is not much work for estate planners in China.

Drucker's Rules

The following are Drucker's Rules for Family Business Management. For additional insight, the reader should refer to Drucker's *Managing in a Time of Great Change*, Chapter 4, "Managing in the Family Business."

Functional vs. Management Work

Drucker suggested there is really no difference between professional management and family-managed businesses when it comes to *functional work*, such as research, marketing, or accounting. On the other hand, when it comes to the management of the family business, different "rules" are required. Without adhering to these rules, Drucker felt that the family business will not survive or prosper.

Drucker's Rules for Family Members in the Business[5]

The first rule is that family members do not work in the business unless they are at least as able as any non-family employee, and work at least as hard.[6]

According to Drucker, family members should not be allowed to work in the family business unless they are as capable as non-family employees. They should only be allowed to stay in the business if they qualify on their own merit, not because they are family members. Respect is also a critical dimension concerning the family member in the business. Family members need to command respect based on their own merit and performance. If family members in the business cannot command respect, they should not be in the company. I once worked on a case where the son of the founder was the CEO of the company and had no respect from the non-family professional management team (marketing, finance, operations, managers, and so forth). Morale suffered and also the performance of the company due to the lack of direction of the company. I arranged for a management buy-out of the son and the company, using a leveraged employee stock ownership plan (ESOP), and the company is now doing very well, managed by non-family professional managers. The major issue was lack of respect, reinforcing Drucker's views.

Drucker continued with his rules by commenting that family members who are not willing to work, no matter what their educational background and capability, should not be allowed in the family business. Also, if the family member is not of top management caliber, with the potential of eventually being able to become part of the leadership of the company, he should actually be paid a stipend to stay away from the business. Some also suggest that family members not be allowed to be hired into entry level positions and ideally, should have spent several years gaining practical experience working in another business before joining the family firm.

With respect to promotions, family members should never be given a preference if there is a more qualified and better performing non-family member in management. Finally, over time, family members will elect not to enter the business, and the company will eventually become totally professionally managed by non-family members. This then leads us into a discussion of the non-family professional manager.

Rules for Non-Family Managers[7]

The second rule: No matter how many family members are in the company's management, and how effective they are, one top job is always filled by an outsider who is not a member of the family.[8]

With respect to top management, Drucker suggested that at least one senior management position always be filled by a non-family professional manager. A somewhat humorous example cited by Drucker of this rule is the Mafia where the second in command to the Godfather, the *consigliore* (attorney), is not a member of the family and may not even be a Sicilian.[9]

The third rule for the family business is that unless the family business is really small, key staff positions should also be filled by non-family members. Drucker reasoned that family members cannot have all the knowledge and expertise required in all of these areas.

The non-family members in top management should be given rewards and incentives that make them feel like "owners" or as Drucker commented, "they need full citizenship in the firm."[10] After all, it is their commitment to the family business that allows the business to grow and continue to be successful. These rewards can be in the form of stock options, stock bonus plans, "phantom stock" and other creative incentives to retain the commitment and motivation of the non-family manager. Without these incentives, there is the danger of the non-family manager or managers becoming frustrated and electing to start their own businesses and becoming competitors.

Another important rule for the non-family manager is to not mix business with the family. Here, Drucker felt there is a danger in becoming too personally involved in the family and losing perspective of the business if the non-family manager attempts to become too close to the family. Therefore, the non-family manager should generally avoid family social gatherings unless it is a special event he or she has been invited to.

Succession Planning

Succession planning, who will take over the leadership of the family business, is a critical decision that should not be left to the last minute. Drucker advised that this decision should be trusted to an outside advisor who is neither part of the family nor part of the business.

Part Two: Drucker's Rules for Exit Strategies and Management Succession

The family business needs to plan for its eventual change in character. Drucker estimated that after two generations, "the family will only be beneficiaries of the business, not bosses." As an example, studies have shown that 80 percent of family businesses in the United States never get to the second generation.[11]

Part Two will deal with the extremely important issues of succession planning and discuss the various exit strategy alternatives available to the family business.

> *The average life expectancy of a family business is 25 years. The stumbling block is management succession.*[12]
>
> Paul J. Lim

Research on Owners of Privately Held Businesses[13]

Several years ago, a leading accounting and consulting firm conducted a study on the owners of privately held and mostly family-owned businesses and discovered the following.

1. *Do Not Know the Business's Value:* 65 percent of business owners did not know what their company was worth. In other words, they are unaware of the Fair Market Value of their business and what they could get for the business if selling the business was an exit strategy they wanted to consider. Knowing the value of the business is also important if the owner is considering other exit strategy alternatives, such as passing the business on to family members.

2. *No Exit Strategy or Succession Plan:* 85 percent of the business owners surveyed did not have an exit strategy or succession plan. The owners had not given any consideration to how or when they will eventually retire and who will take over the management of the business. This is often attributed to their reluctance to accept their own mortality—they will live forever, and the fact that their personal identity is intertwined with the business—they will lose their identity if and when they leave their business. Many owners are unable to "give up their baby," similar to a father's concerns when his daughter gets married and he must give the bride away at the wedding ceremony. There are those owners who feel that by remaining in control of the family business, this will provide them control and influence over the other family

members. Many business owners may "officially" retire only to reappear and meddle in the running of the business.

3. *Majority of Owner's Net Worth Is In the Business*: 75 percent of the business owner's net worth was tied up in their business. There is a *Prudent Man Rule* that suggests that not more than *20 percent* of an individual's personal wealth should be tied up in any one investment. Obviously, most business owners have disregarded this rule. Having equity in the business is all well and good, but how does one convert this into cash and personal wealth for one's retirement?

4. *No Personal Financial and Estate Planning*: 25 percent of senior generation owners had not done any estate planning to minimize their taxes or determine how to convert the equity they have in their businesses into personal wealth and liquidity. It is one thing to pass the family business on to a son or daughter, but in so doing, how does the father get compensated for the hard work and dedication he put into starting and growing the business over the years? It is estimated that between 2001 and 2017, $12 trillion in wealth will be transferred from one generation to another that will be the greatest transfer of wealth ever, much of this transfer involving family businesses.[14] In discussing succession planning in the family business with my students in China, how the older generation cashed-out so to speak was not considered to be an issue—they just leave the business to the next generation.

Six Exit Strategies

Richard Rodnick, the founder and former chairman of the Geneva Companies, a merger and acquisition firm in the United States, has a rule that the time to develop an exit strategy is the *day you start the business*. As an example of practicing this rule, Rodnick had an exit strategy that he would sell the Geneva Companies after five years from the date he started it, which he did when he sold the company to the Chemical Bank of New York for more than $30 million. Some would argue that this rule does not allow the owner to get full value for the company—that if he held on to the company for several more years, he might get considerably more money for the business. To counter this argument, there is another interesting quotation.

When Bernard Baruch, an individual who amassed a personal fortune in the mid-1900s was asked how he became so wealthy?—he replied, "I always sold too soon."[15] Let us briefly review the various exit strategies available to the business owner and then deal with succession planning as part of the exit strategy alternatives.

You develop an exit strategy the day you start the business.[16]
Richard Rodnick, founder and former chairman,
the Geneva Companies

Six Exit Strategy Alternatives

There are six main exit strategy alternatives available to the business owner to consider, excluding liquidation of the business. The first five deal with strategies to consider when there are no family members qualified or interested in taking over the management of the business, and the last strategy deals with succession planning where there are family members who potentially could take over. Actually, there are situations in the first five strategies where family members may still continue to manage the day-to-day operations of the company, but will no longer have a significant percentage of its ownership.

One: Selling to Outsiders   This exit strategy involves selling the business to outsiders through a direct sale or possibly a merger where the other party gains a majority interest in the new business combination. Although it may be called a merger, usually for the owner's ego—"We merged with a multinational giant who is 100 times our size"—most of these transactions are actually acquisitions.

Two: Selling to Insiders—Management and Employees   Selling the business to its non-family member management and employees is another strategy that is usually considered. Often times, management may be disenchanted with the company's lack of direction when the owner-founder loses energy and enthusiasm for growing the business. The owner-founder continues to lead a good life in terms of personal compensation and perks, but has become conservative and averse to taking unnecessary risks. Thus, the company begins to age in a negative sense, often resulting in the loss of market share. Management may feel new leadership can turn the situation around if they had the opportunity. The problem with considering this exit strategy however, is how management and employees can raise the financing required to acquire the business. Passing the hat around, so to speak, and asking management and the employees to contribute some of their personal savings to acquire the company generally will not even raise enough money for a downpayment on the acquisition.

There are some creative ways and corporate financing techniques available for management and employees to acquire the business, such as the Employee Stock Ownership Plan (ESOP) that have been successfully used in the United States and UK, but are generally unknown in China and many other parts of the world. In my merger and acquisition class, selling to "insiders" ranks low in terms of potential buyers for the business unless an ESOP can be structured. China has now implemented its own version of an ESOP but so far lacks the tax advantages that are associated with ESOPs in the United States.

Three: Selling to a Partner or Other Shareholders   If the owner-founder has other partners or shareholders he might consider selling his interest in the business to them. Two issues arise here that need to be dealt with to implement this strategy. First, what is the value of the shares to be sold, and do all shareholders agree on the value? This typically can be resolved by using an outside professional business valuation firm to establish the fair market value of the business and to value the shares. Second, as in the case of selling to management and employees, how will the other shareholders raise the financing to acquire the owner-founder's shares? Agreeing to be paid out of future profits is a typical method. However, this leaves the owner-founder at considerable risk if the new management makes poor business decisions that negatively impact the business. Ideally, the shareholders should borrow the money to cash out the owner-founder and repay the lending institution from the future profits of the business. The ESOP as previously mentioned also has distinct tax advantages when used for buying out other partners or shareholders.

Four: Selling to Equity Funds and Private Investment Groups   Equity Funds and Private Investment Groups (PIGs) can be an attractive exit strategy; in fact, recapitalization is one of the best strategies to consider. Equity Funds and PIGs typically invest in a portfolio of businesses that meet their investment criteria (type of business, industry, geographic location, size in revenues, and so on) and will usually acquire a 60 to 80 percent ownership, sometimes higher, in the business.

One of the major criteria of Equity Funds and PIGs is that there must be a strong management team in place in the business as they are typically not interested in running the day-to-day operations of the business, but only in providing strategic direction at the board level. There should also be a certain degree of synergy with their existing portfolio of businesses such as same or related industry, market served, technology used, and so on. If there are family members who are capable of, and interested in managing the business, this is an excellent way to meet the personal and business objectives of the owner-founder by allowing him to receive a significant payment while management and the remaining percentage of ownership in the business can be transferred to the next generation. There are many funds and PIGs, ranging in size from GE Capital to smaller enterprises that manage pension and retirement funds and look for opportunities to invest those funds. It should be noted that these deals, contrary to Drucker's Rules that are mentioned in Chapter 7, are done for financial reasons although business strategy is considered with respect to synergy with the equity group's existing portfolio of companies. Equity Funds and PIGs are typically in the deal for five to seven years and have their own exit strategy in terms of a possible IPO or selling their portfolio to an interested buyer.

Five: Selling to the Public: Initial Public Offering (IPO)   Although there are some very large family businesses as mentioned in Part One of this chapter, the typical family-owned business is generally too small to seriously consider an IPO as an exit strategy alternative. As such, I will not discuss the IPO in detail other than to mention it is a time consuming and expensive process.

Six: Transfer Ownership to Other Family Members—The Succession Plan   Succession planning is essential to ensure the continuity of the business, particularly if there are family members interested in, and capable of managing the business. Succession planning when there is a single heir, son or daughter, is the least complicated model, if he or she desires to enter the business, and has the ability to eventually run it. The models get more complicated when there are multiple heirs, older vs. younger children, sons vs. daughters, inactive family members, the surviving spouse of the owner-founder, in-laws, and unrelated (non-family member) successors.

When there are multiple heirs, succession planning should involve two entities in the planning process, a family council and an outside advisor. Here, Drucker strongly advocated the role of outside advisors in succession planning.[17] The role of the family council is to first define the responsibilities and qualifications required for the successor in terms of knowledge, skills and experience. David Bork in *Family Business, Risky Business* suggests the following criteria be considered when identifying potential successors:[18]

- Three to five years' employment in a job or jobs that have depended on competence, skill and sustained performance, rather than on family-based relationships. Many also suggest that this experience should have been gained outside of the family business.
- Experience in directing the activities of others.
- Recognition for demonstrated competence on the job.
- Evidence and ability to manage relationships, both with peers and with supervisors.
- Evidence of the ability and willingness to take initiative on the job.
- Evidence of having been a valued employee with legitimate contributions to make.

The next step for the family council is to then identify possible successors, either family members or non-family professional managers, but not to make the selection themselves. This should be left, as Drucker suggested, to an outside, non-family advisor who can provide an objective perspective and eliminate the chance of potential conflict among the family members. As part of the selection process, it is also important to make it clear to everyone involved that they are not required to join the family business.

With respect to the spouse eventually becoming a successor if the owner-founder passes away, this depends on how much involvement the spouse has had in the business prior to the founder's death. If there is another partner, or partners, they may not want the spouse involved in the business. This potential problem can be resolved with a "buy-sell" agreement established between the partners at the time of the formation of the business, outlining how a partner's share in the business can be purchased in the future. These buy-sell agreements are generally funded by company paid life insurance on each partner. In the event of a partner's death, the life insurance proceeds are used to buy out the surviving spouse who typically inherits the share in the business. If the surviving spouse is from a second or third marriage, this can also create concerns among the children as to who will inherit the business upon the owner-founder's death—that if the business is left to the spouse, the children will be cheated out of what they feel is rightfully theirs. Proper estate planning and prenuptial agreements can eliminate these concerns and avoid conflict within the family.

Once the successor has been identified, it is important to have a developmental plan for the individual to gain the necessary knowledge and experience to take over the management of the business. The extent of the developmental plan will obviously vary depending on the age and experience of the potential successor. The son or daughter entering the business after working elsewhere in a first job will require considerably more development as compared to a non-family professional manager who is already performing in a key management position as suggested by Drucker in Part One. Drucker also stressed the need for defining the performance expectations and desired results as the successor progresses through various management levels in the organization. The owner-founder must also be patient, and allow for some mistakes to be made by the successor and use them as learning experiences.

Summary and Closing the Drucker Gap

The first part of this chapter outlined Drucker's Rules for managing and growing the family-owned business and the second part dealt with how to ensure its continuity through proper succession planning. In order to close the Drucker gap, various exit strategies available to the owner-founder when there are no apparent family members interested in eventually managing the business were briefly discussed. I conclude with Drucker's two key points relative to succession planning and exit strategies:

- Don't leave this important task until the last minute.
- Use objective, non-family advisors to assist in the selection process.

The key takeaways from this chapter are:

1. *Exit Strategy*: if you are a family or small business owner, do you have an exit strategy?
2. *Succession Planning*: assuming you will not live forever, how will the continuity of the business be preserved? Do you have a succession plan?
3. *Outside Advisors*: Do you have a knowledgeable outside, non-family member, advisor on your Board?

Assessment Tool and Case Studies

The following Assessment Tool that can be used in Succession Planning. There are also two case studies that are used in our MBA and Executive Development Programs. Both cases deal with succession planning and exit strategies for the family business.

Succession Planning & Assessment Tool

PART ONE—MANAGEMENT & KEY STAFF ASSESSMENT

Description

- This tool allows you to assess the present executives, management and key staff of the organization and the roles they perform in the organization. It will assist you in determining the quality of your present management and key staff, their potential for advancement, and the developmental needs required to prepare them for advancement.

Assessment

- The continuity of management and key personnel is critical to the success of every organization. It is important to assess the management and key staff of the organization in order to determine if the necessary talent presently exists to accomplish the organization's Mission. This also provides insight as to whether potential "talent gaps" exist and what additional talent may be necessary to develop internally, or recruit into the organization.

Instructions

The following is a "Confidential Management & Key Staff Assessment Form."

As a guideline, individuals to be assessed should include the Chief Executive Officer, direct reports, and other managers and key staff essential for the continuity of the organization.

Please make as many copies of the enclosed form as may be necessary and complete an assessment for each of your executives, managers and key staff that you are considering in your organization's Succession Plan.

Confidential Management & Key Staff Assessment

NAME:_____

POSITION:_____

CIRCLE A NUMBER ON THE SCALES BELOW.

1. Compared to others in the organization at the same level, this individual's performance and results are consistently:

1	2	3	4	5	6	7	8	9
	Lower			Average			Higher	

2. Compared to others in the industry doing the same job, this individual's performance and results are consistently:

1	2	3	4	5	6	7	8	9
	Lower			Average			Higher	

3. The methods (management and leadership style, management practices) this individual uses to accomplish the above results are:

1	2	3	4	5	6	7	8	9
	Poor			Average			Excellent	

4. This individual has the ability (knowledge, skills and experience) to perform in the role required of this position:

1	2	3	4	5	6	7	8	9
Low Ability			Average Ability			High Ability		

5. This individual has the willingness (personal motivation and commitment) to perform in the role required of this position:

1	2	3	4	5	6	7	8	9
Low Willingness			Average Willingness			High Willingness		

6. In order to improve this individual's effectiveness and performance in the present position, this individual's training and development needs are:

1	2	3	4	5	6	7	8	9
Needs Help			Moderate			None Required		

7. How much development is required to prepare this individual for promotion to the next-highest position?

1	2	3	4	5	6	7	8	9
Needs Help			Moderate			None Required		

8. How critical would the loss of this individual be to the future success of the organization?

1	2	3	4	5	6	7	8	9
No Loss			Some Loss			Critical Loss		

ADD THE SCORES FOR EACH QUESTION AND TOTAL HERE:_____
REFER TO THE ASSESSMENT SCORES ON THE NEXT PAGE.

Management & Key Staff Assessment Scores

Score	Effectiveness	Development Needs
64–72	Highly Effective	Provide continuous learning through formal executive/management training and development to gain insight on newer concepts and exchange of ideas with a peer group. Consider special assignment in preparation for next higher position.
57–63	Effective	What development needs could this person benefit from the most in order to improve effectiveness and prepare for a higher position?
49–56	Above Average Effectiveness	Identify the questions on the Assessment that lowered this individual's overall score. What development needs should be provided and in what areas?
41–48	Moderately Effective	Identify the questions on the Assessment that lowered this individual's overall score. What development needs should be provided and in what areas?
32–40	Below Average Effectiveness	Considerable development required to improve this individual's effectiveness depending on "willingness" to perform and motivation for self-development (See Question 5 score).
Below 31	Ineffective	Why is this person here?

Diagnosis—Questions Where Scores are Lower than 5

Instructions

Review all questions on the Management & Key Staff Assessment where the individual scored below 5, and explore the issues pertaining to those question.

Question 1: Performance Compared to others in the Organization.

What development does this individual need to improve on personal effectiveness and performance compared to others at the same level in the organization?

Question 2: Performance Compared to others in the Industry.

What development does this individual need to improve on personal effectiveness and performance compared to others in the industry?

Question 3: Management and Leadership Style and Management Practices.

What development does this individual need to improve on management and leadership style and personal management practices?

Question 4: Knowledge, Skills and Experience.

What development does this individual need to gain more knowledge, skills and experience to improve personal effectiveness and performance?

Question 5: "Willingness"—Personal Motivation and Commitment.

What development does this individual need to improve on "willingness" to perform and personal motivation and commitment?

Question 6: Training and Development Needs.

What other training and development needs does this individual need to improve on personal effectiveness, the effectiveness and performance of other employees, and the impact this individual could have on improving the organization's effectiveness?

_____

Question 7: Development for Next Position.

What is the next position this individual should be considered for and what is needed to develop him/her to be ready for that position?

_____

Question 8: Loss to the Organization.

If losing this person is not critical to the organization's future success, why is he/she here? Would development improve this person's value to the organization, and if so, what kind?

_____

PART TWO—SUCCESSION PLANNING

Only complete this part if the individual's assessment score was 57 and above.

1. Next Positions (Advancement)

Indicate for what position or positions this individual should be considered for advancement.

1._____   2._____
3._____

Readiness for Advancement (Check when this Individual would be Ready for Advancement to the above Positions).

Ready Now ( )   Ready in One Year ( )   Ready in Two Years ( )
Ready in Three Years ( )

Next Positions (Developmental)

Indicate what Developmental Positions or Special Projects this individual should be assigned to in order to prepare him/her for advancement.

1._____   2._____
3._____

Source: Copyright © 1997. The Coto Group, Inc. All Rights Reserved.

Case 1: The Great Wall Travel & Tour Company

THE UNWANTED WIDOW

Background

The Great Wall Travel and Tour Company is an established, private company located in Beijing specializing in arranging tours throughout China for international tourists. The company was founded in 1986 as a partnership between Henry Lee and William Wang (each owning 50 percent of the company). Until 2003 and the SARS crisis in China, the company grew steadily in sales, profits and the number of employees. Over this period, the company opened branch offices in Shanghai and Hong Kong, as well as in London and San Francisco. Initially focusing on international tourists from the West and other Asian countries, the company expanded its services to arrange travel tours for Chinese tourists to visit other countries as the Chinese economy grew rapidly and income levels increased allowing more Chinese to travel.

The Situation

The year 2003 was a total disaster for the Chinese tourism industry as a result of the SARS crisis—billions of dollars were lost. Great Wall Travel lost a considerable amount of money during this period and was forced to close its Shanghai, San Francisco and London branches. It also laid off over half of its employees in its Hong Kong and Beijing offices. Although the crisis ended in May, tourism in China did not return to the levels of previous years. The company suffered another blow because Chinese tourists were not welcome in other countries during this same period, also due to SARS. While the government promised to provide aid to this sector, Great Wall Travel did not receive any relief in the way of government funds although it could borrow money at more favorable rates. The reduction in tax rates for the industry was also of no help, since the company lost money and no taxes were due.

To complicate the situation, the stress of attempting to keep the business alive during this period affected William Wang's health, and at the age of 55, he had a heart attack and passed away. Mr. Wang left his half ownership in the company to his 48-year-old wife, Julia Wang.

Julia Wang was semi-active in the business, occasionally leading tours of Chinese tourists to the US and Europe. She considered these tours to be more of a vacation than work. She tended to run up considerable personal expenses on these trips for clothes, cosmetics and other personal items, which she charged to the company as business expenses. This always irritated the other partner, Henry Lee, and he would often complain to Mr. Wang about this. She would also take advantage of special promotions that various airlines, hotels and resorts throughout the world would occasionally offer the company to promote their facilities for tourists. This created a great deal of dissatisfaction among regular employees who thought they were entitled to some of these free trips. Other than these tours and promotional trips, Julia was seldom seen in, or worked in the company's Beijing office. Julia graduated from Peking University, where she studied English. She spent another year studying in Europe where she learned French. However, she had no business management training.

The Meeting

After Mr. Wang's funeral, Julia scheduled a meeting with Mr. Lee. At the meeting, Julia advised him that she would like to become more active in the business and now, as a 50 percent partner, expected to be included in all decisions relative to company operations. She would use her husband's office and secretary, but only wanted to lead an occasional tour of her choice as before and would be the liaison with international airlines, hotels and resorts. Mr. Lee could continue with running the day-to-day operations of the company as long as she was consulted on any major decisions that had to be made and was in agreement with them. Furthermore, she insisted that her son, who studied at the London School of Economics, be made the company's Chief Financial Officer. The company's present financial officer, who had been with the company for 10 years, would have to be let go. This would serve two purposes; the son would manage the company's finances to ensure Julia's interests were protected, and the position would also groom him to take over her role when she no longer wanted to be active in the business. Furthermore, she advised Mr. Lee that her first business decision was that all future Chinese tours to Europe would be coordinated by her, and Air France would be the airline used for many of these tours.

Knowing in advance that Mr. Lee would not be very excited about her demands, she offered him an alternative: he could buy her 50 percent interest in the company for US$2 million and she would officially retire from the business. She advised Mr. Lee that she expected his answer within two weeks. In the meantime, she would be leading a tour to Paris and would also shop for some new "business" clothes she expected the company to pay for.

Mr. Lee's reaction was calm, and replied "that he would consider these alternatives and would schedule another meeting to discuss this further when she returned from Paris."

After his office door closed, he slammed his fist on his desk so hard he broke two fingers and had to have his hand put into a cast.

Now What?

The last thing in the world Mr. Lee needed was Julia coming into the business. Half or more of the employees would leave if they knew she would be more active in the business.

Letting go of the financial officer was not an option. He was Lee's nephew and he was grooming him to take over his part of the business when he decided to retire. Furthermore, it was known that Julia's son was incompetent.

The company does not have US$2 million to buy her out. Where did she get that number from anyway? Maybe between now and 2008, when the Olympics are staged in Beijing, the company could save enough money to buy her out—but that is five years from now and he didn't want Julia around that long.

Case Analysis and Discussion

What should Mr. Lee do now?
How could this situation been avoided?

Notes to the Instructor

This case may be used to reinforce the concepts presented in this chapter and the need for succession planning. Other topics that can be introduced here would include the Buy-Sell Agreement funded with company-owned life insurance and the need for a business valuation to determine the value of the company, each partner's ownership value, and the amount necessary to be funded by life insurance. The use of a leveraged ESOP to buy out another shareholder would also be an alternative to consider in this situation. The structuring of partnerships is another topic that can be discussed. A 50/50 partnership is a recipe for disaster. You can have a 50/50 profit split, but a 51/49 decision-making split.

Case 2: Atlanta Pipe, Valve & Supply Company

CASE STUDY IN EXIT STRATEGIES

Background: The Company

Atlanta Pipe, Valve and Supply Company is a privately-owned company, founded in 1969, and is a distributor of pipes, industrial valves and fittings (PVF) used primarily in process industries (paper mills, food and beverage processing plants, refineries and chemical plants). The company also provides value-added engineering and maintenance services that include design, installation and safety testing. In addition, the company has exclusive distribution agreements for the southeastern United States with several of the largest industrial valve manufacturers in the United States and Europe.

The company has been very successful and has grown to become the largest PFV distributor in the state of Georgia with over US$75 million in annual sales. Overall, the company has been profitable although profits in some years have been somewhat lower due to the cyclical nature of some of its major customers and the industries they serve.

The Situation

Ownership Structure of the Company

Henry Brown, the founder of the company, died several years ago. Surviving him are Ann Brown, his wife, 67, and chairman of the company, who owns 51 percent of the shares; Steve Brown, son, 45, and president of the company, who owns 15 percent of the shares; Lucy Brown, daughter, 38, and vice president, who owns another 15 percent of the shares; and a number of other children and grandchildren who are not active in the business, but share in its profits each year. They own the remaining 19 percent of the shares. There are also three key managers who have been with the company for many years and have played a major role in helping to make the company successful and grow.

Personal Objectives of Family Members

Ann Brown, Chairman

She would like to retire and get her money (value of her shares) out of the company. The vast majority of her personal wealth is tied up in the company.

She wants to make sure that all children and grandchildren are
treated fairly.

Steve Brown, President

He would like to continue to grow the company, primarily by
making strategic acquisitions of competitors in other states. How
to get the capital to make these acquisitions is a problem.
He also resents the fact that he works very hard and that
the inactive children, who make no contribution, share in the
company's profits each year.

Lucy Brown, Vice President

She is not married and is still interested in playing an active role in
the company.
She also resents the inactive children sharing in the profits of the
company each year.

Three Key Managers (Non-family Members)

They would like to share in the ownership of the company for the
contribution they have made over the years.
They have approached Ann Brown and have requested she gives
them each a five percent ownership interest in the company.
They have indirectly suggested that without this ownership, they
might leave the company and go work for a competitor or start
their own company and become a competitor.

Valve Manufacturing Companies

The valve companies, with which the company has the exclusive
distribution agreements with, have been urging Steve Brown to
expand more aggressively into other areas of the Southeast.

Unless they obtain wider distribution and sales, they have indicated they may terminate their exclusive agreements with the company and seek other distribution channels or perhaps sell directly to
the end-user.

Case Analysis

You are a management consultant specializing in mergers, acquisitions and other financial services. You have been referred to Ann
Brown by a friend who feels that, based on your knowledge and

experience in this area, you might be able to assist her and the others (family and non-family members) in achieving their objectives.

You have met with Ann Brown and Steve Brown and reviewed everyone's objectives. She has now asked you for recommendations.

Would you recommend selling the company? Why, why not and to whom — type of buyer?

Would you recommend seeking a private investment group/equity fund investor? Why, why not?

What other recommendations would you make?

What are the next steps you would recommend to be taken if you were retained to assist her and the company?

Notes to the Instructor

Although this case is presented in Chapter 8, it can also be used in the discussion of mergers and acquisitions as discussed in Chapter 7. There are many approaches to resolving the various parties' business and personal objectives in this case from an outright sale to a recapitalization from a private equity group, which would be the best alternative in terms of meeting almost everyone's objectives. A leveraged ESOP would require too much debt and not meet the business objectives of the son in terms of acquiring a competitor.

Endnotes

1. Peter F. Drucker, *Managing in a Time of Great Change* (New York: Truman Talley Books/Plume, 1995), 57.
2. Norman M. Scarborough and Thomas W. Zimmerer, *Effective Small Business Management*, 7th ed. (Upper Saddle River, NJ: Pearson Education, Inc., 2003), 615.
3. Ming-Jer Chen, *Inside Chinese Business: A Guide for Managers Worldwide* (Boston: Harvard Business School Press, 2001), 19–44.
4. Peter F. Drucker, *Management: Tasks, Responsibilities, Practices* (New York: Harper & Row, 1973), 725.
5. Peter F. Drucker, *Managing in a Time of Great Change* (New York: Truman Talley Books/Plume, 1995), 52–57.
6. Ibid., 52.
7. Ibid., 53–54.
8. Ibid., 53.
9. Ibid., 54.

10. Ibid., 54.
11. Scarborough and Zimmerer, *Effective Small Business Management*, 7th ed., 615.
12. Paul J. Lim, "Putting Your House in Order," *US News and World Report*, (December 10, 2001), 38.
13. The Author Anderson/Mass Mutual American Famil Business Survey, 1977, www.massmutual.com/fbn/index.htm.
14. Scarborough and Zimmerer, *Effective Small Business Management*, 7th ed., 615.
15. Charles E. Kirk, "Market Wisdom from Bernard Baruch," *The Kirk Report* (June 5, 2008), 1.
16. Richard Rodnick, At the *"How to Sell Your Business for the Most Profit Workshop,"* (Costa Mesa, CA, June, 1984).
17. Peter F. Drucker, *Managing in a Time of Great Change* (New York: Truman Talley Books/Plume, 1995), 56.
18. David Bork, *Family Business, Risky Business: How to Make it Work* (New York: AMACOM, 1986), 122–123.

Drucker and the Next Society

THE SOCIAL SCIENTIST

What has already happened that will make the future?[1]

Introduction

This chapter presents Drucker's observations on what he had identified as the Next Society, as discussed in one of his later books, *Managing in the Next Society*, with additional insight from his earlier books, *Managing in a Time of Great Change* and *Management Challenges for the 21st Century*.[2] Drucker also commented on the Five Certainties on which to base strategy, which closely correspond to the issues covered in this chapter.

I have included this chapter to demonstrate a recurring theme of Drucker's, observing the external environment and in particular changes taking place in society at large. These changes have major implications on strategy as well as opportunities for innovation. These observations of the Next Society truly reflect Drucker's view of himself as a social scientist. Although he clearly identified these significant issues, here we will also see some Drucker gaps that needed to be closed.

Drucker and the Next Society

First, it would be helpful to describe some of the factors that lead Drucker to categorize the Next Society. He commented, "In the decade of the 1990s, I became aware that society was changing," which motivated the writing of *Managing in the Next Society*.[3] What did he observe that led him to describe the Next Society? Here I will review some of his comments on the major changes that will comprise the Next Society.

1. *Fourth Information Revolution:* The impact of information on business and society, particularly the Internet and e-commerce.
2. *Changing Demographics:* Populations are aging throughout the world, and birthrates are declining, resulting in fewer young people. Drucker forecasted that many countries in the developed world would see their populations decrease over the next several decades. Changing demographics will see the continued movement from rural to urban areas, but also a wide resistance to immigration. Many of these demographic changes are already taking place in China as well.
3. *Steady Decline in Manufacturing:* Drucker predicted that there will be a steady decline in manufacturing as a provider of wealth and jobs. According to Drucker, economically, manufacturing is becoming marginal in developed countries. This has actually been occurring for the last decade throughout the developed world.
4. *Transformation and Splintering of the Workforce:* The workforce in developed countries is transforming from manual to knowledge workers, into two groups—younger and older employees, and into other groups such as full-time employees and outsourced employees and consultants. The need to work beyond normal retirement age is also developing. The implications for organizations are that old management practices will no longer be applicable to managing this new diverse workforce.
5. *Political Instability and Social Unrest:* Drucker predicted that this would be the norm throughout the world in the next several decades of the 21st century.

Applying Drucker

After considering Drucker's question, "What has already happened that will make the future?" consider the following questions:

1. What do these accomplished facts mean to our business?
2. What opportunities do they create?
3. What threats?
4. What changes do they demand—in the way our business is organized and run, in our goals, in our products, in our services, in our policies?
5. What changes do they make possible and what will likely be the advantages?
6. What changes in industry and market structure, in basic values (such as the emphasis on the environment), and in science and technology have already occurred but do not yet have a full impact?
7. What are the trends in economic and societal structure? How do they affect our business?[4]

Issues Impact Assessment

At the end of this chapter, you will find an Issues Impact Assessment tool that is used in our executive development programs in China. Although the titles on the worksheet refer to China, it can be used in any country and may be useful to complete as you review the major factors identified in the Next Society in terms of the potential impact each has on your organization and on you personally. Completing this exercise will allow you to apply some of Drucker's concepts and ideally will make this chapter more meaningful for you.

The following is a brief discussion of these factors. In fact, Drucker was not actually predicting the future; he stated: "Irreversibly, the Next Society is already here."[5]

The Fourth Information Revolution

For those of you who have never read a Drucker book or heard one of his lectures, he typically included a discussion of history. The following is a brief illustration of his writing and teaching style. To arrive at the main point, Drucker often felt it was necessary to take us around the world and back some 6,000 years.

Drucker's first observation was the Information Revolution that he described as being the world's Fourth Information Revolution starting in the 1950s. According to Drucker, the first revolution was the invention of writing in Mesopotamia (now Iraq) some 5,000 to 6,000 years ago, and then in China several thousand years later. The second revolution occurred between 1300 to 500 B.C. with the invention of the written book in China, and 800 years later, in Greece (although the Greeks had been writing for many centuries before books were invented). The third information revolution took place between 1450 and 1455 with Gutenberg's invention of the printing press and movable type. Although one might conclude that the fourth information revolution started with the microchip and computers, Drucker's view was that the Internet and e-commerce are the major impacts of the new revolution. As a result, distance has been eliminated and in Drucker's words, "One consequence is that every business must become globally competitive even if it manufactures or sells only within a local or regional market. Competition is not local anymore—it knows no boundaries."[6]

Changing Demographics: Declining Birthrates and Aging Populations

Demographics will not only be the most important factor in the Next Society, it will also be the least predictable and least controllable one.[7]

According to Drucker, by far the greatest impact on society will come from the changing demographics of the developed nations as well as the developing nations such as China and India both in terms of the aging populations and declining birthrates resulting in fewer young people. These changes will pose different business opportunities as well as enormous social problems.

Aging Populations

Drucker wrote in the *Next Society* that it is estimated that by the year 2030, 50 percent of Japan's and Germany's populations will be over 65 years of age. In 2005, Japan reported that the ratio of people aged 65 and over reached 21 percent of the total population, beating Italy's 20 percent. At the same time, the ratio of people aged 15 or younger in the total population was the world's lowest at 13.6

percent, surpassing Bulgaria's 13.8 percent. Japan's population, now about 127 million, declined in 2006 for the first time since 1945. The Japanese government reported that Japan's population would shrink by half in less than a century unless something was done to reverse falling birthrates.[8] The same trends are occurring in China. It is estimated that by the year 2020, 248 million Chinese will be 60 years and older and by 2040, 437 million people, almost one-third of the population, will be 60 or older in China.[9]

Declining Birthrates

The most important single new certainty—if only because there is no precedent for it in all of history—is the collapsing birthrate in the developed world.[10]

A birthrate of 2.1 children per female is considered optimal for replacing an aging workforce. Fertility rates have been on the decline in industrialized nations for decades, as Drucker observed, and they are now becoming a serious economic problem. Japan's fertility rate fell to a record low of 1.25 in 2005. The United States has a fertility rate of two children per female and is one of the few industrialized nations with a rate that high.

Drucker had also observed that the birthrates in developed countries are not sufficient to replace their populations. As an example, he forecasted that by 2050, Germany's population will decrease from its present 82 million people to between 70 million and 73 million people, and Japan's population will decrease from its present 127 million people to 95 million. The same trends, are evident in Italy, France, Spain, Portugal, the Netherlands, and Sweden.[11]

1.3 Billion and Counting and Trends Within Trends

China is also the exception as its population is forecasted to increase at a rate of approximately 10 million people per year over the next decade although the government has announced a Zero Population Growth goal to be reached by 2030.[12] To put this increase into perspective, this is essentially creating another Australia every two years. With respect to demographics, Drucker suggested to look for trends within trends. As an example, although the trend of an aging population can be observed in China, the ratio of men to women in

China has also been changing. The one-child policy implemented by China in the 1980s has accomplished the goal of limiting population growth to some extent; however, the ratio of 119 male births to 100 female births will create a surplus of 30 million males in the next decade (normal rate is considered to be 103 to 107 of one sex to 100 of another).[13]

We Need More Kids: "Bucks for Babies"

An article in the *Wall Street Journal* reported the growing number of countries that are offering cash and other incentives for people to become parents to deal with their declining birthrate and population problems.[14] Germany is considering a program to make it economically easier for women to bear children by proposing to pay women 67 percent of their salaries with a ceiling of approximately $23,000 for a 12-month parental leave. Men will also be eligible for a two-month payment, or a total of 14 months per couple. Australia began offering bonuses to people who had babies, increasing the bonus to about $3,000 in 2006 and reported that the program has resulted in increasing the average births per female from 1.76 to 1.82. Japan has also created a number of government sponsored schemes, such as cruises for young people, in hopes that they would meet, get married and have families. One city, in Japan has even offered mothers a bonus of $10,000 for having a third child, in hopes of reversing the trend of the declining population in the city. The governments of other countries such as France and Singapore have also offered incentives if women will have more children. As a result, France's fertility rate has steadily risen by increasing tax exemptions for parents with children, increasing its fertility rate to 1.9, far better than any other European Union country. Even Shanghai, one of the largest cities in China, which now has the highest percentage of older people at 20 percent of the population, is encouraging women to have more children.[15]

The Chinese Way: "Cultural Economics"

Beijing has allowed "selected and qualified" only-child couples to have a second child. This is not out of the goodness of their hearts but an economic necessity, and it relies on the Chinese tradition of children taking care of their elderly parents—because financially, the government will not be able to.[16] One of China's other large cities, Guangzhou has also followed suit.[17] One problem is that China will see a shortfall of workers by 2030 as the working age population of those between 15 and 64 will only grow at a rate of four percent per year while those between 50 and 64 will increase by 67 percent between 2005 and 2030.[18] What this means is that the ratio of workers (those contributing to China's social security program of sorts) to the retired has steadily declined from 10:1 in 1990, to 3:1 in 2003 and projected to be 2.5:1 in 2020. This is combined with 25 Chinese provinces that have an estimated cumulative pension deficit of nearly US$1 trillion.[19] With 325 million Chinese reaching 65 and retiring in 2030 and not much in the pot, "the have another kid policy" is perhaps one of the few ways out of a problem that makes the discussion about the US Social Security funding problems seem like a nonevent. The UK faces similar problems with a reported $98 billion pension shortage and is considering raising the age to become eligible for pensions to 69.[20]

The Need for Immigration

Declining populations in developed countries will create a need for the immigration of workers. Drucker estimated that Germany would need one million immigrants a year by 2030 to fill vacant jobs, and Japan is considering allowing in 500,000 Korean immigrants each year for a stay of up to five years. Singapore, Spain, Portugal, Greece and Finland relaxed their immigration laws in response to their declining populations, the UK is reported to be recruiting Poles and other Easten Europeans, and Russia has been reported to be recruiting Indians to settle in Siberia. South Korea, which has a fertility rate of 1.1 births per woman, is blaming a shortage of workers for a decline in new manufacturers, and its businesses are asking for more immigration. Sony had called for more immigration in 2004, and businesses in Germany have called for the government to promote the immigration of more skilled workers.[21] Although immigrants will be needed to fill jobs, Drucker felt they might not be easily assimilated into their new societies, resulting in social tensions and friction.

These demographic changes will also force businesses to rethink their strategies. Catering to the youth market of the last several decades, which sustained growth, may no longer work as the number of younger people decline. Companies may have to think of two segmented markets, an older-age market and a smaller, but more affluent, youth market. Companies will need to really examine changing demographics and their impact on business, and this must be done straight away since as Drucker observed, these changes are taking place now.

The Steady Decline in Manufacturing

Drucker also observed the following major changes taking place in the manufacturing sectors of developed countries. First, labor costs as a percentage of total manufacturing costs have declined from 30 percent of total manufacturing costs to 12 to 15 percent of total manufacturing costs in the last 40 years. The implication of this, according to Drucker, is that developing countries will no longer be able to compete solely on the basis of cheap labor costs. How this will complicate China's strategy to create more labor-intensive manufacturing industries to deal with its enormous unemployment problem will be an interesting situation to watch closely. Second, manufacturing output will double in developed countries by 2020, but at the same time, due to information technology, manufacturing employment will decrease. As an example, manufacturing employment as a percent of the total workforce in the United States has already decreased from 30 percent to 15 percent in the last 40 years, and manufacturing employment is estimated to comprise less than 10 to 12 percent of the workforce by 2020.

The same trend of decreasing manufacturing employment can be seen in developed countries in Europe as well as in China. Drucker concluded that the manufacturing sector would be a declining producer of wealth in terms of the percentage of a country's GDP. Coupled with this will be increased protectionism as countries attempt to protect their domestic manufacturing industries and workers' jobs. Despite China's accession to the World Trade Organization (WTO) in 2001, it continues to experience US protectionism efforts relative to its steel, electronic appliances, furniture, textiles and other industries through the execution of the "safeguard" provisions agreed to by China as a requirement for its WTO membership. At the same time, China continues to provide subsidies to its domestic impacted industries that are also used to foster protectionism.

The Splintering of the Workforce

As a result of the changing demographics, workforces will be comprised of young workers and older workers. People will continue to work beyond the normal retirement age as a result of better healthcare on the positive side, and on the negative side, decreasing retirement benefits (poor pension plan performance as a result of the global economic crisis) that would otherwise have allowed them to retire. Already countries are considering increasing the retirement age as the number of workers who are contributing to government-sponsored retirement plans such as Social Security in the United States is declining, while the number of retirees is increasing. The employee mix of an organization will change to a combination of full-time employees and outsourced employees who will belong to a human resources staffing company, or they may be independent contractors. They will also be knowledge workers, and this latter mobile workforce will present challenges to human resources departments, since existing policies do not take into consideration the splintering of the workforce as Drucker described. Managing and leading non-employees will create the need for creative leadership on the part of management to ensure the retention of these groups, along with their motivation, commitment and performance. As Drucker pointed out, they will have to be treated as "partners" not employees, and few managers know how to do that today.

The 21st Century and Political Instability and Social Unrest

Drucker said the first several decades of the 21st century would see political instability and social unrest. One need not elaborate on this—just look around the world.

Closing Some Drucker Gaps

Each of Drucker's observations that he identified in the Next Society attests to his view of himself as a social scientist and have proven to be very accurate. However, in a number of cases, he omitted both *what to do* as well as the *how to* do it. Following is a brief review of the issues Drucker identified in the Next Society and how to close these gaps and more readily apply his concepts.

Fourth Information Revolution

Drucker identified this revolution and the significance of the Internet in marketing but did not expand on what organizations should do about this or how to do it. He went on to say, "The traditional multinational may very well become obsolete. They will be killed by e-commerce. The e-commerce delivery of goods, services, repairs, spare parts and maintenance will require a different organization than that of any multinational today. It will require a different mind-set, a different top management, and in the end, different definitions of performance—and the way performance is measured." He went on to add, "Under e-commerce, delivery will become one area in which a business can truly distinguish itself—it will become the decisive competitive factor even where brands seem to be entrenched. And no existing multinational and altogether, very few businesses are organized for it. Very few even think that way."[22] Drucker left us hanging in terms of what these different organizations should look like and what kind of different management they will require. I had to rely on other contributors in the field of marketing and on the extensive literature on the use of the Internet to close the Drucker gap. The business model of Dell, the computer company, initially appeared to be a good place to start, and I incorporated a number of Harvard cases relative to Dell in the China programs.[23]

Although China has surpassed the United States in the total number of Internet users (there were an estimated 298 million Internet users in China at the end of 2008, a dramatic increase from only 8.9 million in 2000 and a meager 620,000 in 1997),[24] it has been suggested that it will take over a decade for China to achieve the same Internet revenues.[25] Culturally, Internet marketing may also face some high hurdles to overcome in China, as the Chinese prefer more face-to-face interactions, feeling the product, and also having the opportunity to negotiate the price down.

Changing Demographics and the "Starbucks Economy"

Drucker pointed out the many problems countries will face as a result of these changing demographics as well as their impact on the composition of markets from a business perspective. Closing this Drucker gap required more input from the marketing discipline, including identifying and responding to the needs of these market segments and target markets. Mark J. Penn in an *MSN.com* article (August 2007) "Trend surfing—The Critical 1%," added some additional insight on changing demographics in the United States and their marketing implications. He commented, "Never has marketing been more oriented toward youth and yet our society has never been older. Never have we been so obsessed with emotional marketing while consumers have become feature oriented, combing through hundreds of pages of websites when making purchasing decisions. Never has family life been so strongly depicted as the center of our lives while people are choosing to work more and more, even after they achieve affluence." He went on to add that the "traditional landscape of class, age, religion and geography is giving way to a whole new array of choice based on shared personal tastes and convictions. We are moving away from the Ford economy, where the idea was to mass merchandise on a low-cost, standardized basis, to the Starbucks economy, where the organizing principal is to improve personal satisfaction based on the niching of America."[26]

Trends Within Trends

Drucker also suggested that we have to be aware of trends within trends. The example he cited was the unexpected baby boom in the United States in the 1980s and early 1990s that was later attributed to the increased birth rates of immigrants."[27] Although we focused on China's aging society, there is still a huge market segment of over 90 million that were born in the 1980s and are now having children of their own. In fact, the population growth of China is forecasted to actually be closer to 16 million to 22 million per year until 2016 as a result of this generation having their own children. The result is that one-third of China's population consists of babies under three years old.[28] Applying Drucker then, several segments can be identified that present marketing opportunities for consumer products and services, from the increasing older population to the younger generation and their children. Another huge segment consists of the estimated 30 million Chinese that are moving from the rural areas to the cities each year, a trend that will continue for the next 10 years, resulting in over half of the population living in the larger cities by 2010.[29] This would be the equivalent of everyone in California moving to another state each year.

Summary

As you review the various chapters in this book, keep Drucker's observations on the Next Society in mind, as they have a direct impact on strategy, sales and marketing, innovation, and many of the other topics covered in this book. The key takeaway here would have to be changing demographics and the opportunities and problems this will create (see the attached Next Society Issues Impact Assessment Tool.)

As in the case in real estate and retail where there are three reasons for success—location, location and location—in the case of strategy, Drucker taught us to think of demographics, demographics and demographics.

Next Society Issues Impact Assessment Tool

An Issues Impact Assessment tool was added in our programs in order to facilitate closing some of the Drucker gaps. The tool allowed the participants to transfer some of the broad observations of Drucker relative to the Next Society into the participants' own environment. The key takeaway here is to allow the participants to identify potential opportunities as well as threats to their organizations and to them personally.

The Next Society and China: Issues Impact Assessment

Instructions

1. This Issues Impact Assessment is designed to allow you to reflect on the issues covered in this chapter and assess their potential impact on Chinese organizations (both inside and outside of China), Management Practices and on you personally.

2. Identify an issue that was covered in this chapter and complete the assessment. An example is provided for you.
3. List what you feel the impact this issue will have on Chinese organizations both inside and outside of China.
4. Will this issue present opportunities or threats? What kind?
5. What might the impact of this issue have on you personally?
6. There are no right or wrong answers in terms of completing this assessment.

	CHINESE ORGANIZATIONS		OPPORTUNITIES & THREATS		YOU
Issue	Impact Inside China	Impact Outside China	Opportunity	Threat	Personal Impact
Aging Population of China	Healthcare and other support needed for older people will increase.	May attract foreign competitors— Assisted living industry.	Healthcare and medicine. Assisted living facilities. Live-in assistant services. Other?	Increased social burden and costs to government if issue cannot be addressed through private enterprises.	How to care for older parents and at same time, pursue career in other city? Apartment is too small to accommodate parents.
	How to fund retirement programs of projected older people when numbers of younger people are declining.	May attract foreign competitors— financial services firms—individual retirement accounts.	Financial services— retirement planning.	Same as above	How to support older parents if no retirement plan in place?

Endnotes

1. Peter F. Drucker, *Managing in a Time of Great Change* (New York: Truman Talley Books, 1998), 43.

2. Much of what is contained in this chapter is an updated version of my *Business Beijing* magazine article, Robert W. Swaim, Ph.D., "The Drucker Files: Drucker on the Next Society and China—Part I," *Business Beijing* (November 2003).

3. Peter F. Drucker, *Managing in the Next Society* (New York: Truman Talley Books, 2002).

4. Peter F. Drucker, *Managing in a Time of Great Change* (New York: Truman Talley Books, 1998), 41–43.

5. Peter F. Drucker, *Managing in the Next Society* (New York: Truman Talley Books, 2002), xi.

6. Ibid., 13.

7. Peter F. Drucker, *Managing in the Next Society* (New York: Truman Talley Books, 2002), 251.

8. "Japan Elderly Population Ratio Now World's Highest," *China Daily* & *Reuters* (June 30, 2006).

9. "Aging Population Test Social Security," *China Daily* (December 13, 2006).

10. Peter F. Drucker, *Management Challenges for the 21st Century* (New York: HarperCollins Publishers, Inc., 1999), 44.

11. Peter F. Drucker, *Managing in the Next Society* (New York: Truman Talley Books, 2002), xi. 242–243.

12. "Zero Population Growth," *Beijing Review* (July 31, 2003).

13. "Population to Peak at 1.5 Billion in 2030s" *China Daily* (June 23, 2006).

14. Mark Fritz, "Cash Incentives Aren't Enough to Lift Fertility," *Wall Street Journal* (August 17, 2006).

15. "Shanghai Addresses Aging Issue" *China Daily* (June 25, 2006).

16. "Only Child Parents Encouraged to Have Second Baby," *China Daily* (September 29, 2006).

17. "Only Child Parents Urged to Have Two Kids" *China Daily* (November 10, 2006).

18. "Working-Age Population Set to Decline'" *China Daily* (September 1, 2006).

19. Gordon G. Chang, *The Coming Collapse of China* (London: Arrow, The Random House Group Limited, 2001), 180–181.

20. "UK Pension Age May Be Raised to 69," *China Daily* (December 1, 2005).

21. Peter F. Drucker, *Managing in the Next Society* (New York: Truman Talley Books, 2002) 263–269.

22. Peter F. Drucker, *Managing in the Next Society* (New York: Truman Talley Books, 2002). 57–58.

23. "The Power of Virtual Integration: An Interview with Dell's Michael Dell," *Harvard Business Review*, Reprint 98208 (1998); and "Matching Dell," *Harvard Business School*, Reprint 799-158 (June 6, 1999).

24. "China Boasts 298 mln Internet Users" *China Daily* (January 13, 2009).

25. "China to Take Decade to be No. 2 Internet Market in Revenues," *Google-Forbes.com* (March 17, 2006).

26. Mark J. Penn, "Trend surfing: The Critical 1%." *MSN.Com* (August 28, 2007).

27. Peter F. Drucker, *Managing in the Next Society* (New York: Truman Talley Books, 2002), 250–251.

28. "Baby Boom," *China Daily* (May 8, 2006).

29. "Half of China to Live in Cities by 2010," *China Daily* (November 7, 2006).

Planning and Managing Organizational Change

The organizations likely to suffer the most are those with the delusion that tomorrow will be like yesterday.[1]

Part One: Drucker and the Change Leader

This book so far has dealt with strategy, organic growth and external growth. Often times, in order to implement the business's strategy it may necessitate changes in the organization such as in its structure, technology, people, including a more frequent change, that of the CEO. Change can be presented as an opportunity or as something to be feared and resisted, depending on how the change effort is managed.

This chapter will present some of Drucker's views relative to change as well as my own as a pundit that are based on my practical experience coupled with teaching the graduate Organization Development Program at the University of San Francisco for several years. As in the previous chapters, this is an abstract of an article I wrote for *Business Beijing* magazine that was directed at managing change in Chinese organizations. However, the concepts are generally applicable anywhere.[2]

Why Change?

Drucker wrote that in today's rapidly changing environment, managers must be able to anticipate, plan and lead change efforts in their organizations. Managers must also be able to create an organizational environment where change is seen as an opportunity, not a threat to be resisted. As he stated, "The organizations likely to suffer the most are those with the delusion that tomorrow will be like yesterday."

This chapter reviews Drucker's requirements for change, what change policies he felt are needed in an organization, and the importance of having a change budget. Here we look at leading change as another necessary function of management. In addition, we will examine what organizations can change—and why—the importance of maintaining continuity with change, and the eight errors that contribute to change effort failures.

Ground Rules for Survival

According to Drucker:
- "Unless it is seen as the task of management of the organization to lead change, the organization will not survive." As Arie de Geus commented in *The Living Company,* "The average life expectancy of a multinational corporation—Fortune 500 or its equivalent—is between 40 and 50 years."[3] He added that people live longer than most organizations.
- In a period of rapid structural change, the only ones who survive are the change leaders.
- A central 21st century challenge for management is to make the organization a change leader.[4]

Reinforcing Drucker

If the twentieth century was one of social transformations, the twenty-first century needs to be one of social and political innovations.[5]

In our MBA and Executive Development Programs, we cited Drucker's major observations relative to change:

1. *Demographics:* Aging populations and declining birthrates
2. *Changing Workforce:* From manual to knowledge work, younger and older employees, full-time employees to part-time, outsourced contract employees, and so forth
3. *Information Acceleration:* Increasing information supply and the impact of the Internet
4. *Instability and Uncertainty:* Political and economic uncertainty
5. *Globalization:* The impact of globalization and structural changes

Drucker had previously written about change when describing what he called "A Century of Social Transformation" in his 1995 book, *Managing in a Time of Great Change.* There he commented, "No century in human history has experienced so many social transformations and such radical ones as the twentieth century."[6] Arie de Geus asking in *The Living Company,* reinforced Drucker's views on change. "But can fundamental change be brought about by foresight? In practice, this can happen only if a company's managers can see the signals for change in time—before the situation has deteriorated to the point where the company is losing options. *In short, to act with foresight, the company must act on signals, rather than on pain.*"[7] Some of the key points from de Geus are:

Anticipating Change

- Identify opportunities and threats
- Stimulate change to take advantage of opportunities
- Be alert and responsive
- Act on signals—not pain

Taking the Mystery Out of Change

Before addressing Drucker's views on how to become a Change Leader, it is important to take the mystery out of change by understanding *why* organizations change and *what* organizations can change. It is also crucial to note what organizations should not change.

Why Organizations Change

Organizations change for a number of different reasons. They can either react to these reasons or be ahead of them. These reasons include:

1. *Crisis:* Obviously September 11 is the most dramatic example of a crisis that caused countless organizations, and even

industries, such as airlines and travel, to change. The crisis at the accounting firm, Arthur Andersen, and its involvement in the Enron scandal obviously created many changes as the organization attempted to survive. The subprime credit crisis, the decline in home values and increased foreclosures, the dramatic increase in oil prices and gasoline prices at the pump, have combined to create demands for change in numerous areas. These include more government control over crude oil futures speculators, more fuel efficient autos, and more domestic sources of energy versus depending on foreign energy, just to name a few suggested changes.

2. *Performance Gaps:* The organization's goals and objectives are not being met, or other organizational needs are not being satisfied. Changes are required to close these gaps. Huge performance gaps in the US auto industry have created the need for many changes including structural changes.

3. *New Technology:* Identification of new technology and more efficient and economical methods to perform work. Are there actually more fuel-efficient autos, such as the one that supposedly runs on air, already in existence that are being kept off of the market by the Big Three auto makers in the United States?

4. *Identification of Opportunities:* Opportunities are identified in the marketplace that the organization needs to pursue in order to increase its competitiveness.

5. *Reaction to Internal and External Pressure:* Management and employees exert pressure for change. External pressures come from many areas, including customers, competition, changing government regulations, shareholders, financial markets, and other factors in the organization's external environment. Consider the pressure domestic airlines are under as a result of the increase in the price of jet fuel, forcing many changes such as a reduced number of flights, additional charges for suitcases, increased ticket prices, and a decrease in the number of cities served.

6. *Mergers and Acquisitions:* As discussed in Chapter 7, Mergers and Acquisitions are new business combinations that often create changes in a number of areas. These changes involve attempting to integrate the two companies successfully and create the benefits that initially made the union attractive.

7. *Change for the Sake of Change:* Often times an organization will appoint a new CEO. In order to prove to the board and shareholders he is doing something, he will make changes just for their own sake.

8. *Sounds Good:* Another reason organizations may institute certain changes is that other organizations are doing so (such as the previous quality circles and re-engineering fads). It sounds good, so the organization tries it.

9. *Planned Abandonment:* Changes as a result of abandoning declining products and markets, and allocating resources to innovation and new opportunities.

What Organizations Can Change

What organizations can change fall into the following broad areas:

1. *Mission, Vision, Strategy:* As discussed in Chapters Two and Three, organizations should continually ask themselves: "What is our business, and what should it be?" Answers to these questions may lead to changes in the organization's mission (the purpose of its business), its vision for the future (what the organization should look like), and its competitive strategy.

2. *Technology:* Organizations can change their technology (for example, the way they produce whatever they sell) in order to increase efficiency and lower costs.

3. *Human-Behavioral Changes:* Training can be provided to managers and employees to provide new knowledge and skills, or people can be replaced or downsized. Downsizing is probably one of the more difficult changes and challenges Chinese SOEs will face as they restructure in an attempt to improve their competitiveness.

4. *Task-Job Design:* The way work is performed in the organization can be changed with new procedures and methods for performing work (Taylor's Scientific Management).

5. *Organizational Structure:* Organizations can change the way they are structured in order to be more responsive to their external environment and their marketplace (Drucker's decentralization). In addition to changes in reporting relationships as

depicted on the organization chart, this also includes where decisions should be made in the organization (centralized or decentralized).

6. *Organizational Culture:* Entities can attempt to change their culture, including management and leadership styles, and their values and beliefs. Of all the things organizations can change, this is by far the most difficult and time consuming to undertake. Chinese SOEs will be faced with changing their cultures that have been ingrained by a planned economy to a market orientation as they attempt to compete more effectively in the global economy. Remember change may take time, attempting to change a culture can best be illustrated by the following quote:

> *The British created a civil service job in 1803. The job called for a man to stand on the cliffs of Dover, overlooking the English Channel with a spyglass.*
>
> *He was supposed to ring a bell if he saw Napoleon and the French Navy coming. The job was abolished in 1945.*[8]

I cited the above quotation in an executive development program I was conducting in London in the early 1980s, and one of the English participants corrected me: "The job was not abolished—they gave him a phone."

These then are the major elements that organizations can change. It is important to note that changes in one of these elements will usually have an impact on another element. As an example, changing technology may require changes in the human-behavioral area (new knowledge and skills on how to use the technology.)

Part Two: Drucker's Insight on Change

The next part of this chapter will highlight what organizations should not attempt to change, why many efforts to change fail, the requirements for change and becoming a change leader, the policy of organized improvement, and Drucker's views relative to the need of a change leader's budget. While the first part dealt with establishing a broad framework for the discussion of change, this section will include a number of Drucker's observations relative to change with an additional discussion from the field of organization development (the planned management of change.) It is important to mention that my views on organization development (OD) differ significantly from the traditional "process approach" OD school. The premise of process consultation is to facilitate the clients in becoming self-sufficient in solving their own problems through self-discovery. I focus on planning and managing complex organizational change using the Action Research Model that will be described later in this chapter. I have also included a case study to illustrate that approach.

What Organizations Should Not Change

When you introduce change, it's very important to maintain continuity and the commitment to fundamental values, which don't change.[9]

According to Drucker, there are a number of things that organizations should not change.[10] These are mainly in the human-behavioral area and include:

1. *Need for Recognition:* Employees need to be recognized for their contribution. Although changes may be required in the organization, employees must be assured that they are doing some things right, and that the changes being made are neither a result nor reflection of their performance.
2. *Need for Respect:* Regardless of what changes may be required, individuals in the organization must continue to be treated with respect. One way of providing this is to continually communicate why the change or changes are necessary.
3. *Need for Trust:* Employees must continue to have trust in their management. One way of maintaining this when change efforts take place is to communicate to employees what will be preserved, and a reminder that the changes are consistent with the organization's mission, objectives, vision and strategy.
4. *Need to Feel Productive:* According to Abraham Maslow and his Hierarchy of Needs Theory, people strive for self-actualization,

the need to be able to utilize their knowledge and skills in performing meaningful work. Although changes may be taking place, there needs to be continuity with respect to people's work. Changes that are being implemented must appear to be consistent with the direction and vision of the organization and individual contributions.

5. *Need to Grow:* Organizations must continue to provide their managers and employees with an opportunity to learn and grow. Change can be a very positive opportunity to provide personal learning and growth opportunities.

Eight Reasons Why Change Efforts Fail

Before discussing what organizations need to do to become Change Leaders, it is useful to review the errors that organizations frequently make that hinder the success of their change efforts:

1. *Not Establishing a Great Enough Sense of Urgency:* Opportunities are lost because the organization fails to establish a sense of urgency as to why the change is needed.
2. *Not Creating a Powerful Enough and Guiding Coalition:* Organizations fail to assemble a group with enough power and prestige to lead the change effort, which also may not have top management's commitment and full support.
3. *Lacking a Vision:* Organizations fail to create a Vision for the future to help direct the change effort. For example, what will be different after the change? What will be preserved? What are the strategy and objectives for achieving the Vision?
4. *Undercommunicating the Vision:* Organizations fail to communicate a Vision for the future. What will the organization look like as a result of the change? The Vision has to be presented as an opportunity—not a threat.
5. *Not Removing Obstacles to the New Vision:* Systems, policies, or structures that seriously undermine the Vision are not dealt with and removed.
6. *Not Systematically Planning and Creating Short-Term Wins:* Individuals are not recognized or rewarded for performance improvement as a result of their change efforts.
7. *Declaring Victory Too Soon:* Organizations fail to monitor the progress of their change efforts and evaluate results. Often

victory is declared when the change has not been totally implemented.

8. *Not Anchoring Changes in the Organization's Culture:* Organizations fail to have employees accept the change as the way things will be done from then on, and as a result they revert to their old familiar ways of doing things.

Drucker's Requirements for Becoming a Change Leader

Having reviewed why and what organizations can change, what not to change, and the errors organizations frequently make when initiating change, the following are Drucker's observations on how organizations can become "Change Leaders" in the fullest sense. Drucker cited the following requirements which the organization needs:[11]

1. Policies to make the future
2. Systematic methods to look for and anticipate change
3. To know the right way to introduce change
4. Policies to balance change and continuity

Policies to Make the Future

Drucker was unequivocal in saying that organizations need to "abandon yesterday" and free resources from being committed to maintaining what no longer contributes to performance, and no longer produces results. He said, "It is not possible to create tomorrow unless one first sloughs off yesterday, for to maintain yesterday always commits the organization's scarcest and most valuable resources and—above all—its ablest people to non-results."[12] Therefore, the first policy needed is that of Planned Abandonment as covered earlier.

Policy of Planned Abandonment   This policy starts out with the question: "If we do not do this already, would we, knowing what we know now, go into it?" If the answer is "No," the reaction must be: "What do we do now?"[13] Drucker argued that abandonment is the right action if a product, service, market, or process still has a few good years of life. Organizations tend always to overestimate how much life is still left.

Drucker thought differently: "They are not dying, they are dead." Dying products, services or processes always demand the greatest care and greatest efforts—but they tie down the most productive people. Organizations must therefore systematically review their products and services and so forth, and abandon those that no longer contribute to results. Organizations should have an Abandonment Report and regular management meetings to determine what needs to be abandoned. Planned Abandonment was also covered in detail in chapter 6.

Policy of Organized Improvement   The second policy required of Change Leaders is one of Organized Improvement. Essentially this refers to the previous discussion of What Organizations Can Change. Here Drucker pointed out the need for being able to define performance in a given area.[14] Once performance is defined, gaps can be identified, and decisions can be made if the performance gap is such that changes are required. This policy tends to deal with the topic of organizational effectiveness versus strategy as Michael Porter differentiated and was briefly covered in Chapter 3.

Exploiting Success   According to Drucker, many organizations are so dominated by a focus on problem solving that it undermines their ability to be flexible and innovative. Most organizations squash creativity. Here the organization needs to identify opportunities. As Drucker said, "Organizations need to starve problems and focus on opportunities."[15]

Regular operating reports received by management should be accompanied by an Opportunity Page outlining identified opportunities that the organization might pursue. Employees also need to be encouraged to look for changes that can be exploited as opportunities for different products, businesses, processes and services.

Policy of Systematic Innovation and Creating Change   The fourth policy required is one of Systematic Innovation, that is, a policy to create change and make the entire organization see change as an opportunity. In *Innovation & Entrepreneurship,* Drucker cited many windows of opportunity an organization should systematically explore. The one offering the most opportunities for innovation, he felt, were analyzing the reasons for "Unexpected Successes and Unexpected Failures."

Piloting

Neither studies nor market research nor computer modeling are a substitute for the test of reality. Everything improved or new therefore first to be tested on a small scale, that is, it needs to be PILOTED.[16]

Drucker's brief discussion of the need for piloting essentially addressed one of the Change Strategies to consider when planning a major change effort. Here, Drucker confined his discussion to the introduction of new products.

The Change Leader's Budget

According to Drucker, in order to be a Change Leader, the organization needs a Change Leader's Budget. Where the organization has an operating budget of 80 to 90 percent of all expenditures, it should also have a Change Leader's Budget for the future.[17] This would be 10 to 12 percent of all expenditures, and focus on future products, new services, new technologies, the development of markets and customers, distribution channels, and the development of people.

The budget should be maintained for the future to exploit successes when the organization is experiencing both good and poor financial performance. Competition is likely to reduce its spending when the industry is having difficult times; therefore, maintenance of the budget through these periods can create an opening.

Change and Continuity

Change should also be accompanied by continuity. Education and communications are extremely important relative to changes the organization plans to implement. Part of these communications must include what is going right in order to reinforce morale, protect self-worth, build credibility and reduce potential resistance. In addition to describing the Vision (what the organization will look like after the change), it is important to communicate what will be preserved. Equally important is communicating the relationship or linkage between the planned change and the overall direction of the organization. It is imperative that the change be consistent with the organization's mission, vision, and values. These views of Drucker were supported by Arie de Geus when he said, "Every organization must have enough stability to continue to function satisfactorily and still prevent itself from becoming too static or stagnant to adapt to changing conditions."[18]

To try to make the future is highly risky. It is less risky however, than not to try to make it.[19]

Parts 1 and 2 Summary

Implementing the business's strategy may require changes in a number of areas, from how work is performed, to structure and where decisions are made in the organization, to leadership at the top, and so forth.

In Parts 1 and 2, I shared some of Drucker's thoughts on the importance of change, and how organizations can become, according to Drucker, Change Leaders. I have focused on the policies he suggested organizations need to establish in order to achieve this. Drucker stressed that genuine Change Leaders focus on tomorrow, not yesterday, and pursue opportunities for innovation. *How* to plan and lead the change effort and what change strategies and tactics to utilize were largely omitted here by Drucker. In order to close this gap, it was necessary to turn to the Behavioral School and the many tools available from the field of Organization Development that deal with planning, implementing and managing change efforts.

Part Three: Planning and Managing Complex Organizational Change

Parts 1 and 2 discussed *why* organizations must change and *what* they can do to change and incorporated a number of Drucker's views on the subject. I have selected the Action Research Method from the field of Organization Development (OD) as the most practical for those responsible for planning and implementing a major change effort. I have also added a diagnostic tool that can be used in planning a change effort and in particular, assessing who are the people that will be impacted by the change effort and if there will be potential resistance from them to the planned change.

Change Leaders

With respect to the Change Leaders, I discussed the alternatives of using outside Change Leaders or consultants, an internal Change Leaders that might be from the OD Department or a manager or staff member assigned to the project, or using a combination of both. Each alternative has its advantages and disadvantages as described below.[20]

External Change Leader (Outside Consultant)

- *Advantage:* No axe to grind. Can be objective because not involved in internal company politics.
- *Disadvantage:* Not familiar with the organization and may require time to become familiar with the organization and its practices.
- *Disadvantage:* Usually cannot follow up on the implementation of the change effort.

Internal Change Leader

- *Advantage:* Knows the organization and the key players (unless recently hired).
- *Disadvantage:* May not be objective because of internal politics. May favor one group to the exclusion of others in the planned change.

If the change effort being contemplated is a large one and may impact the entire organization, using a combination of an external and internal Change Leader may be the best approach. This combines the expertise in change management of the outside consultant with the knowledge of the organization of the internal Change Leader. With respect to selecting the internal Change Leader, this should be a person who has credibility and respect in the organization and is known for getting results.

The Action Research Model

There are number of popular change models in OD literature including Kurt Lewin's *Three Step Process* the Lippitt, Watson and Westley *Phases of Planned Change;* and the *Action Research Model,* which I selected as the most practical.[21] Once again, I am positioning the discussion here as though dealing with a complex organizational change. There are many changes a manager might make that do not require the complete application of the Action Research Model that is described in Table 10.1.

The following briefly describes each of the steps in the Action Research Model. For a more detailed discussion see the Harvey and Brown book, *An Experiential Approach to Organization Development.*[22] The case at the end of this chapter will also illustrate each of these steps.

Table 10.1   The Action Research Model for Managing Change

1. Scouting	6. Implementation
2. Entry	7. Evaluation
3. Data Collection	8. Stabilization
4. Diagnosis	9. Termination
5. Action Planning	

Action Research Step 1: Scouting

Awareness of a Need for Change, the first step, involves the client (senior executive) becoming aware of a problem (Performance Gap) and a perceived need for change although he may not be aware of the real problem or what changes are needed. This might also include being aware of an opportunity to be pursued that may also require some changes to be made (see Table 10.2).

Table 10.2   Scouting: Awareness of a Need for Change

Client	Change Leader
1. Performance gaps recognized and an awareness of a need for change	1. Meet with client
2. Contacts and meets with the change leader (internal or external)	2. Discuss awareness, readiness and commitment for change
3. Discuss awareness of need for change and readiness for change	3. Verify power and authority to implement change
4. Assignment given to change leader and commitment made for change	

The client may next meet with a Change Leader (internal or external) to review the situation, including an awareness of a need for change and the client's readiness for change. The Change Leader verifies the client's readiness and commitment to change and also that the necessary power and authority exists to approve the change effort. This would include determining the resources that would be made available for the change (Drucker's Change Budget). Based on this discussion, the Change Leader accepts the assignment and proceeds to Step 2.

Tasks and Change Tools Used   Tools that the Change Leader uses in the first step are depicted in Table 10.3.

Table 10.3   Scouting Tasks and Change Tools

Tasks	Change Tools
1. Awareness of a need for change (Problem)	1. Define Performance Gap
2. Awareness of a need for change (Opportunity)	2. Preliminary Assessment of Change Equation*
	3. Define Source of Innovation
	4. Preliminary Assessment of Change Equation

*The change equation is a diagnostic tool used in assessing a change effort and will be described later in this chapter.

Action Research Step 2: Entry (Establish Contract)

Establish Contract Step 2 involves establishing a contract between the client and the Change Leader that details the work to be performed and expected results. This would include:

1. Defining the assignment and how it will be performed
2. Defining the expected results and when the results will be delivered
3. Determining what additional resources and support may be required
4. Exploring the problem or opportunity to be pursued further
5. Communicating the Change Leader's objectives to the organization

With respect to establishing a contract, this would generally be a consulting contract with the external Change Leader that would include fees, and so forth. A contract with the internal Change Leader might be a Work Plan outlining all the tasks to be completed with respect to the change effort. Item 5 above is important since if the organization's members understand the Change Leader's objectives and their potential involvement in the process, a higher degree of commitment for the eventual change can be built. (see Table 10.4).

Tasks and Change Tools Used

Table 10.4   Entry: Tasks and Change Tools

Tasks	Change Tools
1. Define how assignment will be performed	1. Analysis of Change Equation: Identify impacted groups
2. Determine support required	2. Consider appropriate strategies and tactics to use
	3. Identify impacted groups to involve in process

Diagnostic Tool: The Change Equation

Before continuing with a description of the Action Research Model, it would be helpful to discuss a tool that can be used early on in analyzing and planning the change effort. An excellent diagnostic tool for assessing a change effort is the Change Equation as depicted in Figure 10.1. It is important to note for the mathematically inclined that the equation is used for illustrative purposes and cannot be quantified. The elements of the equation include C or the desired change, F or the situation in the future (desired state or vision) as a result of the change, N or the situation now, P or the plan of how to get from the now to the future, and R or potential resistance to the change. It should be noted that the R could also be denoted as PL or perceived loss. That is, what those who will be impacted by the change effort perceive they will lose as a result of the change (power, prestige, benefits, reporting relationships, authority and responsibility, and so forth).

If the sum of the future minus the present is positive, and multiplied by the change plan is greater than the potential resistance, the change effort will be successful.

Managing the Equation

The following is a discussion of each element of the equation and how the Change Leader can manage it.

$$C = (F-N) \times P > R$$
$$\text{Change} = (\text{Future} - \text{Now}) \times \text{Plan} > \text{Resistance}$$

Figure 10.1   The Change Equation Diagnostic Tool

Change Equation Step 1: Managing the "N"   The first step in managing the Change Equation deals with "N" or the present or situation "Now." The Change Leader must create dissatisfaction with the present situation and create an awareness of a need for change. As an example, "Customers are complaining about our products' poor quality. We are losing sales and good customers as a result. If this continues, we may have to close the plant, lay off workers, etc., etc." The job here is create as much dissatisfaction with the present situation as possible (deficits or (–)). The Education and Communication and Involvement and Participant Tactics are recommended here. Share information with those who will be impacted by the change, such as results from customer surveys, task forces, focus groups and so forth. The more *negative* information that can be provided as to why the need for change the better. A classic example of this application was the Broadway musical of the 1950s, the *Music Man* starring Robert Preston. Preston played the part of a salesman in the Midwest who sold instruments and uniforms for children to form bands. In one scene he sang about a pool table in the town of River City and how the presence of the pool table was corrupting the children, distracting them away from their studies and chores. His song, "Trouble in River City" was an excellent example, of his managing the "N" and creating dissatisfaction with the present situation. Of course, he eventually went on to describe the "F" and how the trouble would be removed with the creation of a boys' band in River City, the change he desired. From this brief example, it can also be seen that the Change Equation directly applies to selling and can be used to assess a selling situation. The only difference in the Change Equation for this application is the "R," which deals with removing the buyer's "risk" in doing business with your company vs. the one he is presently dealing with.

It is also important to acknowledge what is going right and that not everything needs to be changed. This is important to reinforce morale, protect others' self-worth, build credibility in the Change Leader, and helps to reduce resistance.

Change Equation Step 2: Managing the "F"   Managing the "F" presents a Vision for the future—what will things be like after the change. Here it is necessary to show the benefits of the change as well as what will be preserved. The goal is to create and present the value (+) of moving to the future, that deficits (–) will be removed, organizational needs will be satisfied, and value will be obtained. Also, convert any potential perceived loss (resistance) into gain.

In communicating the Future, the communications campaign should include:

- Whether the way people work will change
- What new skills may be required and how they will be provided
- Whether people will have to behave differently
- Whether the change will present a good opportunity for the people or there may be some negative consequences
- Link the change effort to show consistency with the organization's Mission, Vision and Values
- How the change supports the organization's business direction and objectives
- Focus on people—they need to feel valued and included

Figure 10.2 illustrates how the first two elements of the Change Equation (Now and Future) should be managed.

Change Equation Step 3: Managing the "R"   Managing the "R" deals with those who will be impacted by the change effort and overcoming potential resistance or perceived loss or what people think they will lose as a result of the change effort. The Participation and Involvement Strategies and Tactics are most appropriate to use here—involving those who will be impacted by the change or representatives of those groups in the change planning process.

The "R" and Resistance to Change   Before going on to the next step in managing the Change Equation it will be useful to briefly review why there is resistance to change efforts. The major sources of resistance to change include:

$$C = (F-N) \times P > R$$
$$\uparrow \quad \uparrow$$
$$(+) \ (-)$$
Benefits Deficits

Figure 10.2   Managing the "F" & "N"

Uncertainty about the Causes and Effects of the Change

- People avoid uncertainty (risk)—established procedures are well known and predictable.
- Lack of trust—distrust of any changes instituted from above.
- Need new skills—may need to learn new skills or information.
- Could have an initial negative impact on performance and impact rewards (compensation, promotion).
- Negative performance—change may be interpreted as not doing present job well.

Unwillingness to Give Up Existing Benefits (Perceived Loss)

- Unwillingness to give up tasks and relationships.
- Loss of power, prestige, salary, quality of work and other benefits (security).

Awareness of a Weakness in Changes Being Proposed

- Potential problems overlooked by initiators of the change ("We tried this before and it didn't work").
- Plan to introduce the change considered to be too complicated, costly and time consuming. May also disrupt current operations.

Lack of Credibility of the Change Leader

- Change Leader may not be respected by the organization or have credibility.
- Has this person been able to produce results before?
- What experience does the Change Leader have in previous change efforts?

Increasing Resistance to Change   All of these factors contributing to resistance or perceived loss will increase if:

- Change is seen as threatening if it is not perceived as helpful.
- Change will be opposed by the impacted group unless they have specifically requested it.
- Change will be opposed by management as a real or imaginary threat to their prestige and authority unless they have specifically requested the change.

- Group opposition is usually more than the sum total of individuals' opposition $(2 + 2 = 6)$.
- Magnitude of the change—the greater the change, the greater the opposition by the affected groups.

These factors that increase resistance can be potentially reduced by communicating the benefits of the change and that there is also continuity with the change. This comes from managing the elements of the Change Equation. The greater the prestige of the manager supporting the change effort, or that of the Change Leader, the greater influence he or she can exert for the change. Providing information as to the "N" and "F" and the "P" can substantially reduce this resistance. Involving members of the affected groups in the planning process can also create internal pressure for the change.

Change Equation Step 4: Managing the "P"   As pointed out, having an incomplete plan can contribute to resistance to the change effort. Therefore, it is essential that the plan meet the following criteria:

1. The plan must not be complicated and must be easily understood.
2. The plan must be perceived as doable and present the credibility of the Change Leader.
3. The plan must not consume large amounts of time or resources or be disruptive to operations.
4. The plan must indicate what will be preserved.

Other criteria include involving those who will be affected by the change effort in the planning process and communicating that the plan will be successful and produce the desired results.

Elements of the Plan   The change effort plan should include the following elements:

1. *Description of the "N" and "F":* What the organization looks like today and what you want it to look like after the change.
2. *Communications Plan:* Informing everyone about the change, as well as keeping them up-to-date as your change effort evolves.
3. *Recognition Plan:* How you will celebrate successes and reward those employees that support you and your change effort.

4. *Guidelines:* Defining processes, roles, and responsibilities in order to reduce conflict and potential power struggles.
5. *Measurements:* Identifying accountability and tracking success.

There are many benefits to having a good change effort plan. First, it acts as a roadmap and lets everyone know where we are going, how to get there, and when have arrived. Second, it is a communications tool that lets everyone know why the change is needed, clarifies any misunderstandings, tells employees what they need to do, and what they can expect of you. Third, it is a marketing tool to help sell the employees on the change effort. Other benefits include a quality assurance tool to provide quality control of the change effort, a credibility builder to let employees know you are in charge and in control, and a resistance reducer providing evidence that the change effort will be a success.

As can be seen, the Change Equation can be a good diagnostic tool in analyzing and planning a change effort. Experienced Change Leaders use this tool early in the process to help determine what groups might be affected and potentially resist the change effort and thus select the appropriate change strategies and tactics.

Action Research Step 3: Data Collection

The next step in the change process is Data Collection—gathering information about the problem or opportunity to be pursued. There are many sources to consider, similar to performing market research as depicted in Table 10.5.

Action Research Step 4: Diagnosis

After data has been collected, the next step is a diagnosis and providing feedback to the client on the part of the Change Leader as depicted in Table 10.6.

Table 10.5   Data Collection: Tasks and Tools

Tasks	Change Tools
1. Gather information about the problem or opportunity	1. Secondary research sources
	2. Focused interviews and focus groups (submit issues for discussion in advance)
	3. Feedback instruments (questionnaires and surveys)
	4. Participation and Involvement Strategies and Tactics

Table 10.6   Diagnosis: Tasks and Tools

Tasks	Change Tools
1. Definition of "real problem" or issues relative to the opportunity	1. Focus and Problem Solving Groups (Participation and Involvement Tactic)
2. Preliminary recommendations for change	2. Assessment of Change Equation
3. Feedback to client	3. Change Strategies and Tactics
4. Client's commitment to change	

During this step, it is important to provide feedback to the client as to what the "real problem" is and what the Change Leader recommends for change. Here, it is essential to obtain the client's commitment to proceed with the change. Also, prior to going on to the next step, Action Planning, it is important to determine what strategy and tactics will be used to implement the change effort. The following is a brief discussion of the strategies and tactics that are available to use in a change effort.

Change Strategies and Tactics

People are not stressed because there's too much change in organizations but because of the way in which change is made.[23]

Change Strategies   There are three approaches or strategies to consider when planning and managing a change effort. These include a Top Down or Unilateral Approach, A Shared Responsibility–Participative Approach, and a Bottom Up or Pilot Program Approach. It is possible to use all three strategies in one change effort as described below.[24]

Top Down–Unilateral Approach: The CEO issues an order that something needs to be changed (product quality improved, better customer service response, and so on). The advantage of this approach is that change is implemented quickly. The disadvantage is that the decision might have been made in isolation without having complete information.

Shared Responsibility–Participative Approach: Those who might be affected the most are involved in the assessment and planning of the change effort. The advantage is through involvement and participation, potential resistance to change can be decreased, and a sense of ownership will be developed for the change effort. This helps to improve the probability of the employees' commitment to the change and its success. The disadvantage is that a participative approach takes time for people to meet and may not be conducive to authoritative cultures. In addition, the group must have a leader skilled at leading group problem analysis and decision-making meetings to prevent the horse from becoming a camel.

Bottom-Up–Pilot Program Approach: Perhaps the change being contemplated will have an impact on the entire organization. If the organization is large, it might be best to test the change in one location in the form of a Pilot Program (Drucker's Piloting). The advantage is being able to assess the change effort and make changes that may be necessary to improve its success before impacting the entire organization, or abandoning the change effort if no positive results are achieved. The only drawback to this approach is ensuring that the change effort has the support and commitment of senior management and those in power and is not seen as an individual effort in guerrilla warfare.

As pointed out, these strategies can be used in combination. As an example, the CEO feels a change is required (Top Down). He appoints a Change Leader to study the problem and recommend what changes should be made. The Change Leader forms a group of knowledgeable people, many of whom will be possibly impacted by the change and could resist to be involved in developing the change plan (Shared Responsibility). Part of the eventual change plan is to test it in one of the organization's locations (Pilot Program).

Change Tactics   Although there are a number of tactics that can be used in implementing a change effort, the most effective ones are communications, participation, and facilitation.[25]

Education and Communications: Continuous communications and the sharing of information with those who will be most impacted by the change as to why the change is needed, what will be changed, what will be preserved, how the change effort is consistent with the organization's mission and vision, what the plan for the change will be, and so forth.

Facilitation and Support: Often changes will require new knowledge and skills on the part of those who will be impacted by the change. They need to be advised that they will be provided training and other support needed in order to perform after the change has been implemented.

Participation: This is essentially the same as the Shared Responsibility Strategy of involving those who will be impacted by the change in the planning and implementation of the change effort.

Action Research Step 5: Action Planning

Once the client commits to the change effort, an action plan needs to be developed including identifying what change strategies and tactics will be used. An essential part of the plan includes a communications campaign in terms of communicating the need for change and what changes will be required to eliminate a Performance Gap or to pursue an opportunity, particularly to those who will be impacted by the change. Tools used to accomplish these tasks include the Change Equation, particularly important in assessing those who will be impacted by the change effort and who may resist and the strategies and tactics to use in terms of Education and Communication (see Table 10.7).

Table 10.7   Action Planning: Tasks and Tools

Tasks	Change Tools
1. Mutual development of Action Plan for change effort includes: • Change Required • Implementation Plan • Strategies and Tactics	1. Analysis of Change Equation: • Identify "R" and involve in action planning • Determine change strategies and tactics
2. Develop Communications Campaign—Communications of the Elements of the Change Equation (C, N, F, & P to the organization)	2. Education and Communications Tactics

Action Research Step 6: Implementation

Before proceeding with the change effort's implementation, it is important to ensure that those with the power, authority, and influence in the organization are committed to and support the change effort. It is also essential to gain the endorsement from those with credibility and prestige in the organization when dealing with a complex organizational change. Without this support, and the use of appropriate strategies and tactics for its implementation, the change effort will be resisted and fail. Once again, continued communications via the Education and Communications Tactic is important for reinforcing the need for the change (see Table 10.8).

Table 10.8   Implementation: Tasks and Tools

Tasks	Change Tools
1. Gain commitment from those with power and authority	1. Power, Authority and Influence Assessment
2. Gain endorsement for change from those with credibility and prestige in the organization	2. Participation and Involvement Strategy
	3. Possible Negotiations Tactic
4. Implement Change Plan	4. Change Strategies and Tactics
5. Continue Communications Campaign	5. Education and Communications Tactic

Action Research Step 7: Evaluation

An assessment of progress and results of the change effort must be ongoing. Based on the results, additional diagnosis and modifications to the change plan may be required. Here, the Participation and Involvement Strategies and Tactics may need to be continuously used as tools. Communication continues to be important in terms of keeping the organization apprised of progress of the change effort (see Table 10.9).

Table 10.9   Evaluation: Tasks and Tool

Tasks	Change Tools
1. Assessment and evaluation of the change effort and results	1. Participation and Involvement Strategies and Tactics
2. Further diagnosis may be required	2. Participation and Involvement Strategies and Tactics
3. Modifications to Change Plan	3. Education Communications and Tactic—progress, results, changes

Table 10.10   Stabilization: Tasks and Tools

Tasks	Change Tools
1. Change accepted by organization as a way of life	1. Education and Communications Tactic
2. Change seen as an opportunity—not a threat	2. Education and Communications Tactic

Action Research Step 8: Stabilization

Once the change effort has been successfully implemented, it is important to continue the Education and Communication Tactic to allow the organization and those impacted by the change to accept this as the "way of life"—that we should have been doing this all along. Without this, people will regress to the old ways. They should also see the change effort as an opportunity and not a threat (see Table 10.10).

Action Research Step 9: Termination

Here, the external Change Leader departs while the internal Change Leader ensures the change is stabilized. The internal Change Leader may receive a new assignment, and the process is then repeated.

Common Mistakes in Change Efforts

One of the most frequent mistakes made in managing a change effort is going from Step 1—Scouting, to Step 6—Action Planning and Step 7—Implementation, and ignoring the steps in between. As a result, the proper strategies and tactics are neglected. Also, input from knowledge workers, functional specialists, and those responsible for the results is typically ignored. It is important that all steps in the Action Research Model be completed in sequence, including the use of the diagnostic tool during the early steps.

Part Three Summary

This was a brief description of the Action Research Model for Planning and Implementing a complex change effort. The case study at the end of this chapter will illustrate how each of these steps was actually handled.

The key take-aways from this part are to review the Eight Errors that contribute to change failure and also "what" to preserve in any change effort. The Change Strategies and Tactics as described in this part are also key to consider when contemplating a change effort. Finally, the Action Research Model, if followed, can lead to a more successful change effort. An Assessment Tool is included at the end of the chapter relative to Drucker's Requirements for Change.

I conclude this chapter with my favorite quotation on change:

There is nothing more difficult to carry out, nor more doubtful of success, nor more dangerous to handle, than to initiate a new order of things, for the reformer has enemies in all those who profit by the old order, and only lukewarm defenders in all those who profit by the new order, this lukewarmness arising partly from fear of their adversaries, who have the laws in their favor, and partly from the incredulity of mankind, who do not truly believe in anything new until they have actual experience of it.[26]

Machiavelli

Leading Change Assessment Tool:

Assessing the Four Requirements for Change

Instructions

1. Assess your organization with respect to the Four Requirements for Change.
2. Comment where you feel improvement is necessary, what kind of improvement is needed, and why.

Four Requirements for Change

1. Policies to Make the Future (circle a number)

No Policies			Some Policies			Complete Policies		
1	2	3	4	5	6	7	8	9

IMPROVEMENTS NEEDED: _____
_____
_____

2. Systematic Methods to Look for and Anticipate Change (circle a number)

No Methods			Some Methods			Complete Methods		
1	2	3	4	5	6	7	8	9

IMPROVEMENTS NEEDED: _____
_____
_____

3. Know Right Way to Introduce Change (circle a number)

Don't Know Right Way			Somewhat Know			Completely Know		
1	2	3	4	5	6	7	8	9

IMPROVEMENTS NEEDED: _____
_____
_____

4. Change Efforts and Maintaining Continuity Are Balanced (circle a number)

Not Balanced			Somewhat Balanced			Change and Continuity Balanced		
1	2	3	4	5	6	7	8	9

IMPROVEMENTS NEEDED: _____
_____
_____

Case Study: The Change Process, Analyzing and Planning a Change Effort

OCCIDENTAL PETROLEUM (OXY)

Case Overview

This is an actual change effort that I planned and managed as an External Change Leader for the Occidental Petroleum Corporation (Oxy) of Los Angles, California, in the early 1980s. Referring to the "Action Research Model and Nine Steps for Analyzing and Planning a Change Effort," the following is a brief description of the various activities that were undertaken at each step in the process. Prior to describing each step, a brief background of the company and the external environment at the time is provided.

The Company

At the time of this case, Occidental Petroleum Corporation was the 16th largest US corporation on the Fortune 500 List (revenues of approximately $14 billion) and according to *Fortune* magazine, "The fastest growing company in the United States since *Fortune* began tracking company performance."

Brief History of Occidental Petroleum (Oxy)

It was founded by two oil people in Los Angeles in the 1950s. In search of investment capital to drill their first well (in Beverly Hills, the most exclusive area of Los Angeles which everyone thought was crazy), they found the retired and world-famous entrepreneur, (particularly famous for his relations with every Soviet Union leader since Lenin) Armand Hammer. Hammer invested in the small company for a 50 percent equity interest (initially as a tax write-off), oil was found in Beverly Hills (still a producing field today), and the company got its start.

An Exploration and Production Company Unlike other major multinational petroleum companies such as Exxon, Mobil, Shell, and BP, Oxy was primarily an exploration and production company as opposed to being a totally integrated company that had both refining and retail marketing outlets. Oxy's mission was to explore, find and produce oil and gas, and to sell the products to other oil companies. Its objectives were to find Big Plays, that is, extremely large oil fields with large oil and gas reserves vs. the smaller type oil fields found in the United States. Its focus was therefore on international oil and gas exploration where the opportunities for finding Big Plays were greater than in the United States.

International and Domestic Operations   At the time of this case, Oxy's operations were 95 percent international and only five percent in the United States (primarily in California and Texas). International operations included Argentina, Bolivia, and Peru in Latin America, the North Sea (Scotland, the second-largest Oxy operation and the most profitable), and Libya (Oxy's largest operation but partially nationalized by the Libya Government). Oxy also owned a 50 percent interest in Occidental of Canada. In addition, Oxy established new exploration operations in Australia, China (a JV with CNOOC), Colombia, Madagascar, Oman, Pakistan, and Tunisia. Its exploration and production operations were headquartered in California with Finance, Legal, and Crude Sales and Marketing in Houston, Texas, and its IT Center was in Antwerp, Belgium.

Executives, Management, and Knowledge Workers

All executives and managers of Oxy, including its knowledge workers (petroleum engineers, geologists, geophysicists, and so forth) had extensive experience with other major petroleum companies prior to joining Oxy. What attracted many of these people to join Oxy was the entrepreneurial, fast-paced, nonbureaucratic culture of the company. Decisions were made quickly, risks were allowed to be taken at the local national level, and significant financial resources were devoted to pursuing opportunities. Few, if any, recent college graduates were recruited, as Oxy desired to hire only experienced people. Although the company employed several thousand "national" employees in its various foreign operations, expatriates held most senior management and technical/professional positions. Also, although all executives, managers and technical/professional employees were highly qualified in their respective professions, few, if any, had any formal management training. Later in the assignment and during an interview with the Executive Vice President of worldwide exploration, the Change Leader asked if his function practised management-by-objectives and how were the objectives established? The EVP replied they had an objective, "To find oil" and that was the end of the discussion on management practices.

The External Environment: The Demand for Knowledge Workers

The external environment was quite similar to what could be found globally in 2006. The price of oil per barrel was at an all-time high. This motivated high exploration activity in the United States. "Oil Patch" and "Rig Count" (the number of drilling rigs operating and drilling for oil—a measure of petroleum industry activity) was also at a peak. New, smaller, and independent exploration and production companies were started in a search for new oil sources in the United States.

This increase in a exploration activity also created a large demand for petroleum industry knowledge workers (geologists, petroleum engineers, and so forth). As a result, to attract experienced professionals from the major oil companies, the independent firms offered signing bonuses, extremely high salaries, and a percentage share in any new oil fields that were discovered. Students graduating with Master's degrees in petroleum engineering and the geosciences were also provided the same packages from the major oil companies including stock grants—not options. For those employed in, or about to enter the industry, things were never better.

The Action Research Model

The following discussion describes how each step of the Action Research Model was completed in dealing with this case.

Step One: Scouting, an Awareness of a Need for Change

The CEO of Oxy's Oil and Gas Division sensed a need for change. The company was incurring close to $3 million in external recruiting fees annually, searching for experienced petroleum industry knowledge workers, yet at the same time, the company was losing some of its most experienced people to the new exploration and production companies. The CEO felt that if this trend continued, the company would have difficulty in meeting its growth objectives, as it would lack the necessary human resources to fill the required positions in its expanding exploration and production operations.

The CEO was not sure what the "Real Problem" was, but felt some changes were needed. With that in mind, an External Change Leader was contacted and a meeting was arranged to discuss the client's awareness, readiness, and commitment to change.

During this meeting, it was also confirmed that the CEO had the power and authority to approve a change effort, once recommendations for the necessary change or changes were proposed.

Step Two: Entry, Client and Change Leader Establish Contract

A second meeting was held between the CEO and Change Leader to establish the contract during this phase of the change process. Issues discussed and resolved were:

1. *Define the Assignment:* The assignment was defined as to determine the "Real Problem" and present recommendations to address the problem and possible changes that might be required. The conduct of an extensive needs analysis was agreed to as well as to who was to perform the analysis.
2. *Define Results:* It was concluded that a detailed proposal of what changes might be required in the organization would be submitted to the CEO within six months of the start of the project.
3. *Additional Resources and Support Required:* The CEO committed unlimited resources to the project including the Change Leader being provided additional support staff from Oxy to assist in the project.
4. *Explore Problem:* It was determined that an extensive needs analysis would be performed to explore the problem. Tools used for the analysis are described in Step Three, Data Collection Phase.
5. *Communications of Objectives to Organization:* The Change Leader's objectives were communicated to all senior management and other key management staff throughout Oxy's worldwide operations via a detailed memo from the CEO. The memo also established dates for the Change Leader's meetings with key management and staff and included an agenda of issues to be discussed during these meetings. The Change Leader would visit every Oxy location throughout the world.

Step Three: Data Collection

A number of tools and methods were used with respect to collecting data relative to the "Real Problem." These included secondary research, use of questionnaires, and focused one-on-one and group interviews.

Secondary Sources of Information Prior to conducting the on-site interviews, the Change Leader reviewed various internal documents to gain insight into the organization's culture and management practices. The following is an excellent example of why the organization did not believe in bureaucracy and volumes of paperwork. Oxy constructed the Piper-Alpha oil platform off the coast of Scotland in the North Sea. The platform was built to withstand 90-foot waves and eventually became the most productive off-shore platform in the world—producing 250,000 barrels of oil per day from 27 deep sea wells with no artificial lift (oil flowed freely from the wells to the surface without the assistance of pumping). Oxy originally budgeted $350 million for the construction of the platform. The final cost of all construction work on the platform exceeded $900 million.

When the accounting people (Big "A's") asked for justification of the over one-half billion overrun, a two-page report was prepared and summarized as follows:

1. *Point One:* Oxy did not anticipate the difficult weather conditions encountered in the North Sea.
2. *Point Two:* Oxy overestimated the productivity of the largely union member U.K. labor force.
3. *Point Three:* The Piper-Alpha platform produces an estimated $10 million dollars per day in revenue. By spending the extra money, the platform became operational 20 days ahead of schedule and produced an additional $200 million in revenue the accountants did not forecast.
4. *Point Four:* Oxy engineers could have perhaps done a better job in planning.

The report was filed away, and no one ever questioned the cost overrun again, and the "A's" (Administrators) stayed out of the "Es'" (Entrepreneurs) and "Ps'" (Producers) way.

Other secondary sources such as annual reports, shareholder-meeting presentations by Hammer, and other documents were reviewed to gain greater insight into Oxy.

Focused Interviews—Senior Corporate Headquarters Executives and Key Staff Following secondary research, focused interviews were scheduled with the key executives at Oxy's corporate headquarters in California and Houston. These included the Chairman and CEO—Oil and Gas Division, Executive Vice President of Engineering and Production, Executive Vice President—Worldwide Exploration, Executive Vice President of Finance, Executive Vice President of Latin American

Operations, Vice President of Latin American Exploration, Vice President of Domestic Operations, Vice President of Purchasing, Chief Legal Counsel, President of Oxy Crude Sales (the sales and marketing arm of the company), President of the Permian Corporation (a major subsidiary involved in oil transportation), CEO of Canadian Occidental Petroleum Corporation, and the Vice President of Administration (including Human Resources Management). Additional interviews were held with their key direct reports such as Chief Petroleum Engineer, Chief Drilling Engineer, Chief Mechanical Engineer, Chief Geologist, Chief Geophysicist, R&D Directors, and a number of other senior knowledge workers representing the geosciences.

Assess the Change Equation

A preliminary assessment was made of the Change Equation following these interviews. This assessment concluded that:

"R" and Perceived Loss: The various functional executives considered the managers and knowledge workers in their functions (engineering, geosciences, and so forth) to belong to them no matter where these people worked internationally. They, as opposed to human resources management, made all decisions relative to their people's selection, assignments, promotion, and compensation. HR was there essentially to take care of the paperwork associated with these transactions. They would strongly resist any recommendation and change that would appear to diminish their power and control in these areas.

Corporate Culture: Each senior executive stressed the importance of preserving the organization's culture—that of being a fast moving organization, responsive to change, and without bureaucracy. A war story was told during one interview describing Oxy in the early days and the hiring of its first Human Resources Manager. One of the first tasks the HR Manager took on was to create an organization chart of all Oxy operations since none had previously existed. When the chart arrived on Dr. Hammer's desk he inquired as to who had prepared the chart? When he was advised it was developed by the new HR Manager it was reported that he gave instructions to immediately fire the HR Manager citing this was "bureaucracy."

Employee Questionnaires/Survey: A survey of all employees using a questionnaire was conducted in Oxy's North Sea Operations. The questionnaire attempted to measure a number of issues such as management and leadership styles, compensation and benefits, advancement opportunities, and so forth (factors similar to Herzberg's Two-Factor Theory) and the employees' assessment of these issues. The North Sea Operation was selected since it was considered to be the most successful and profitable Oxy operation and also tended to practice more modern management techniques as compared to other Oxy operations.

Focused Interviews Throughout the World: The Change Leader met with all senior executives and their immediate reports in all of Oxy's worldwide operations. Meetings were held in the United States, Canada, Peru, and Bolivia in Latin America, London and Scotland in the U.K., Belgium, and Libya. Interviews were also held with both expatriates and national technical/professional employees at these locations. Smaller exploration offices were not visited because of their relatively small size (a few geoscientists at the most); however, some were interviewed later when they visited the corporate headquarters in California.

Participation and Involvement Tactic and Education and Communication: All senior executives and international country heads were provided frequent feedback and reports relative to information obtained during this Data Collection Phase. Sources of information were held in confidence (a commitment made to those interviewed) in order that objective and unbiased information (both positive and negative relative to the company and its management practices) could be obtained.

Step Four: Diagnosis

The following tasks were completed in this Phase based on the previous Data Collection Phase:

1. Define the "Real Problem" The "Real Problem" was defined as a lack of a human resources planning and development system. Oxy lacked the visibility of its human resources, including their knowledge, skills, experience, education, job performance (the 16th largest corporation in the Fortune 500 did not have a formal performance evaluation process in place), and career objectives. Lacking this visibility, internal human resources recommendations were typically ignored when it came to job assignments and advancement (unless they had close contact with senior functional executives) in preference for recruiting candidates from the outside. Internal people became discouraged over time, and feeling ignored, they left the organization for other opportunities. It was also a practice that in some less-than-desirable foreign operations, such as Libya and the Amazon jungle of Peru, local managers tried to hide their people and keep them as long as the could, knowing that attempting to attract replacements to these areas was difficult. It was not unusual for an Oxy knowledge worker to resign from one operation, such as Libya, and then apply for a similar job in another Oxy operation, such as the North Sea.

The diagnosis also revealed that Oxy paid excellent salaries and benefits, including a stock purchase plan, and these were not issues as far as Oxy's people were concerned (hygiene factors). This did contribute to a related problem, however. In order to advance and increase one's compensation, knowledge workers were forced to leave their technical/professional areas of expertise and advance into management. Without any management training as previously noted, Oxy gained inexperienced and marginal managers at the expense of losing high-caliber technical/professional people (knowledge workers).

2. Preliminary Recommendations Preliminary recommendations included development of a Functional Human Resources Inventory System. This inventory would contain all managers and knowledge workers in their respective functions (engineering, geosciences, and so forth), both expatriate and national employees, and include information relative to their knowledge and skills, education, job performance, career objectives, and so forth. The inventory would also assess the individual's readiness for advancement and also identify potential next positions and locations.

In addition, a "Dual Career Path" system would be developed to allow technical/professional employees to advance within their areas of functional expertise and with compensation comparable to if they had taken the management path. As such, the Chief Petroleum Engineer (the highest individual contributor in that particular function) could earn as much as the Vice President of an international Oxy operation.

3. Feedback to Client The Preliminary Recommendations and Action Plan were submitted to and discussed with the CEO. All parts of the Change Equation were described in detail—the situation now ("N"), the desired future state as a result of the change ("F"), the plan ("P") of how to get from "N" to "F," and the strategies and tactics to be used to reduce potential resistance and perceived loss ("R").

4. Client's Commitment to Change The CEO accepted the recommendations and suggested several next steps. This included meeting individually with the senior executives to explain the proposed changes and inviting all international executives to a meeting to review the proposed changes. This obviously was using the "Shared Responsibility—Participation and Involvement" and the "Education and Communications" strategies and tactics in addition to the CEO's "Top Down" decision.

5. The Meeting   A meeting was held with all senior executives and top international operating managers to present and review the plan. Although the initial resistance was dealt with, in that senior functional executives would still have control over their people (the Functional Human Resources Inventory would be prepared by Human Resources to give them greater visibility of the organization's human resources and they still made the job assignment and advancement decisions), another unforeseen "R" surfaced. As a key part of developing information for the inventories, job performance information was required. The problem, as previously stated, was that Oxy, although being the 16th largest corporation on the Fortune 500, did not have or believe in traditional performance evaluations. Many thought this was bureaucracy and were opposed to developing an Oxy system. The outcome of the meeting was a request to have the Change Leader study this issue and recommend how it could be dealt with to overcome the new "R."

6. Bottom-Up Pilot Program   Using the Participation and Involvement Tactic, meetings were held with the senior management and human resources and training staff of Oxy's North Sea Operations to plan a Pilot Program and test a performance evaluation system. The North Sea was selected for the Pilot, since it had high visibility and credibility in the organization due to its success, and its current Vice President of Operations was identified as being the new Executive Vice President of Worldwide Operations and Engineering once the incumbent retired within the next year. It was also determined that "Facilitation and Support" would also be required in the way of a training program, since most managers lacked the necessary skills to conduct performance evaluation and career planning meetings with their employees. The Pilot proved to be successful, and an Action Plan was finalized to implement the proposed changes in all Oxy worldwide locations.

Step Five: Action Planning and Step Six, Implementation

The following elements were included in the Action Plan to implement the change effort:

1. Communications Campaign A professional video introducing the program (to be called Oxy OD for Oxy Organization Development Program) was produced. The video was in both English and Spanish for the Latin American Operations. The video would be used to introduce the program to all managers and knowledge workers throughout the world in small meetings. Brochures describing the objectives of the program and how the program would work were also developed.

2. Participation and Involvement HR and Training Managers were trained how to both introduce the program and implement it in their respective operations.

3. Facilitation and Support A comprehensive training program was developed to train all managers in how to implement the program and conduct career development and performance evaluation sessions with their knowledge workers. Over 500 managers were trained throughout the world in less than 90 days.

4. Implementation Following the training program, the process was introduced with interviews, and data collection for building the Functional Human Resources Inventories was started. Information on all managers and knowledge workers was collected after the interviews by local HR Management and forwarded to the Change Leader and his staff for organization.

5. Participation and Involvement and Functional Review Boards Functional Review Boards consisting of senior functional executives in each discipline, as well as senior management representation from the international operations, were formed to review their respective Human Resources Inventories and approve the recommendations relative to career development needs, readiness for advancement, next possible position and location, and so forth. External recruiting would only be allowed if there were no qualified internal candidates for a position that could be found in the Human Resources Inventories.

Step Seven: Evaluation

1. All Functional Human Resources Inventories were developed within six months of the implementation of the program.
2. External search fees for recruiting external candidates were reduced from over $3 million to less than $500,000.
3. Turnover of knowledge workers was significantly reduced within the first years of the implementation of the program. Knowledge workers now knew they had visibility in the organization, regardless of where they were in the world.

The Real Test   The real test of the value of the program came in the early 1980s when Oxy, along with the other petroleum companies, was ordered by President Reagan to remove all of its US citizens from Libya although they would be allowed to continue operations there. The companies were given 30 days to remove their personnel and replace them with whomever they wanted, as long as they did not have a US passport (this was a prelude to the eventual bomb attack on Tripoli.)

Oxy determined that it needed to replace approximately 90 managers and knowledge workers to maintain continuity of operations in Libya. Consulting with the Functional Human Resources Inventories, Oxy was able to identify within 24 hours 90 technical/professional people in its worldwide operations without US passports to restaff its Libyan Operation.

Step Eight: Stabilization

Many comments from senior executives were made after the Libyan crisis relative to the value of Oxy OD. To demonstrate Stabilization, the most significant comments that were made were, "We should have been doing this all along."

Step Nine: Termination

Having successfully completed this change effort, the Change Leader went on to work with various national petroleum companies throughout the world as a consultant in designing and implementing similar programs.

Endnotes

1. Peter F. Drucker, *Management Challenges for the 21st Century* (New York: HarperCollins Publishers, Inc., 1999), 72–93.
2. Robert W. Swaim, Ph.D. "The Drucker Files: Why Your Organization Needs to Be a Change Leader, Parts I & II, *Business Beijing* (May & June 2002).
3. Arie de Geus, *The Living Company:* Growth, *Learning and Longevity in Business* (Boston: Harvard Business School Press, 1997), 1.
4. Peter F. Drucker, *Management Challenges for the 21st Century* (New York: HarperCollins Publishers, Inc., 1999), 73.
5. Peter F. Drucker, *Managing in a Time of Great Change* (New York: Truman Talley books, 1995), 272.
6. Ibid., 213.
7. Arie de Geus, *The Living Company: Growth, Learning and Longevity in Business* (Boston: Harvard Business School Press, 1997), 30.
8. Alan C. Filley, Robert J. House, and Steven Kerr, *Managerial Process and Organizational Behavior,* 2nd ed. (Glenview, IL: Scott, Foresman & Company. 1976), 467.
9. Peter F. Drucker and Peter Senge, "Leading in a Time of Change." *MTS Video* (1999).
10. Peter F. Drucker, *Management Challenges for the 21st Century* (New York: HarperCollins Publishers, Inc., 1999), 90–92.
11. Ibid., 73.
12. Ibid., 74.
13. Ibid., 74.
14. Ibid., 80.
15. Ibid., 82.
16. Ibid., 86–88.
17. Ibid., 88–89.
18. Arie de Geus, *The Living Company:* Growth, Learning and Longevity in Business (Boston: Harvard Business School Press, 1997), 1.
19. Ibid., 73.
20. Donald F. Harvey and Donald R. Brown, *An Experiential Approach to Organization Development* (Englewood Cliffs, NJ: Prentice-Hall, Inc. 1982), 33.
21. Ibid., 53–55.
22. Ibid., 61–67.
23. Peter F. Drucker, *Management Challenges for the 21st Century* (New York: HarperCollins Publishers, Inc., 1999), 72–93.
24. Donald F. Harvey and Donald R. Brown, *An Experiential Approach to Organization Development* (Englewood Cliffs, NJ: Prentice-Hall, Inc. 1982), 61–67.
25. Stephen P. Robbins, *Organizational Theory: Structure, Design, and Applications,* 2nd ed. (Englewood Cliffs, NJ: Prentice-Hall, Inc., 1987), 316–317.
26. Alan C. Filley, Robert J. House, and Steven Kerr, *Managerial Process and Organizational Behavior,* 2nd ed. (Glenview, IL: Scott, Foresman & Company. 1976), 487.

Strategic Planning: The Entrepreneurial Skill

Strategic planning is making decisions today to create a desired future.[1]

What Is Strategic Planning: Drucker's Definition

Strategic planning is the continuous process of making present entrepreneurial (risk-taking) decisions systematically and with the greatest knowledge of their futurity; organizing systematically the efforts needed to carry out these decisions; and measuring the results of these decisions against the expectations through organized, systematic feedback.[2]

The key term here in Drucker's definition is *the continuous process* reinforcing the need for strategic planning not to be an annual event that people endured and attempted to get out of the way so that they could get back to what they thought they should be focusing on—today's operations and problems.

If we were not committed to this today, would we go into it?[3]

This quote is a recurring theme of Drucker's and relates to his concept of Planned Abandonment. Drucker felt strategic planning needed to start with an assessment of where we are today in terms of present products, services, or even business units and to stop committing resources to dying products or businesses. If the answer to the above question is "no"—Drucker suggested asking, "How can we get out—fast?" This is somewhat opposed to other strategies advocated by the Boston Consulting Group (BCG), which sometimes suggests that it is worthwhile to continue to "harvest" rather abandon (see BCG in Appendix A). A decision also needs careful assessment of Net Marketing Contribution as described by Roger Best.

Drucker then described the next step in strategic planning by asking another question.

What new and different things do we have to do, and when?[4]

Here Drucker focused on management, asking, "What do we have to do today if we want to be in some particular place in the future?" He also suggested "that decisions must be made to commit resources to it today."[5]

Drucker's Summary: Strategic Planning

Drucker summarized what he felt was crucial in strategic planning:

1. "First, the systematic and purposeful work on attaining objectives be done.
2. Second, that planning start out with sloughing off yesterday, and that abandonment be planned as part of the systematic ways to attain tomorrow.
3. Third, that we look for new and different ways to attain objectives rather than believe that doing more of the same will suffice.
4. Finally, that we think through the time dimension and ask, "When do we have to start work to get results when we need them?"[6]

Richard J. Vogt in "Forecasting as a Management Tool" defined strategic planning accordingly: "Essentially, strategic planning formulates the purpose of the organization (mission), determines its strategy and translates these two into specific attainable goals (objectives). It gives direction to today's Operations Planning and to tomorrow's development plans that reflect all predictable factors and alternatives appropriately relating to the forecasts."[7]

What Is "Strategic Thinking"?

This can be a difficult concept for managers/students to grasp: Exactly what does one do when one "thinks strategically," and what is supposed to be the outcome of "strategic thinking?" Rudy A. Champa helped to clarify this when he wrote, "Strategic thinking is the type of thinking that determines where the organization is going in the future. By comparison, operational planning determines 'how' the organization will get there." He expanded on this by making the following key points:

> *Strategic thinking determines our vision. It asks the questions: WHAT sort of business are we today? And WHAT sort of business do we want to become in the future? (Similar to Drucker's* "What should our business be?)[8]
>
> Rudy A. Champa

Champa then differentiated between "strategic thinking" and "operational planning":

- "Operational planning", on the other hand asks, "HOW do we achieve our vision?"
- In other words, HOW do we get from the business we are today—to the sort of business that we want to become in the future?"[9] (This reinforces Drucker's focus on objectives.)

According to Mintzberg, he contrasted planning, which is about *analysis,* with strategic thinking, which is about *synthesis* and further commented, "The latter involves intuition and creativity that often cannot be developed on a schedule."[10] Jack Welch discussed the importance of strategic questions in relation to strategic thinking when he wrote in *Jack: Straight From the Gut,* "Five simple questions brought strategic thinking to life for me:

1. What is the detailed global position of your business and that of your competitors' market shares, strengths by product line, and by region today?
2. What actions have your competitors taken in the past two years that have changed the competitive landscape?
3. What have you done in the last two years to alter that landscape?
4. What are you most afraid your competitors might do in the next two years to change the landscape?
5. What are you going to do in the next two years to leapfrog any of their moves?"[11]

Strategic Thinking Versus Operational Planning

As can be seen from the perspectives of Champa and Welch, there is a significant difference between strategic thinking that eventually leads to strategic planning and operational planning, which Drucker did not address. He left out *how* the strategic plan gets translated into operational plans and objectives to guide in decision making at the other levels in the organization.

Arthur A. Thompson, Jr., and A.J. Strickland III were very concise in their definition of a strategic plan: "A strategic plan consists of an organization's mission and future direction, near-term and long-term performance targets, and strategy."[12]

Who Does This and When?

Another question Drucker ignored was "Who is responsible for strategic planning in the organization, and when should this be done?" The following is a general consensus of the pundits relative to where strategic planning should be initiated.

Senior executives should be responsible for defining the business's Mission, Vision, and Strategy Thompson and Strickland wrote, "Ultimate responsibility for *leading* the tasks of forming, implementing and executing a strategic plan for the entire organization rests with the CEO, even though other senior managers normally have significant leadership roles also." They added, "Every company manager has a strategy-making/strategy-implementing role. It is flawed thinking to view strategic management as solely the province of senior executives."[13]

Subsidiary Business Unit, Functional, Area and Operating Managers should be involved in the planning process Peter Rea and Harold Kerzner commented, "Historically, strategy has focused mostly on the top of the organization. However, a strategic issue can emerge from anywhere in the organization and initiative to push it forward can be taken by personnel at any level. The problem of implementation and resistance to change demands involvement from all levels of the organization. Those employees responsible for implementing the plan should be involved in its conception."[14]

Involve Cross Functional Teams in the Process Depending on the nature of the organization, Cross-Functional Teams should be involved in part of the process, particularly with respect to providing the most current information relative to their respective discipline.

Role of the Board in Crafting Strategy

Concerning the role of the Board of Directors in strategic thinking and planning, Thompson and Strickland recommended: "The Board should exercise oversight and see that the five tasks of strategic management are done in a manner that benefits shareholders."[15] Their view was that the Board should not play a hands-on role in formulating or implementing strategy as the Directors generally lack specific industry experience. Their main role is to be supportive critics. On the other hand, Champa suggested that the Board would comprise the "nucleus" of the team that will participate in "strategic thinking" meetings including outside directors who, he felt, can add "an extra dimension in the meetings by way of their external viewpoint and perhaps their wider and more detached perspective."[16] He did suggest however, that their role be similar to that proposed by the other pundits in being a sounding board and critics of the process used during the strategic thinking meeting.

Strategic Planning in Diversified Companies

Although Drucker wrote about diversification, he did not draw any distinction between strategic planning in a diversified company, such as GE, as opposed to a single-business company. Thompson and Strickland noted that in diversified companies there are typically four distinct levels of strategy managers. These include:

1. The Chief Executive Officer and other senior corporate-level executives who have primary responsibility and personal authority for big strategic decisions affecting the total enterprise and the collection of individual businesses into which the enterprise has diversified.
2. Managers who have profit-and-loss responsibility for one specific business unit and who are delegated a major leadership role in crafting and executing a strategy for their business.
3. Functional area managers within a given business unit who have direct authority over a major piece of the business (manufacturing, marketing and sales, finance, R&D, HR management) and whose role it is to support the business unit's overall strategy with strategic actions in their own areas.
4. Managers of major operating units (plants, sales districts, local offices) who have on-the-scene responsibility for developing the details of strategic efforts in their areas and for executing their piece of the overall strategic plan at the grassroots level.

In our Drucker Executive Development Program, the participants found this discussion to be useful since it reinforced the need for managers other than the executives at headquarters to actually formulate their own strategies, including functional missions in support of the overall business's mission. Our pundits also distinguished between strategic planning in the diversified business and in the single-business enterprises by suggesting that the single business enterprises generally needs no more than three of these levels: a business-level strategy manager, functional area strategy managers and operating-level strategy managers.[17]

Finally, the pundits recommended that the strategic process has to proceed more from the top down than from the bottom up. Direction and guidance have to flow from the corporate level to the business level and so on. The rationale here is that lower-level managers cannot carry out their unit's strategy without understanding the company's long-term direction and higher-level strategies.

The Role of Planners: What They Should and Should Not Do

Many large organizations may have a planning department that is responsible for the organization's strategic plans. The following are some guidelines in terms of what these planners should do and not do:

- Research and gather information for decision making (Drucker's "Going Outside").
- Conduct studies of industry and competitive conditions (External Assessment and Industry Assessment, and so on).
- Explore Innovative Opportunities and Strategic Issues to be addressed by Senior Management.
- Provide *support* in revising strategic plans based on new external and internal assessments and changes.
- Develop strategy performance assessment and establish annual review process.

Why Planners Should Not Be Strategy Makers

- Managers may have no commitment to the strategy.
- Managers will not claim responsibility or accountability for poor results—not their plan.
- Managers will defer difficult decisions to the planners.
- Planners typically know less about the company situation compared to line management.
- Strategic planning is usually viewed as an unproductive, "bureaucratic" process.

A Pundit's View of Planners

When Jack Welch took over as GE's CEO, he found an extensive planning department, which he eventually disbanded. He also forced planning down to the business unit level. Regarding this move, he commented, "I took too long to take apart the corporate staff, keeping on economists, marketing consultants, strategic planners and outright bureaucrats much longer than I needed to."[18]

Strategic Planning Pitfalls to Avoid

1. Senior management's assumptions that it can delegate the planning function to a planner.
2. Senior management becomes so engrossed in current problems that it spends insufficient time on long-range planning.

3. The planning process therefore becomes discredited among other managers and staff.
4. Worrying about the height of the waves rather than the direction of the tide?
5. Failure to develop company goals (Vision) as a basis for formulating long-range plans.
6. Failure to assume the necessary involvement in the planning process of line management.
7. Failure to use plans as standards for measuring managerial performance.
8. Failure to create a climate in the company that is congenial and not resistant to planning.
9. Assuming that corporate comprehensive planning is something separate from the entire management process.
10. Injecting so much formality into the system that it lacks flexibility, looseness, and simplicity, and restrains creativity.
11. Failure of top management to review with departmental and vision heads the long-range plans that they have developed (communicating the Vision).
12. Senior management's consistently rejecting the formal planning mechanism by making intuitive decisions that conflict with formal plans (information for decision making).

When to Do Strategic Planning

Most managers are familiar with "operational or business planning" that typically includes establishing short-term objectives, a budget and so forth. Typically, this is an annual event where the unit's plan eventually gets folded into the division or location plan, and eventually into the company's overall annual plan. This is not strategic planning. Thompson and Strickland commented: "Once-a-year strategizing under 'have-to' conditions is not a prescription for managerial or business success. Strategy is something that ought to be modified whenever it is propitious to do so and certainly whenever unfolding events dictate." This might be comparable to changes required as discussed in relation to Drucker's question, "What will our business be?" Thompson and Strickland added, "Annual changes may not be adequate. In today's world, strategy life cycles are growing shorter, not longer. Because of the speed of change in many of today's industries, strategy life cycles are increasingly measured in months and single years, not decades or even five-year plans."[19] They concluded with their views on strategic management as "an ongoing, never-ending process, not a start-stop event that, once done, can be safely put aside for a while."[20]

Types of Strategies

Our various pundits have pointed out that the output of strategic thinking leads to strategic planning and a "strategy," among the other elements that they have included in the strategic plan. Once again, the type of strategy that will be developed will depend on the nature of the organization as previously discussed—single-business or diversified. These can be categorized as a Corporate Strategy and a Businesses Strategy.[21]

Corporate Strategy: This is the strategy for the entire company (single-business company).

The corporate-level executives and the CEO are essentially responsible for its development with input from others such as the Board, depending on whose views we accept—the various pundits' or Drucker's.

Business Strategy: A strategy is developed for each business if it is a diversified company.

This obviously makes sense as each industry the company competes in has its own unique issues that must be considered. As an example, GE is considering divesting its appliance subsidiary, which is in an industry that is highly competitive (based on price) and declining. Here, the Business-Level General Managers are responsible for developing the strategy and plan. This strategy is the same as a corporate strategy in a single-business company. The focus of business strategy is how to build and strengthen the company's long-term competitive position in the marketplace. The Business Strategy is therefore concerned with:

1. Forming responses to changes under way in the industry, the economy at large, the regulatory and political arena, etc.
2. Crafting competitive moves and market approaches that can lead to sustainable competitive advantage.
3. Building competitively valuable competencies and capabilities.
4. Uniting the strategic initiatives of functional departments.
5. Addressing specific strategic issues facing the company's business.

A business strategy is powerful if it produces a sizeable and sustainable competitive advantage; it is weak if it results in competitive disadvantage. It is important to note that these are broad definitions of strategy. The specific strategy that will be chosen may correspond to Michael Porter's Generic Strategies or the various strategies that are too numerous to mention that can be found in current strategic management and marketing literature.

Functional Strategy applies to the organization's functions such as finance, marketing, production and so on. The heads of the organization's major functions are primarily responsible for developing their Functional Strategies.

Operating Strategies are developed for business operating units such as plants, sales districts, regions and departments within functional areas. These are developed by unit managers and lower-level supervisors.

Summary

Drucker's initial observations (1973) relative to strategic planning provided a framework for the topic. Many of his views are applicable today, but require the insight of other contributors to make it more relevant for today's environment. The following two quotes by Thompson and Strickland perhaps best summarize the key points, not only in this chapter, but in this book as well.

Strategic management *refers to the managerial process of forming a strategic vision (What should our business be?—Drucker), setting objectives, crafting a strategy, implementing and executing the strategy, and then over time, initiating whatever corrective adjustments in the vision, objectives, strategy and execution are deemed appropriate (What will our business be?—Drucker)."*

Objectives. *The purpose of objectives is to convert managerial statements of strategic vision and business mission into specific performance targets—results and outcomes the organization wants to achieve" (Differs with Drucker's objectives as strategy).*[22]

Arthur A. Thompson, Jr. & A.J.
Strickland III

Endnotes

1. Peter F. Drucker, *Management: Tasks, Responsibilities, Practices* (New York: Harper and Row Publishers, Inc., 1973), 121.
2. Peter F. Drucker, *Management: Tasks, Responsibilities, Practices* (New York: Harper and Row Publishers, Inc., 1973), 125.
3. Ibid., 126.
4. Ibid., 126.
5. Ibid., 127.
6. Ibid., 128.
7. Richard J. Vogt, "Forecasting as a Management Tool," *Michigan Business Review* (January 1970): 20–24.
8. Rudy A. Champa, *Strategic Thinking and Boardroom Debate* (Mission Viejo, CA, Critical Thinkers Press, 2001), 12–13.
9. Ibid., 12–13.
10. Henny Mintzberg, *The Rise and fall of Strategic Planning* (New York: The free press, 1944).
11. Jack Welch, *Jack, Straight From the Gut* (New York: Warner Books, Inc., 2001) 390.
12. Arthur A. Thompson, Jr. & A.J. Strickland III, *Strategic Management: Concepts and Cases*, 13th ed. (New York: McGraw-Hill/Irwin, 2003), 17.
13. Ibid., 27.
14. Peter Rea, & Harold Kerzner, *Strategic Planning: A Practical Guide* (New York: John Wiley & Sons, Inc., 1997), 1.
15. Arthur A. Thompson, Jr. & A.J. Strickland III, *Strategic Management: Concepts and Cases*, 13th ed. (New York: McGraw-Hill/Irwin, 2003), 17.
16. Rudy A. Champa, *Strategic Thinvking and Boardroom Debate* (Mission Viejo, CA, Critical Thinkers Press, 2001), 110.
17. Arthur A. Thompson, Jr. & A.J. Strickland III, *Strategic Management: Concepts and Cases*, 13th ed. (New York: McGraw-Hill/Irwin, 2003), 22.
18. Jack Welch, *Jack, Straight From the Gut*, 132.
19. Arthur A. Thompson, Jr. & A.J. Strickland III, *Strategic Management: Concepts and Cases*, 13th ed. (New York: McGraw-Hill/Irwin, 2003), 21.
20. Ibid., 18.
21. Ibid., 48–49.
22. Ibid., 6–9.

Strategic Decision Making

A decision to do nothing is still a decision.[1]

Introduction

Drucker defined strategic planning "as the continuous process of making present entrepreneurial *(risk-taking) decisions* systematically and with the greatest knowledge of their futurity; organizing systematically the *efforts* needed to carry out these decisions; and measuring the results of these decisions against the expectations through organized, *systematic feedback.*"[2]

Rudy A. Champa also discussed the Critical Decision Making Processes dealing first with strategy and second with innovation necessary for the business's growth. He spoke of the "development of a *Strategic Blueprint* for the future look of the business, which can be used as a *decision-making filter* to help focus resources and determine choices for future products and markets."[3] Since both Drucker and Champa focused on decision making as an integral component of strategic thinking and planning, this chapter briefly includes some of Drucker's and other pundits' views on the topic.

Drucker on Problem Solving Versus Decision Making

Drucker provided considerable insight over the years on the subject of decision making, starting with the Elements of Decision Making as described in his original book, *The Effective Executive, The Essential Drucker,* and in his last book, *The Effective Executive in Action.* Since these Drucker books are readily available, I have only included an abstract of what I feel are some of the key points he made that relate to decision making and strategy. The reader will not find too many key points on strategy here since much of what Drucker wrote focused on *problem solving,* not *strategic decision making.* What is the difference?

What Are Strategic Decisions?

Chapters 2 and 3 best described the "strategic decisions" concerning strategy the executive must make, starting with Drucker's three key questions:

1. What is our business?
2. What will our business be?
3. What should our business be?

Also reviewed in Chapter 3 was the additional insight of Peter Rea and Harold Kerzner on assessing the feasibility of a particular strategy and the seven guidelines (strategic decisions) to use in the assessment of strategy.[4] Arthur A. Thompson Jr. and A. J. Strickland III also cited the strategic decisions that need to be made that directly relate to strategy in Chapter 3, which they briefly repeated here, because of the clear distinction they make between problem solving and strategic decisions, "A company's strategy represents management's answers to such fundamental business questions as: Whether to concentrate on a single business or build a diversified group of businesses (one of Drucker's strategies)? Whether to cater to a broad range of customers or focus on a particular market niche (Drucker's concentration)?" and a number of other significant strategic decisions that must be made as outlined in Chapter 3.[5] (A list of strategic questions is included as a supplement to this chapter.)

Drucker's Views on Decision Making (A Review)

This chapter will focus on Drucker's advice on "how to determine when a decision is necessary?" and Drucker's Decision Making

Elements and Steps. I have added a Group Decision Making Process as a *how-to* tool at the end of this chapter, which attempts to close some Drucker gaps that are discussed relative to decision making. Once again, the basis for this chapter was two articles I wrote for the *Business Beijing* magazine on Drucker and decision making in 2003.[6] Since I commented that what Drucker described was more applicable to problem solving and generally attributed to closing "performance gaps" (as an example, "Why did we not meet our sales objectives this quarter?"), I will attempt to put his views into a strategic decision-making perspective when possible: in other words, to go beyond Drucker.

What Good Decision Makers Do

According to Drucker, "Good decision makers know that the decision to be made is about the 'right problem,' therefore they know how to define the problem."[7] Drucker felt decision makers also know they may have to compromise to reach an alternative that will be acceptable to various constituencies. This latter view may be an overgeneralization and may depend more on the magnitude of change that occurs when the decision is implemented. Drucker added: "Good decision makers also know that a decision is a commitment to action, it must get people to act and be implemented."[8] Finally, he argued that decision making consists of Elements and Steps, which will be reviewed in this chapter.

Elements of Decision Making

In *The Effective Executive*, Drucker described the following Elements of Decision Making:[9]

1. Determining if a decision is necessary and classifying the situation/problem as generic or unique
2. Defining the problem
3. Satisfying boundary conditions and specifications for the decision
4. Deciding what is right
5. Converting the decision into action
6. Feedback: Is the decision being implemented and is the problem being resolved?

What Is a Decision?

According to Drucker, "A decision is judgment and a choice between alternatives." He went on to say, "It is rarely a choice between what is right or wrong, at best it is a choice between 'almost right' and 'probably wrong'—but more often a choice between two courses of action neither of which is probably more nearly right than the other."[10] Although this may sound as though the decision maker has no idea of what he or she is deciding, these views are supported by earlier research in decision-making theory that have led to the description of two decision-making models, a Rational Model and a Bounded Rationality Model.[11]

The Rational Model of Decision Making

The Rational Model is described as a logical, step-by-step approach to decision making, with a thorough analysis of alternatives and their consequences. The characteristics of this model suggest the outcome will be completely rational (optimized), the decision maker uses a consistent system of preferences to choose the best alternative, the decision maker has complete information and is aware of all alternatives, and the decision maker can calculate the probability of success for each alternative. In summary, the model assumes the decision maker has complete information relative to the problem and unlimited time and resources to explore all possible alternatives that will arrive at an optimum decision.[12]

Problems with the Rational Model

As Drucker has described, decision makers are content to find an acceptable or reasonable solution versus the best or an optimal solution. Often there is either too much or too little information available, or the cost of obtaining the information can be too time consuming and expensive. We are therefore generally confined to the neighborhood of the problem's symptoms as opposed to thinking outside the issue. As such, decision makers typically use their judgment instead of a defined prescriptive model.

Bounded Rationality Model: Satisficing

The Bounded Rationality Model suggests that there are limits upon how rational a decision maker can actually be.[13] The characteristics of this model are that managers suggest the first satisfactory alternative, they are comfortable making decisions without considering all the alternatives, and they make decisions by rules of thumb or "Availability or Representative Heuristics" (judgmental short cuts in decision making).[14] Availability Heuristics are judgments made on available information. As an example, people have a greater fear of flying than driving. There is more press coverage and news when a jetliner with several hundred passengers crashes as compared to auto accidents. If air travel were actually more dangerous, two completely filled 747's would have to crash each week to equal the number of annual auto accident deaths.[15] Representative Heuristics is the tendency to assess the likelihood of an occurrence by trying to match it with a pre-existing category. As an example, managers attempt to predict the performance of a new product by relating it back to a previous product's success.

Executives should be careful during their strategic thinking that their decisions are not "satisficing" and that they are not relying on Availability Heuristics in reaching strategic decisions (for example, IBM executives commenting that "PCs will never replace mainframe computers—they have no memory".)

Satisficing

The concept of satisficing was developed by Herbert Simon many years ago (Classical Management School), suggesting that managers will not select an alternative that optimizes the situation, but will select an alternative that they feel is good enough to solve the problem.[16] The old saying "good enough for government work" generally refers to the concept of satisficing. In summary, managers and organizations feel it may take too much time or cost too much to optimize the situation.

Executives must be aware of this during strategic thinking and when making such important strategic decisions as "What should our business be?" There are too many strategies to consider to be bound by satisficing.

Classifying Decisions: Programmable and Nonprogrammable Decisions

The type of decisions that need to be made can be classified as Programmable and Nonprogrammable decisions. I will add

Drucker's views as to the type of problems that fit these two classifications.

Programmable Decisions

Programmable Decisions are generally simple, routine situations for which people have a decision rule that has been established or known. Policy and procedure manuals, such as suggested by Max Weber (Classical School) in the early 1900s, are designed to allow people in the organization to make programmable decisions without the approval of their superiors. As an example, the secretary when asked to send a proposal to a potential client to arrive the next day knows the organization uses Federal Express and does not have to ask her boss for a decision on which courier to use. A symptom of poor management practices would be where the secretary needs to ask the boss who to use, delegating decision making upward and consuming management time.

Decisions on strategy do not fall under this category.

Nonprogrammable Decisions

A Nonprogrammable Decision is a new situation that requires a decision and creative solution. There are no prescribed rules for this type of decision, and this chapter will focus on Nonprogrammable decisions.

Strategic decisions fall under this category.

Determining If a Decision Is Necessary

As Drucker stated, "A decision to do nothing is still a decision." One of the first questions he suggested the decision maker asks is this: "Is a decision necessary?"[17] The problem with making unnecessary decisions is that it wastes management time and the organization's resources; decisions made when they are not necessary threaten to make other decisions ineffective, and potential confusion can be created in the organization.

Strategic Thinking and the Strategic Management Process require that a number of decisions be made, even if it is not to change a strategy that is working (a decision to do nothing).

Rules from Ancient Greek Medicine[18]

Drucker used an analogy from ancient Greek medicine to determine if a decision is necessary. He asked, "Is surgery needed?" There may be several situations as cited below:

Will the Situation Cure Itself or Stabilize? In a condition that is likely to cure itself or to stabilize itself without risk or danger or great pain to the patient, Drucker stated, "You observe and check regularly, but you don't operate. To perform surgery in such a condition is an unnecessary decision." People may complain about a new policy the organization has implemented; however, complaints will eventually diminish when they get used to the policy and as such, a decision to change the policy again may not be necessary.

An inappropriate strategy will not cure itself, and this Drucker observation is not considered applicable to strategic decision making.

Is the Situation Degenerative or Life Threatening? If the condition is degenerative or life threatening and there is something you can do, Drucker advocated, "You do it quickly. It is a necessary decision despite the risk."

If the executives waited this long for strategic thinking, they have not been monitoring their environment, customers, competition and so on.

Problem in Between? According to Drucker, this is probably the largest single category. This is where the surgeon has to weigh opportunity against risk (life vs. death). It's also where he or she has to make a decision.

Recurring Crisis? Drucker said this was left out of the rule and should be added. One has to fix a recurring crisis, but it should not occur again once it has been fixed. Max Weber recommended developing policies for recurring crises (problems), and his writings from the early 1900s are still applicable.

Most likely there is something wrong with the business's strategy, and perhaps there is a poor fit between the three key assumptions (Drucker's Theory of the Business). A change in senior management may also be a necessary strategic decision.

Drucker suggested acting or not acting ("A decision to do nothing is still a decision."), but do not take half an action. Drucker cited the surgeon who operates and only takes out half of the tonsils (the situation is not cured, only made worse). A better illustration of what Drucker meant here might be a decision that has been made but not implemented. Jack Welch supported Drucker's views here: "Yet 40 years later when I retired, one of my greatest regrets was that I did not act fast enough on many occasions. When I asked myself, how many times should I have held off on a decision? versus how many times do I wish I'd made that move faster? I inevitably found that the latter won almost every time."[19] (*Strategic decisions are too important not to act.*)

Classifying Problems: Generic and Unique Events

Drucker classified problems as Generic Events and Unique Events.[20]

The Generic Event can be answered with a standard rule and principle. It can be considered a Programmable Decision, as previously discussed, and resolved by policy and procedure manuals.

This is generally not applicable to strategic decision making.

Unique Event to Organization/Common in Industry: An event that is generic overall but unique for the organization. Unique events must be treated individually. The executive cannot develop rules for unforeseen exceptional events. As an example, Drucker cited an organization receiving an offer to merge with another company. This is unique to the organization if it has never been approached before, but may be common within the industry, particularly one that is undergoing consolidation.

This will typically require a strategic decision to be made.

Truly Unique Event: The truly unique events are quite rare. Drucker suggested that virtually every problem has been solved already by someone else. Thus the effective decision maker should carefully examine the problem to determine whether it is generic or truly unique. Examples that might be considered truly unique events would be 9/11 and the effects of the SARS epidemic on the Chinese travel industry. On the other hand, since similar events (the attack on Pearl Harbor, the plague, polio) have taken place before, these are therefore not unique, but have not necessarily been dealt with by the present generation of executives and managers. Finally, Drucker commented that events that appear to be unique may really be the first appearance of a new generic problem.

Although interesting, these classifications might fall into the "so what?" category as the decision maker is still left with a problem to be resolved or a strategic decision to be made, whether it's generic or unique.

Selecting the Problem

Other issues affecting decision making deal with how the problem for decision making is selected by the executive. These may include Visible Problems and the concept of Escalation of Commitment, or, as Drucker described, Feeding Yesterday and Starving Tomorrow.

Visible Problems Generally Selected

Decision makers (executives) want to appear competent and on top of problems and as such, it is easier to identify visible and high profile problems. Decision makers will therefore select the problems that are visible to others to prove they are addressing the problems and doing their job. Decision makers will also tend to select problems that are in their own self-interest versus those that are in the interest of the organization as a whole. The problem here is that while management time is being committed to visible problems, less visible, but perhaps more serious problems, particularly strategic decisions, are overlooked or neglected.

Escalation of Commitment: Feeding Yesterday

Another decision-making problem is the tendency to continue to commit resources to a failing course of action, the problem of Escalation of Commitment. This is very similar to Drucker's concept of Feeding Yesterday and Starving Tomorrow. Here, the manager continues to commit resources to a previous decision when the facts suggest the decision was wrong—an increased commitment to a previous decision in spite of negative information, or throwing good money after bad.[21]

Reasons for Escalation of Commitment The reasons for the Escalation of Commitment include the following factors:

1. Basically, the manager feels responsible for the present failure of a previous decision that he or she made.

2. The manager continues to commit resources to prove that the decision was right the first time.
3. The manager is unwilling to appear inconsistent by changing to another course of action—not continuing to commit resources to the failure.
4. The manager cannot differentiate between situations where persistence will pay off and situations where it will not. There is a tendency to believe in the saying "If first you don't succeed—try again."

Executives must be aware of this potential influence on their strategic thinking and strategic decisions. Committing more resources to a failing product line or strategy ("we need to give it time to work) is falling into the Escalation of Commitment trap.

Drucker's Steps in the Decision Making Process

Having determined if a decision is necessary and classifying the problem, the second element of Drucker's model is Defining the Problem.

Defining the Problem as Opposed to the Symptoms of the Problem

Drucker stressed the importance of Defining the Problem: Too often, symptoms of a problem are treated rather than the real problem. Considerable effort should be made in defining what the Real Problem is. According to Drucker, "The wrong answer to the 'Right Problem' can be corrected while a right answer to the wrong problem causes damage."[22]

As an example, an organization may be experiencing a high turnover rate of professional employees (knowledge workers). Management may feel the problem is a compensation system that is not competitive with the marketplace and requests the human resources manager to develop a new compensation system. The Real Problem on the other hand may be management itself and its practices in leading the organization's knowledge workers, or it may be a lack of career opportunities.

Guidelines and Key Questions to Ask

Drucker offered several guidelines and key questions to ask when defining the Real Problem. These include verifying the definition of the problem against observable events. The decision maker should ask, "What is this all about?" "What is pertinent here?" and "What is key to this situation?"

Here there is a possible blending of Drucker's problem-solving approach and strategic decision making. As an example, returning to his Theory of the Business, the problem might be identified as being the wrong strategy.

Specification of the Decision: Establishing Boundary Conditions

The third Element of Drucker's model deals with Establishing Boundary Conditions for the Decision.[23] A simpler explanation of Boundary Conditions is the establishing of the objectives and goals for the decision and allowing for the effects of the decision to be measured. According to Drucker, these are key questions that need to be asked in order to determine what the decision is to achieve:

- What does the decision have to accomplish?
- What are the objectives the decision has to reach?
- What are the minimum goals the decision has to achieve?
- What are the conditions the decision has to satisfy?

These specifications could be readily transferable to strategic thinking and strategic decision making, even though initially put forth by Drucker for problem solving.

What Is Right?

Key issues the decision maker needs to keep in mind here include:

- The difference between what is right and what is acceptable
- Anticipating the need to eventually compromise
- Not signaling your willingness to compromise in advance

According to Drucker, "effective decision makers do things right, not what is acceptable—they do not ask what will be acceptable?"[24]

The decision maker must also be willing to eventually compromise relative to the decision that is being made, in order to overcome potential resistance of various constituencies. This involves negotiation and it is important for the decision maker not to advise others in advance of his willingness to do this. Once it has been identified that you are willing to negotiate, more people impacted by the decision will also want to negotiate and potentially compromise the desired decision (the horse becomes a camel).

Doing "what is right versus what is acceptable" applies to strategic thinking and strategic decision making; however, compromising on the business's vision and strategy may not be in the best interest of the organization. Furthermore, compromising with what and with whom? Is GM compromising in its strategic decisions to close many of its US plants?

Converting the Decision into Action

Another famous quotation of Drucker is: "A plan that is not implemented is not a plan—but only a good intention."[25] In order to ensure the decision will be implemented, the decision maker must ask additional questions:

Who has to know of this decision? It is important to inform those who will be impacted by the decision (refer to Chapter 10, "Planning and Managing Organizational Change," which discusses how the Participation and Involvement Strategies and Tactics are used to involve those people who would be impacted by a change/decision in the planning process). By involving those people in the decision-making process, implementation of the decision will have a higher probability of success since those who were involved in the process will have a sense of ownership and commitment to the decision. This is a better approach than just sending out a memo of what decision has been made.

What Action Has to Be Taken and Who Has to Take it?

This is essentially developing an Action Plan of what has to be done, when, and who will be responsible for the implementation of the decision.

What Does the Action Have to Be So That People Who Have to Do It Can Do It?

The Action Plan should also include what support and resources people who will be responsible for its implementation may require. Will they need additional funding, people, special knowledge and skills, coordination with other departments for information and co-operation, and so on?

Feedback

The decision maker needs to build feedback systems into the decision and Action Plan:

- How and when will progress toward resolving the problem be evaluated?
- What information will be needed, and when, to evaluate progress?
- Do not rely on just reports; it is important to get out and observe what action is taking place.

Most of these comments would also be applicable to strategic thinking, strategic decision making, and strategic planning.

Other Decision Making Guidelines

In addition to the Elements of Decision Making as described by Drucker, he offered several other guidelines to improve the effectiveness of decision making. These included focusing on "Opinions Rather Than Facts," "The Importance of Developing Disagreement" and "Involving Others."

Opinions Rather Than Facts

Drucker argued that one has to start with "opinions," not "facts."[26] His rationale was that people tend to look for facts that support the conclusion they have already reached. Opinions on the other hand, allow for the testing and the eventual exploration of facts that are necessary to make the opinion tenable.

Perhaps the most important Drucker concept here is that by seeking opinions, it allows for the generating of alternatives for consideration. Alvin Toffler, in *Revolutionary Wealth* (2006),[27] includes an interesting discussion on "truth filters" and what sources people rely on to believe, which relates to what Drucker advocated here. On the other hand, can facts always be ignored at first as Drucker suggests? As an example, water pollution in China is a serious problem. Fact: There were 162 water pollution accidents (industrial waste discharged into rivers contaminating the water supply of many Chinese cities) during the first eight months of 2006 alone.[28] In dealing with this problem, should decision makers ignore these facts and instead seek opinions like, "I think we have a water pollution problem in China"?. This Drucker gap was closed with a concept called "suspending judgment" that will be reviewed later in this chapter.

Develop Disagreement

According to Drucker, "'The First Rule' of decision making is one does not make a decision unless there is disagreement."[29] He argued that disagreement allows alternatives to be considered, offers differing viewpoints, and stimulates the imagination and development of new ideas. The decision maker then needs to explore why others disagree. The views of Mary Parker Follett, an earlier contributor to management theory, and her discussion of constructive conflict perhaps influenced Drucker's thinking here.[30]

Developing disagreement is not always an easy task for those involved in group problem analysis and decision making. This can be best illustrated by the concept of Group Think, as put forth by Irving L. Janis of UC Berkeley in the early 1970s. Janis described the problems groups have in making decisions when there is a strong desire to maintain the cohesiveness of the group. He described how group members may withhold dissent or differing points of view (self-censorship) in order to preserve the cohesiveness of the group, which can lead to poor decisions.[31] I would also disagree with Drucker on developing disagreement as the First Rule. The first job of decision makers is to define the "real problem," after which there may be disagreement relative to the various alternatives that are generated by the group to resolve the problem.

Getting Others to Buy the Decision

Another guideline from Drucker deals with how to get others to buy or accept the decision. Here he cited the Japanese model of building consensus to the decision or pre-selling the decision to the organization. Two models of decision making are used to expand on his point, the Western—Short-Long Model and the Eastern—Long-Short Model.

The Western—Short-Long Model   This model suggests that the process of making a decision in Western countries, particularly in the United States, is made relatively quickly, or in a short period of time. On the other hand, in many cases those who are impacted by the decision have been left out of the decision-making process and may therefore not understand or resist the decision. As a result, considerable time must be spent in "selling" the decision to the organization and delaying its implementation.

The Eastern—Long-Short Model   This model is characteristic of the Japanese model described by Drucker, who during his career spent a considerable amount of time consulting with companies in Japan. Here, considerable time is devoted to first defining the question and then developing a consensus for the decision or pre-selling it.[32] Once this consensus has been developed and the eventual decision accepted by the organization, its implementation is considerably shorter than the Western Model. This is similar to the Participation and Involvement Strategy and Tactics described in Chapter 10.

Forced Participation

Finally, Drucker mentioned Forced Participation or having people who will have the responsibility for implementing the decision or who could sabotage it to participate in the decision-making discussion.

The executives should involve those who can contribute useful information to the strategic thinking and strategic decision making process. However, the final decision will rest with the CEO.

The Drucker Gap

In this chapter it was necessary to include the contributions of others from the Classical and Behavioral Schools to support many of Drucker's views with the *why*. Drucker did not discuss the advantages and disadvantages of group versus individual decision making, on which there is considerable research and literature. It was necessary to adapt Drucker's views on decision making, which pertained more to problem solving than to strategic decision making.

I have included a detailed Group Problem Analysis and Decision Making Process to supplement the discussion of Drucker's concepts on decision making as it provides a track to follow during a strategic thinking and strategic decision making session.

Group Decision Making—An Open Systems Approach

The Group Decision-Making Process, an Open Systems Approach, was developed to close the Drucker gap with respect to his views on decision making. I borrowed from both the Classical and Behavioral Schools in attempting to provide more clarity to Drucker's approach, and I offer a more concise and easier to follow *how-to* tool for managers to use in leading group problem analysis and decision making discussions. The literature with respect to group decision making is extensive, and I will avoid a lengthy discussion of the research that suggests higher quality decisions can be reached by groups versus individuals although it may take longer than individual decision making.[33] It is important, however, that the group has a process to follow, which is described below. I have also indicated where Drucker's observations and elements fit in this process. Finally, I suggest the Open Systems Approach is applicable to strategic thinking, planning, and decision-making sessions.

An Open Systems Approach

An Open System is described as an organization that receives inputs from its outside environment (raw materials such as coal, for example), transforms them (manufactures a product, electricity), and provides outputs to the outside environment (sells and delivers the product, energy). Outputs could also be beneficial or harmful, such as carbon dioxide emissions from a coal burning power plant. Few, if any organizations can be considered to be Closed Systems in that their external environment does not impact them so we will focus on the Open System. This Transformation Process is helpful in problem analysis and decision making, as it allows decision makers to look at the organization from a process or value chain perspective, similar to the approach taken in Six Sigma (Classical School).

The Organization's Subsystems

In Open Systems Theory, an organization is comprised of a number of subsystems. These include the Mission, Vision and Values Subsystem; Management Subsystem; Human, Social, and Cultural Subsystem; Structural Subsystem; and the Technological Subsystem.[34] The Open Systems Problem Analysis and Decision-Making Approach examines all of these subsystems to determine what the "real problem" might be and also to assess what the impact of a particular decision might be on the various subsystems of the organization. This will become clearer as the "Process" is described. These subsystems are briefly described below and are also depicted in Table 12.1.

Mission, Vision and Values: This subsystem describes the purpose of the organization, or as Drucker would ask, "What is our business?" The Vision the organization has for the future, "What should our business be?" and the Values and Beliefs that are shared in the organization.

Management Subsystem: The management practices and leadership style of the organization's management (executive, managers, supervisors and so forth).

Human, Cultural and Social Subsystem: The people in the organization, their knowledge, skills, values and beliefs, and how combined they contribute to the organization's culture.

Table 12.1   Elements of Open Systems Theory

Organizational Subsytems	Task Environment	General Environment
Mission and Vision	Customers	Legal and Regulatory
Management	Suppliers	Natural Resources
Human, Social and Cultural	Competitors	Economic, Political and Society
Structural	Technology	Culture, Values, Beliefs
Technological		Climate

Structural Subsystem: There are two dimensions of this subsystem. One deals with reporting relationships as depicted on the organization chart. The other deals with decision making, where decisions are made in the organization, and if the organization is responsive to its external environment.

Technological Subsystem: The technology used to perform work, produce information and so on.

Task and General External Environments

In Open Systems Theory, the organization's external environment that it interacts with consists of both a Task and General Environment.

The Task Environment   The Task Environment includes the organization's customers, suppliers and competitors, or those closest to the organization, with which it interacts most frequently. Also included are changes in technology that may be impacting the industry.

The General Environment   This is the environment the organization operates in and includes the legal and regulatory element, natural resources, economy (macro and micro), society including demographics, education, culture, values and beliefs, and climate.

The Open Systems Problem Analysis and Decision Making Process considers all of these elements when analyzing a problem. Some may or may not apply to each situation, but it provides a comprehensive checklist and roadmap to follow.

Steps in the Open Systems Process

The Open Systems Problem Analysis and Decision-Making Approach consists of 12 steps as depicted in Table 12.2. Each step also includes a checklist of key questions that should be asked relative to that element.

1. *Strategy Determination:* The early identification of a problem or symptom of a problem. Key questions that should be asked by the decision maker include:
    * What is our goal or objective?
    * Identify the Performance Gap, the differences between our goal and objectives and the actual results.

Table 12.2 Steps in the Process

1. Strategy Determination	7. Identifying Alternatives
2. Strategy Analysis Phase	8. Evaluating Alternatives
3. Meeting Opening and Facilitation	9. Decision Making
	10. Action Planning
4. Gathering Information	11. Evaluation and Control
5. Impact Analysis	12. Concluding the Meeting
6. Defining the Problem	

- Is the gap important? (Similar to Drucker's "Is a decision necessary?")

2. *Problem or Strategy Assessment:* Key questions to ask if the decision maker concludes a decision is necessary:
   - Is emergency action required? (Get the people out of the burning building and then find out how the fire started.)
   - Is a group problem analysis meeting necessary? Does the decision maker have enough information about the "real problem" to make the decision or would input from others be useful?
   - Who are the right people to ask who have relevant information, knowledge and expertise about the situation (Drucker's Getting Opinions)?
   - Who might be impacted by a decision, and do they have the power to resist (Drucker's Need for Compromise)?
   - Who else has the power, authority and influence for approving the decision? Should they be invited?
   - What will be the right time and place for the discussion?

3. *Opening the Meeting & Establishing the Rules of Conduct:* When all meeting participants are present, the decision maker should establish the Rules of Conduct for the meeting. Once the organization gets familiar with this process, this can be done with a quick reminder in future problem analysis and decision-making meetings.

Opening the Meeting

- State the Goal and Performance Gap. ("Our sales objective for this quarter was $50 million, and we came in at $30 million, a gap of $20 million.")

- State the objectives for the meeting. ("To find out what contributed to the Performance Gap and correct it.")
- Deal with issues, not people. (We are not here to blame people for the gap.)

Stating the Rules of Conduct and Meeting Facilitation: Rules of Conduct can be distributed to all the meeting participants and quickly reviewed by the facilitator:

- Everyone should listen.
- Don't talk at the same time, and avoid side conversations.
- You want to define the "real problem" (Drucker's "What is the question?").
- You want to explore alternatives.
- Suspend judgment: Do not evaluate alternatives until all inputs are received. If someone gets put down by the group, say, because he was considered to be impractical, this will inhibit other members of the group from contributing their thoughts and restrict creativity.

4. *Gathering Information (Drucker's Generic or Unique Event)*: This next step deals with gathering information relative to the issue or Performance Gap. Here, the subsystems of the organization and the organization's Task and General Environments should be explored, depending on the complexity of the issue. The following is a brief checklist of the questions that might be asked as each subsystem and the environmental elements are explored:

Mission and Vision Subsystem: Key Questions

- *Mission:* Is this the right business to be in? *Note:* An Industry Attractiveness Assessment Tool was also developed to assist in answering this question and can be found in Appendix A.
- *Revised Mission:* What is changing that should cause us to rethink our Mission?
- *Vision:* Is our Vision for the future appropriate? What should our business be?
- *Strategy:* Is our Strategy working or needs to be revised?

Additional Strategic Questions are enclosed at the end of this chapter for reference in strategic thinking and planning sessions.

Management Subsystem: Key Questions

- Are Management Style and Practices contributing to the problem?
- What other management or supervisory actions may be contributing to the problem?
- Does management know what to do?
- What is our information flow? Does information get to the right place—in time for action to be taken?
- What are the systems, procedures and policies involved? Are they appropriate or creating obstacles to performance?

Human Subsystem: Key Questions

- Do people have the ability (knowledge and skills) to perform effectively?
- Do people understand what they are supposed to do (Role Clarity)?
- Do people receive frequent feedback on their performance?
- Do people have the willingness to perform? What are the reward systems and consequences for their performance (positive, neutral, negative)?
- Do people get rewarded for not performing?

Structural Subsystem: Key Questions

- How is work organized?
- What are the working conditions and plant layout?
- Do people have authority and responsibility for results?
- Where are decisions regarding work made? Where should they be made?
- Should we be organized differently?

Technological Subsystem: Key Questions

- Is there something wrong with our technology?
- Do we have the proper equipment, raw materials and supplies?
- Is the equipment functioning properly? Is it being maintained?

- Are the systems and procedures for using the equipment proper and known?
- Have we made any recent changes in technology or how work is performed?
- Is there better technology available?

External Task Environment: Key Questions

- *Customers and Suppliers:* Are they contributing to the problem?
- *Competition:* Is competition doing anything that has an impact on the company that could be contributing to the problem?
- *Social/Political Factors:* What social/political factors are having an impact on the organization?
- *Technology:* Are there any changes in technology that have an impact on the organization?

External General Environment: Key Questions

- *Legal/Regulatory:* Are any present or pending government or other regulations influencing the situation?
- *Natural Resources:* Could this be contributing to the situation (increased oil prices)?
- *Climate Conditions:* Do any changes in climate conditions have an impact on the organization? *Note:* This has nothing to do with global warming. Temperature fluctuations in a manufacturing process could impact tolerances and so forth.
- *Economy:* What changes in the macro and micro economy may have an impact on the organization?
- *Culture:* Does culture have any influence in contributing to the problem (foreign operations)?
- *Education Levels and Demographics:* What influence does the education system and demographics of the population have on the problem?
- *Political/Sociological:* Does the present political system and society have any impact on the problem?
- *Technology:* Are changes in technology having an impact on the problem?

5. *Impact Analysis:* Once an assessment has been made relative to the organization's subsystems and external environment,

the next step is to perform an Impact Analysis. In other words, has a change in one subsystem had an adverse impact on another? As an example, new technology (Technological Subsystem) has been introduced to manufacture a product; however, the employees have not been properly trained in the proper procedures of how to use the technology (Human Subsystem). A key question to ask here—is one or more subsystems impacting another subsystem(s)? Look for impacts and relationships.

6. *Defining the Problem:* The object of the first five steps in the Open Systems Approach is to assist the group in defining the "Real Problem" as opposed to the symptoms of the problem (Drucker's Defining the Problem). Returning to the first example of high turnover of knowledge workers, an assessment of the organization's subsystems might have revealed that (1) the organization's technology is not current or state-of-the-art—knowledge workers, particularly those in IT will gravitate to organizations with the latest technology in order to continue their self development—and (2) the organization lacks a career planning system and therefore knowledge workers see limited opportunities in the organization for advancement and growth. In stating the "Real Problem" then, the conclusion should include

- *The Goal:* What are we trying to achieve?
- *The Obstacle:* What obstacle or obstacles are in the path of the goal that need to be removed?

7. *Identifying Alternatives:* Once the Real Problem has been identified, the next step in the process is to consider what alternatives will resolve the situation. Here, the decision maker who is leading the group problem analysis discussion establishes some additional rules.

- Statement of Restrictions: State what possible alternatives cannot be considered because there are certain restrictions that are imposed. In our example, the organization cannot go out and replace all technology because of budget and capital constraints.
- Request Alternatives: The decision maker now opens the meeting to alternatives from the group. The decision

maker should avoid stating his or her thoughts first, since if he or she is in an authority or power position, this could bias the group or limit the offering of other alternatives from the group members.

- Suspend judgment: List the alternatives on a flip chart but do not assess their merits at this time. Suspend judgment until all group members have had an opportunity to express their views and suggestions. Criticizing one alternative before others have had an opportunity to contribute their suggestions may cause some to withhold their input so as not to be put down by the group.

8. *Evaluating Alternatives:* Once all alternatives have been put forth by the group, each should then be evaluated by asking the following questions:

- How will this alternative help resolve the problem and achieve the goal?
- How will this alternative not help?
- What future problems might this alternative cause?
- What will be the impact of this alternative on other subsystems?

9. *Decision Making:* The next step is to make the decision and select the alternative that meets your criteria (Drucker's Make the Right Decision). An additional consideration is to make sure that those with power, authority and influence are committed to the decision if the nature of the decision is beyond the scope of the decision maker's authority and requires blessings from above.
Can't Reach a Decision: Not all problems can be resolved in one meeting. The group may need more time to sleep on it. Adjourn the meeting and reschedule another time to meet to reconsider the problem. Perhaps additional research may be required (facts as opposed to opinions).
Revise the Goal: Was the goal of $50 million in sales for the quarter realistic? If not, perhaps the solution to the problem and the "Performance Gap" is to revise the goal.

10. *Action Planning:* One of Drucker's famous quotes is most applicable here.

A plan which is not implemented is not a plan . . . but only a good intention.[35]

In action planning, it is important for the decision maker to clarify the following in order that everyone understands the plan and what part they will play in its execution.

- What will you do and when?
- What will the others do and when?
- Do they have the resources to do what you want them to do (knowledge, skills, information, budget and so forth)?
- What support and coordination with other departments in the organization may be necessary?
- What controls and feedback system will be established to evaluate progress (Drucker's Feedback)?
- Confirm everyone's understanding of their part in the plan by having them repeat it back during the meeting before you adjourn.
- Set times for evaluating progress and when you will meet again.

11. *Evaluation and Control*: The evaluation and control system that is put into place to monitor progress should provide timely feedback and information. The key is to know what is happening while it is happening. Key questions the decision maker needs to ask include:

- Is progress being made?
- What corrective action must be taken?
- Should the Plan be revised?

12. *Concluding the Meeting*: Once the Action Plan is understood, the decision maker should thank all of the participants for their contributions and adjourn the meeting. The minutes of the meeting and the Action Plan should be prepared after the meeting and distributed to all of the meeting participants and others who may be impacted by the decision.

Chapter Summary

This chapter attempted to adapt Drucker's views on decision making, which were originally focused on problem solving, and apply them to strategic thinking and strategic decision making. A number of concepts from decision theory were included to reinforce Drucker's views on the topic. A key take-away should be the need for defining the "*real problem*" even in a strategic decision making context. Too often, symptoms of the problem are confused with what the real problem actually is, and by treating symptoms, the problem is never corrected. Executives involved in strategic thinking and strategy determination should be aware of the numerous issues that can lead to poor decisions such as Escalation of Commitment, Group Think and other obstacles. The Open Systems Problem Analysis and Decision-Making Approach has been included to provide a clearer path and tool for implementing Drucker's views on decision making.

The following are some questions that need to be considered in strategy determination, some are covered earlier.

Strategic Decision Making Supplement
STRATEGIC MANAGEMENT QUESTIONS

Drucker's Three Key Questions

1. What is our business?
2. What will our business be?
3. What should our business be?

Drucker's Theory of the Business Assumptions

- What its business is?
- What its objectives are?
- How it defines results?
- Who its customers are?
- What the customers value and pay for?
- What do we assume about the market?
- Is the market still what we think it is?

- Who is our distribution channel? What do they pay for?
- Non-customers: Why don't they buy from us? What are they willing to pay for? What is value to them?

Drucker's Core Competencies Assumptions

- What are we good at?
- What are the abilities and knowledge we depend on in order to conquer and maintain our leadership in the market?
- What are the things we know how to do better than our competitors and with less effort?
- In what things are we really excellent, and in what things would we have to be?

Drucker's Assumptions About Mission

- What is our Mission?
- What does it have to be?
- What results are we trying to achieve?
- How are we going to measure them, or at least value them?

Drucker's Additional Questions About Mission

- Customer Needs: WHAT is being satisfied?
- Customer Groups: WHO is being satisfied?
- Technologies Used, Functions Performed and Unique Capabilities (Core Competencies): HOW are customer needs being satisfied?
- What is the Mission of the business?
- Is the Mission appropriate for the current environment, or does it need to be redefined?

Drucker's What Will Our Business Be?

Market Potential and Market Trends

- How large can we expect our market for our business to be in five or 10 years—assuming no basic changes in market structure or technology?
- What will be the factors that will determine this development?
- What changes have taken place or are taking place in the environment that will have an impact on our present customers, products and services, and industry?

Changes in Market Structure

- What changes in market structure are to be expected as the result of economic developments, changes in fashion or taste, or moves by competition?

Innovation

- What innovations will change the customer's wants, create new ones, extinguish old ones, create new ways of satisfying his wants, change his concepts of value, or make it possible to give him greater value satisfaction?

The Consumer

- What wants do the consumers have that are not being adequately satisfied by the products or services offered today?

Drucker's What Should Our Business Be?

- What changes in the environment can be observed that have an impact on characteristics, Mission and Purpose of the business?
- What opportunities are opening up or can be created to fulfill the Purpose and Mission of the business by making it into a different business?
- How to build these anticipations into the Theory of the Business, into objectives, strategies and work assignments?

Drucker's Strategic Vision

- Does it chart an organization's future strategic course and define the business composition in three to five years?
- Does it identify business activities to be pursued?
- Does it define the business's future market position?
- Does it define its future customer focus?
- Does it define the kind of organization the business wants to become?

Vision for the Future

- What should our business be?

Drucker's Concept of Planned Abandonment (Products and Business Units)

Are they still viable?
Are they likely to remain viable?
Do they still give value to the customer?
Are they likely to do so tomorrow?
Do they still fit the realities of population and markets, of technology and economy?
If not, how can we best abandon them, or at least stop pouring in further resources and efforts?

Aging Population

- Will the steady growth in the number of older people continue to provide market opportunities—and for how long?
- Will their income still be high (developed countries) or go down?
- Will they continue to spend freely as they have been?
- Will they continue to want to be "young" and spend accordingly?

Industry Analysis

- Should we be in this or another industry?
- Is the industry growing, stable, or declining?
- How easy or difficult is it for others to enter or leave the industry?
- Knowing what we know now, would we do this?

External Environment Assessment

- What changes are or will take place in the following areas: Customers and Non-customers (changing needs), Competitors (competitive analysis), Technology, Suppliers, Government Regulations, Demographics and Society Changes and so forth?

Assessment of Innovative Opportunities and Potential Risks

- Based on the External Environment Assessment, what Innovative Opportunities should the organization prioritize and pursue?
- What Risks or Threats should the organization be aware of and attempt to minimize?

Internal Assessment (Core Competencies and Capabilities)

- Do we have the resources (capabilities) to compete?
- What other resources are needed and when?

- What weaknesses do we have in key competitive areas that we need to address?
- What strengths (core competencies) do we have that we should take advantage of?
- Establishment of Long-Term Objectives (Three to Five years)
- What long-term objectives need to be established now in order to achieve our Vision?

Strategic Alternatives and Decision

- What is the best competitive strategy that will allow us to accomplish our objectives and achieve our Vision?
- What are the competitive strategies to consider?

Strategic Plan

- How are we going to document how we will get there (the Strategic Plan)?
- What resources will we need, how will we be organized?
- Who should do this?

Implementation of the Plan and Leading Change

- What changes may be necessary in the organization?
- Who will plan, lead and implement organizational change?
- Are we achieving our objectives?
- Are we receiving the right information when we need it for decision making?

Test of Strategy

- The organization attains its original objectives.
- The organization experiences rapid growth (doubles or triples its size in a relatively short period of time).
- Unexpected success or failure (own or a competitor's.)
- The firm's sales are growing faster, slower, or about the same pace as the market as a whole, thus resulting in a rising, eroding, or stable market share.
- The company is acquiring new customers at an attractive rate as well as retaining existing customers.
- The firm's profit margins are increasing or decreasing, and how well its margins compare to rival firms' margins.

- Trends in the firm's net profits, return on investment, and economic value added, and how these compare to the same trends for other companies in the industry.
- The company's overall financial strength and credit rating are improving or on the decline.
- The company can demonstrate continuous improvements in such internal performance measures as unit cost, defect rate, scrap rate, employee motivation and morale, number of stock outs and customer back orders, fewer days of inventory, and so forth.
- How shareholders view the company based on trends in the company's stock price and shareholder value (relative to the market value added of other companies in the industry).
- The firm's image and reputation with its customers.
- Is the company regarded as a leader in technology, product innovations, e-commerce, product quality, short times from order to delivery, having the best prices, getting newly developed products to market quickly, or other relevant factors on which buyers base their choice of brands.

Guidelines for Assessing the Feasibility of a Given Strategy

1. Does the strategy focus on the environment? (According to Rea and Kerzner, the purpose of strategy is to help the organization respond to environmental opportunities/threats.)[36]
2. Does the strategy create or sustain a competitive advantage? (Does the company serve customers in ways that are difficult for competitors to match and similar to Porter's views?)
3. Does the strategy match organizational capabilities/constraints? (There needs to be a fit between the strategy and the organization and its culture and talent.)
4. Does the strategy maintain strategic flexibility? (The strategy helps to manage some risks by remaining flexible—deals with Drucker's "What will our business be?")
5. Does the strategy focus on the fundamental strategic question? (Having the ability to resolve strategic issues that were raised during strategic thinking.)
6. Does the strategy allow for the analysis of financial resources and constraints? (Source and use of funds—pay dividends to shareholders or reinvest in R&D?)
7. Does the strategy allow management to think systematically?

Strategic Objectives: Another Point of View

- Winning additional market share
- Overtaking competitors on product quality or customer service or product innovation
- Achieving lower overall costs than rivals
- Boosting the company's reputation with customers
- Winning a stronger foothold in international markets
- Exercising technological leadership
- Gaining a sustainable competitive advantage
- Capturing attractive growth opportunities

Crafting Strategy

- Whether to concentrate on a single business or build a diversified group of businesses (one of Drucker's strategies)?
- Whether to cater to a broad range of customers or focus on a particular market niche (Drucker's concentration)?
- Whether to develop a wide or narrow product line (Drucker's specialization and diversification)?
- Whether to pursue a competitive advantage based on low cost or product superiority or unique organizational capabilities (Drucker's knowledge competencies)?
- How to respond to changing buyer preferences?
- How big a geographic market to try to cover?
- How to react to newly emerging market and competitive conditions?
- How to grow the enterprise over the long term?

Other Market Analysis Questions

1. Who buys?
2. Where is it bought?
3. What is it being bought for?
4. Who is the non-customer? Why does he not buy our products?
5. What does the customer buy all together?
6. What share of the customer's total spending—disposable income, discretionary income, or discretionary time—goes on products, and whether the share is going up or down?
7. What do customers—and non-customers—buy from others? What satisfaction do they give that they cannot get from our products?

8. What product or service would fulfill the satisfaction areas of real importance—both those we now service and those we might serve?
9. What would enable the customer to do without our product or service? (This is more closely associated with substitute products: gas prices forcing people to buy smaller cars vs. SUVs, using public transportation more, and so on.)
10. Who is not competing against us—and why? (Who else might enter the industry and become our competitor?)
11. Who are we not competing against? (Possibly identifying opportunities outside our industry.)

Endnotes

1. Comment made by Drucker at the Claremont Graduate School Ph.D. Program, Fall 1976.
2. Peter F. Drucker, *Management: Tasks, Responsibilities, Practices* (New York: Harper and Row Publishers, Inc., 1973), 125.
3. Rudy A. Champa, *Strategic Thinking and Boardroom Debate* (Mission Viejo, CA, Critical Thinkers Press, 2001), 11.
4. Peter Rea, Ph.D., and Harold Kerzner, Ph.D., *Strategic Planning: A Practical Guide* (New York: John Wiley & Sons, Inc., 1997), 59–60.
5. Arthur A. Thompson, Jr., and A.J. Strickland III *Strategic Management: Concepts & Cases.* 13th ed., 10.
6. Robert W. Swaim, Ph.D., "The Drucker Files: Is a Decision Necessary? Parts I & II." *Business Beijing* (July & August 2003).
7. Peter F. Drucker, "The Elements of Decision Making." *Corpedia 8104.* On-line program (2001).
8. Peter F. Drucker, *The Effective Executive* (New York: Harper & Row, 1967), 136–137.
9. Ibid., 122–123.
10. Ibid., 143.
11. Fremont E. Kast and James E. Rosenzweig, *Organization and Management: A Systems and Contingency Approach* (New York: McGraw-Hill, Inc. 1979), 368–370.
12. Ibid., 368.
13. Ibid., 370.
14. Stephen R. Robbins, *Organizational Behavior*, 8th ed. (Upper Saddle River, NJ: Prentice-Hall, Inc. 1998), 111–112.
15. Ibid., 111.
16. Herbert A. Simon, "Administrative Decision Making." In: *Management Classics* (Santa Monica, CA: Goodyear Publishing Company, 1977).

17. Peter F. Drucker, *The Effective Executive* (New York: Harper & Row, 1967), 155.
18. Peter F. Drucker, "The Elements of Decision Making." *Corpedia 8104*. On-line program (2001).
19. Jack Welch, *Jack: Straight from the Gut* (New York: Warner Books, Inc. (2001), 398.
20. Peter F. Drucker, *The Essential Drucker* (New York: HarperCollins Publishers, Inc., 2001), 241–260.
21. Stephen R. Robbins, *Organizational Behavior*, 8th ed. (Upper Saddle River, NJ: Prentice-Hall, Inc. 1998), 112–113.
22. Peter F. Drucker, "The Elements of Decision Making." *Corpedia 8104*. On-line program.
23. Peter F. Drucker, *The Essential Drucker* (New York: HarperCollins Publishers, Inc., 2001), 245–247.
24. Ibid., 247–249.
25. Comment made by Drucker at the Claremont Graduate School Ph.D. Program, September, 1978.
26. Peter F. Drucker, *The Essential Drucker* (New York: HarperCollins Publishers, Inc., 2001), 251–254.
27. Alvin and Heidi Toffler, *Revolutionary Wealth* (New York: Alfred A. Knopf, 2006).
28. "China Seas One Water Pollution Accident Every Two to Three Days", *Xinhua News Agency* (September, 2006).
29. Peter F. Drucker, *The Essential Drucker* (New York: HarperCollins Publishers, Inc., 2001), 254–256.
30. Mary Parker Follett, *Management as a Profession* (New York: McGraw-Hill Book Company, 1927).
31. Iving L. Janis, *Victims of Group Think* (Boston: Houghton Mifflin, 1972).
32. Peter F. Drucker, *Management: Tasks, Responsibilities, Practices* (New York: Harper & Row 1973), 466–470.
33. Stephen R. Robbins, *Organizational Behavior*, 8th ed. (Upper Saddle River, NJ: Prentice-Hall, Inc. 1998), 267.
34. Fremont E. Kast and James E. Rosenzweig, *Organization and Management: A Systems and Contingency Approach* (New York: McGraw-Hill, Inc. 1979), 107–120.
35. Comment by Drucker during a Ph.D. class at the Claremont Graduate School, September 1978.
36. Peter Rea and Hardd Kerzner, *Strategic Planning: A Practical Guide* (New York: John Wiley & Sons, Inc., 1977). 59 –60.

Strategic Management Application Tools

Application Tools

A number of Strategic Management Application Tools are included here to allow the reader to transfer Drucker's concepts to their own organizations and to close some of the gaps as discussed. Some tools were specifically developed while others were added from other contributors such as the Boston Consulting Group (BCG) Strategy and GE Models. These tools and instructions in this Appendix include:

The Industry and Market Tools

These tools have been included to answer a number of Drucker's suggested questions, such as *Should we be in this business? What will our business be? Who and where is the customer? What trends are taking place in the marketplace?*

1. Industry Attractiveness Assessment Tool
2. What Will Our Business Be Form Assessment
3. Market Growth Matrix
4. Business Market Segmentation Assessment

Internal Capabilities and Competitive Assessment

These tools address the internal (core competencies) and mission assumptions of Drucker's Theory of the Business as well as competition.

  5. Strategic Competitive Capabilities Assessment
  6. Competitive Advantage Index
  7. Planned Abandonment Assessment
  8. Values and Mission Assessment (The Theory of the Business)

Strategy and Marketing

These tools present an overview of strategies made popular by the Boston Consulting Group and GE. A more comprehensive discussion of strategies was also included in the Drucker Strategy MBA course.

  1. BCG Strategy Matrix and Assessment
  2. GE Strategic Planning: A Practical Guide
  3. Planning Channel Architecture Matrix

1. Industry Attractiveness Assessment Tool[1]

INSTRUCTIONS

  1. Review each Element below and complete the Assessment of Your Company's Industrys Attractiveness Form below by circling the appropriate score.
  2. Total your scores and refer to the Score Interpretation key on the next page to determine your present industry's attractiveness. Also complete this assessment for industries your company is considering entering.

Element	High	Moderate	Low
Market Size	Large Market (5 points)	Medium Market (7 points)	Small Market (10 points)
Market Growth Rate	Fast Growth (10 points)	Some to No Growth (5 points)	Declining Growth (0 points)

Element	High	Moderate	Low
Number of Competitors	Many Competitors (0 points)	Moderate Number of Competitors (5 points)	Few Competitors (10 points)
Strength of Competition	Strong Competition (0 points)	Moderate Competition (5 points)	Weak to No Competition (10 points)
Industry Capacity	Over Capacity (0 points)	Capacity = Demand (5 points)	Demand Greater Than Capacity (10 points)
Industry Profitability	Highly Profitable (10 points)	Moderately Profitable (5 points)	Little Profit to Unprofitable (0 points)
Entry Barriers	Difficult to Enter Industry (10 points)	Moderate Costs to Enter Industry (5 points)	Easy to Enter Industry (0 points)
Exit Barriers	High Costs to Exit —(0 Points)	Moderate Costs to Exit —(5 points)	Low Costs to Exit (10 points)
Type of Products	Expensive (10 points)	Differentiated (5 points)	Commodity (0 points)
Threat of Substitutes	Great Threat (0 points)	Some Threat (5 points)	Little to No Threat (10 points)
Technological Changes in the Industry	Rapid Changes (0 points)	Moderate Changes (5 points)	Few to No Changes (10 points)
Capital Investment Requirements	High Capital Investment Required (10 points)	Moderate Capital Investment Required (5 points)	Small Capital Investment Required (0 points)
Integration Activity	High Activity (0 points)	Moderate Activity (5 points)	Little to No Activity (10 points)
Economies of Scale	Large Economies of Scale Required (0 points)	Moderate Economies of Scale Required (5 points)	Little Economies of Scale Required (10 points)
Product Innovation	Rapid Innovation (0 points)	Moderate Innovation (5 points)	Low Innovation (10 points)

Element	High	Moderate	Low
Supplier Impact	High Impact (0 points)	Moderate Impact (5 points)	Little to No Impact (10 points)
Government Regulations That Have Negative Impact	Highly Regulated (0 points)	Somewhat Regulated (5 points)	Few Regulations (10 points)
Government Regulations That Have a Positive Impact	Highly Regulated (10 points)	Moderately Regulated (5 points)	Few Regulations (0 points)
Power of Customers	Considerable Power (0 points)	Moderate Power (5 points)	Little to No Power (10 Points)
Total Points in Each Column			
Total Points			

Score Interpretation

The Industry Attractiveness Scores will range from five to 190 points. Attractiveness can be interpreted as outlined below:

Scores of 151 to 190 Points   The industry is unusually attractive. If you are in it, invest heavily for leadership. If you are not in it, you may find it difficult to enter without making an acquisition of a company already in the industry, but if there is a practical way in, enter it with both.

Scores of 121 to 150 Points   This industry is attractive. If you are in it, consolidate your position, and gain or maintain market leadership. If not, consider entry if it is closely related to your existing business and you have the expertise or can share costs with your existing business.

Scores of 91 to 120 Points   The industry is neither attractive nor unattractive. Competitive position is the key here.

Scores of 61 to 90 Points   The industry is not very attractive, but it is possible for segment leaders and very well run companies to a make a reasonable return or make a living if a privately-owned company.

Scores of 31 to 60 Points   This is an unattractive industry. If you are not the market leader, sell the business or diversify into an industry that you have experience with.

Scores of 5 to 30 Points   A very unattractive industry—try to get out of the industry, abandon fast. If you are still reporting profits or anyone is foolish enough to buy the business, sell.

2. What Will Our Business Be? Assessment Form

INSTRUCTIONS

1. Complete an assessment of *your own company* relative to the Four Factors that can have an impact on "What will our business be?" (things that have or are happening that will have an impact on the industry and your company that may change your Mission).
2. Attempt to determine what the impact of that Factor will be on your company in the short term.

Factors	What Has or Is Taking Place?	Potential Short-Term Impact on Your Company?
Market Potential:		
• Growing Trend and Factors Affecting This?		
Market Trend:		
• Changes in Market Trend?		
Changes in Market Structure:		
• Economic Developments?		
• Changes in Fashion?		
• Changes in Taste?		
• Moves by Competition?		
Innovation:		
• Change Customer's Wants?		
• Create New Wants?		
• Extinguish Old Ways?		
• Create New Ways of Satisfying Wants?		
• Change Concept of Value?		
• Provide Greater Value?		
The Consumer:		
• Wants Not Now Being Satisfied?		

3. Market Growth Matrix

INSTRUCTIONS

1. *Situation Now:* Provide examples of industries that are *presently* either growing fast, have slow growth or are stable, and those that are declining.
2. *Future Situation*: Provide examples of industries that will be either growing fast, have slow growth or will be stable, or will be declining in the next three to five years.

Market Growth Rate	Now	Next 3 to 5 Years
FAST GROWING INDUSTRIES		
SLOW GROWING OR STABLE INDUSTRIES		
DECLINING INDUSTRIES		

4. Business Market Segmentation Assessment: Major Segmentation Variables[2]

INSTRUCTIONS

1. Review each of the variables below as they may apply to your organization.
2. Discuss your conclusions in terms of how you might segment the business market with others in your organization.

Market Segmentation Variables	Your Company
Demographic	
1. *Industry:* Which industries should be served?	
2. *Company size:* What size companies should we serve?	
3. *Location:* What geographic areas should we serve?	
Operating Variables	
4. *Technology:* What customer technologies should we focus on?	
5. *User or nonuser status:* Should we serve heavy users, medium users, light users, or nonusers?	

6. *Customer capabilities:* Should we serve customers needing many or few services?

Purchasing Approaches

7. *Purchasing-function organization:* Should we serve companies with highly centralized or decentralized purchasing organizations?

8. *Power structure:* Should we serve companies that are engineering, finance, marketing, etc. dominated?

9. *Nature of existing relationships:* Should we serve companies with which we have strong relationships or go after the most desirable companies?

10. *General purchasing policies:* Should we serve companies that prefer leasing? Service contracts? Systems purchases? Sealed bidding?

11. *Purchasing criteria:* Should we serve companies that are seeking quality? Service? Price?

Situational Factors

12. *Urgency:* Should we serve companies that need quick and sudden delivery service?

13. *Specific application:* Should we focus on certain applications of our product rather than on all applications?

14. *Size of order:* Should we focus on large or small orders?

Personal Characteristics

15. *Buyer-seller similarity:* Should we serve companies whose people and values are similar to ours?

16. *Attitudes towards risk:* Should we serve risk-taking or risk-avoiding customers?

17. *Loyalty:* Should we serve customers that show high loyalty to their suppliers?

5. Strategic Competitive Capabilities Assessment[3]

INSTRUCTIONS

1. List in the first column of the table below the Strategic Competitive Capabilities (SCCs) needed to compete in your industry (Product Quality, Service, Competitive Price, Inventory Availability, Delivery, Credit Terms, Distribution Channels, Experienced and Knowledge-able Sales People, etc.). List the *most important* SCCs first.
2. *Competitive Comparison:* Compare your SCCs to that of your major competitors in the next three columns. Place a number in the columns from one to 10 (1 being very poor compared to the competitor, 10 being much stronger than the competitor).
3. *Action:* In the last column indicate what action your company should take to exploit SCCs where you are much stronger than your competitors, and what action should be taken where you are much weaker than your competitors.

Strategic Capabilities Assessment

Strategic Competitive Capabilities (SCCs)	Competitor	Competitor	Competitor	Action To Take— Use as an Advantage or Improve SCC

6. Competitive Advantage Index: Your Company versus Major Competitors[4]

PART I. INSTRUCTIONS

1. Complete the Competitive Advantage Index for your major competitors or a major competitor in your marketplace.
2. Assign a "Weight" in terms of *Relative Importance* in your marketplace for each of the *Factors (Product Quality—50%; Service Quality—30%, etc.)* Weights should add to 100% for each major category.
3. Rank each Factor on a scale from 0 (*Much Poorer than competitor*) 3 (*Equal to competitor*) to 6 (*Much Better than competitor*).
4. Multiply the Relative Importance Percentage times the Factor Score and record in the Factor Score Column. Ignore the decimal percentage (50% weight × 5 score = 250)
5. Total all Factor Scores and record in the Total Category Advantage Score.

Matrix I

Competitive Advantage Factors	Relative Importance (%)	0	1	Much Poorer 2	Equal To 3	Much Better 4	5	6	Factor Score
Differentiation Advantage									
Product Quality									
Service Quality									
Brand Image									
Relative Price									
Differentiation Advantage Score	100%								
Cost Advantage									
Unit/Variable Costs									
Transaction Costs									
Marketing Expenses									
Operating/Overhead Expenses									
Cost Advantage Score	100%								
Marketing Advantage									
Market Share									
Brand Awareness									
Distribution/Channels									
Sales Coverage & Sales Force									
Marketing Advantage Score	100%								

PART II. INSTRUCTIONS

1. Assign a "Weight" in terms of Relative Importance in your marketplace of each of the Three Major Sources of Competitive Advantage (Cost—0.40, Differentiation—0.40 and Marketing—0.20, etc.) in the table below. Weights should be expressed as percentages (0.40, 0.20, etc.) and add to 1.0 for each major source.
2. Insert your Factor Score for each Category from Matrix I.
3. Multiply the Relative Weight times the Factor Score, and insert in the Overall Score Column. (0.40 Cost Advantage Weight x 300 Factor Score = 120 Overall Score)
4. Divide the Overall Score by the Maximum Score for each Category, and insert a Percent of Maximum in the last column. (120 Cost Advantage Overall Score/240 Maximum Score = 50%)

Source of Competitive Advantage	Relative Weight	Factor Score	Overall Score	Maximum Score	Percent of Maximum
Cost Advantage				240	%
Differentiation Advantage				240	%
Marketing Advantage				120	%
Total	1.00			600	%

Assessment & Discussion Questions

Competitive Advantage (Percentage Maximum Scores in the 70% Range And Above)

1. Discuss where you feel your company has a competitive *advantage* and why.
2. How can your company make use of this advantage in the marketplace as part of its marketing strategy?

Competitive Disadvantage (Percent Maximum Scores in the 40 Percent Range And Below)

1. Where is your company at the most competitive *disadvantage*?
2. If important (relative weight), what should be done to correct this?

7. Planned Abandonment Assessment

INSTRUCTIONS

Select a product(s) or service(s) that your company presently provides.
    Complete the Assessment below to determine if these product(s) or service(s) should be abandoned.

Products/services	Assessment
List the Product(s)/Service(s) in the next column.	Product(s)/Service(s):
What percentage of the company's total sales does this product(s)/service(s) represent? List in the next column.	Percent of Total Revenues?
What percent of the company's total gross profit does this product(s)/service(s) represent? List in the next column.	Percent of Total Gross Profit?
Are the products/services still viable?	
Are they likely to remain viable?	
Do they still give value to the customer?	
Are they like to give value in the future? If so, for how long?	
Do they still fit the realities of the population, markets, technology, and the economy?	
If not a viable product/service, how can the company best abandon them?	
How can the company stop pouring further resources and efforts into this product/service?	
If the product/service were abandoned, what would it be replaced with?	
How long would I take to get the replacement to the market?	

8. Values and Mission Assessment

The Theory of the Business: The Mission

Peter Drucker proposed the concept of the Theory of the Business that is comprised of three main elements:

1. The Mission
2. The Assumptions about the Environment
3. The Core Competencies of the Business

This Assessment allows you to assess your own organization's Values and Mission.

Scoring the Questions   For each question, assign a value of 0 to 10 *using only even numbers* as follows:

0—VERY POOR: There is an almost complete lack of this concept. Its absence or wrong approach may lead to important problems or risks for the business.

2—POOR: There is a significant imbalance. The inherent problems or missed opportunities can lead to significant losses.

4—AVERAGE: This position of mediocrity or lack of study/focus leads the business to difficulties, in a weak position with some competitors and is an important source of missed opportunities.

6—ABOVE AVERAGE: The score is starting to be acceptable. This is an aspect to assess, and is a good idea to review it and improve the assessment.

8—GOOD: The matter is well focused, and there is a consciousness that it can be improved when there is time available or when the business desires perfection.

10—EXCELLENT: This score is reserved for those cases where something very tangible has been reached that gives the firm a competitive advantage or has achieved its objectives.

Score each of the following statements according to your assessment of your organization. Then total the scores to arrive at your organization's Value and Mission Assessment.

Values and Mission Questionnaire

1. In our organization, there is a corporate culture that brings people and teams of people together, and this culture arises from explicit values that are not merely preached by top management but are practised on a daily basis.
   SCORE:_____

2. Senior management is the most logical one to make coherence between their actions and the values of the organization. In other words, there is total consistency between what is said should be done and what is actually done.

   SCORE: _____

3. The Mission of the organization is oriented outwards, to customers, to the market, and we avoid the mistake of orienting the Mission towards what we know how to do or what we like.

   SCORE: _____

4. The Mission clearly defines the Purpose of the Business, without ambiguity and is written down in a simple, clear, and direct manner, so that it may be fully understood by all the members of the organization.

   SCORE: _____

5. The Mission is centered on a single purpose, although in reality it covers a *very wide* range of tasks.

   SCORE: _____

6. The Mission is centered on giving Value to the customer or consumers, instead of concentrating on financial gain. The only realistic way of obtaining results is to give Value to the customers and not the other way round, as some people think.

   SCORE: _____

7. The Mission, although it clearly states our purpose, leaves the doors open to necessary future innovation or changes in the external environment.

   SCORE: _____

8. The Mission is reviewed *every year*, in the current situation of change. To review it every three or five years is too dangerous. Drastic events affect almost all business sectors and all countries, very quickly.

   SCORE: _____

9. The Mission is *operative* but also has a sufficient portion of dreams to motivate people to achieve.

   SCORE: _____

10. The policies and objectives of the organization are consistent with the Mission and are in fact inspired by it.

    SCORE: _____

11. The Mission is very *original* and contains a high degree of *differentiation* with respect to what any competitor could establish. In each business sector, many businesses produce and sell similar products but do it in very different ways and meanings. If a business emulates its competitors' efforts 100 percent, its possibility of progress is very slim.

    SCORE:_____

12. The leaders of the organization obtain the commitment of their team to achieve the Mission.

    SCORE:_____

TOTAL YOUR SCORES FOR ALL QUESTIONS:_____

Values and Mission Assessment

Total Scores	Assessment
94–120	Good to Excellent
74–92	Above Average to Good
50–72	Average to Above Average
26–48	Below Average to Average
12–24	Poor to Below Average
0–10	Poor

Based on your Values and Mission Total Score, answer the following questions:

Do we need any adjustments in our Values and Mission? Which ones?

_____

_____

_____

What should we do better?

_____

_____

Where should we act?

_____

_____

_____

9. BCG Strategy Matrix and Assessment[5]

INSTRUCTIONS

List your company's product or products to be assessed below (at least two products or services):

Product One:

_____

Product Two:

_____

Product Three:

_____

Indicate what the product(s) is according to the BCG Model on the Matrix below (Star, Cash Cow, Problem Child, Dog: see Product Classifications on the next page).

Review the Strategies recommended by the BCG Model for this product classification, and compare it with the strategy your company is implementing or should be implementing.

Product	Classification	BCG Strategies	Our Company's Strategy (Now or Should Be)
	Star	1. Maintain Market Dominance 2. Invest in Process Improvements 3. Maintain Price Leadership 4. Use Excess Cash to Invest in Other Parts of the Business (Innovate)	
	Cash Cows	1. Protect Market Share 2. Reinvest Earnings for Product Development (Innovation)	
	Problem Children	1. Invest Heavily to Increase Market Share 2. Increase Market Share Through Acquisition 3. Divest, Harvest, or Abandon 4. Focus on Market Niche and Develop a Competitive Advantage	
	Dogs	1. Focus on Markets That Can Be Dominated 2. Harvest—Cut Back All Support to Generate Cash Over the Remaining Life of the Product 3. Divest—Sell 4. Delete From the Product Line (Abandon)	

BCG Model Product Classifications[6]

BCG Product Classification	Characteristics	Our Products
Stars	1. High Growth and Enduring Competitive Advantage 2. High Quality and Central to the Firm's Mission 3. Market Leader 4. Good Growth Potential 5. Profitable 6. Large Investment Required to Finance Growth	
Cash Cows	1. Limited Growth Potential but Enduring Competitive Advantage 2. Profitable Products 3. Generate More Cash than Needed to Maintain Market Share	
Problem Children	1. Growth Potential or Enduring Competitive Advantage 2. Either Low Quality or Not Central to the Firm's Mission 3. Growth Potential 4. Poor Profit Margins 5. Significant Investment Required	
Dogs	1. Limited Growth Potential and Lacking Competitive Advantage 2. Limited Quality and Product Not Central to the Firm's Mission 3. Operate at Cost Disadvantage 4. Few Options to Grow at a Reasonable Cost 5. Market Not Growing	

10. GE Strategic Planning: A Practical Guide[7]

	Competitive Position: HIGH	**Competitive Position: MEDIUM**	**Competitive Position: LOW**
Market Attractiveness: HIGH	**PROTECT POSITION** • Invest to grow at maximum digestible rate • Concentrate effort on maintaining strength	**INVEST TO BUILD** • Challenge for leadership • Build selectively on strengths • Reinforce vulnerable areas	**BUILD SELECTIVELY** • Specialize around limited strengths • Seek ways to overcome weaknesses • Withdraw if indications of sustainable growth are lacking
Market Attractiveness: MEDIUM	**BUILD SELECTIVELY** • Invest heavily in attractive segments • Build up ability to counter competition • Emphasize profitability by raising productivity	**SELECTIVITY/MANAGE FOR EARNINGS** • Protect existing program • Concentrate investments in segments where profitability is good and risk is relatively low	**LIMITED EXPANSION OR HARVEST** • Look for ways to expand without high risk; otherwise, minimize investment and rationalize operations
Market Attractiveness: LOW	**PROTECT AND REFOCUS** • Manage for current earnings • Concentrate on attractive segments • Defend strengths	**MANAGE FOR EARNINGS** • Protect position in most profitable segments • Upgrade product line • Minimize investment	**DIVEST** • Sell at time that will maximize cash value • Cut fixed costs and avoid investment meanwhile

COMPETITIVE POSITION

11. Planning Channel Architecture Matrix[8]

INSTRUCTIONS

Review the Marketing Channels and Methods on the Matrix below and determine which ones should be used by your company to accomplish the Demand-Generation Tasks (Lead Generation, Qualifying Sales, Pre-Sales, and so on).

3. PLANNING CHANNEL ARCHITECTURE MATRIX

INSTRUCTIONS

Review the Marketing Channels and Methods on the Matrix below and determine which ones should be used by your company to accomplish the Demand-Generation Tasks (Lead Generation, Qualifying Sales, Pre-Sales, etc.) Rank each Method in order of importance; 1,2, 3, etc. for each of the Demand Generation Tasks.

DEMAND-GENERATION TASKS

Marketing Channels & Methods	Lead Generation	Qualifying Sales	Pre-Sales	Transaction Management Fulfilment	Post-Sales Service	Account Management
Internet						
National Account Management						
Direct Sales						
Telemarketing						
Direct Mail						
Retail Stores						
Distributors						
Dealers & Value Added Resellers						
Advertising						

Source: Adopted and modified from Philip Kotler, Marketing Management, 11th ed. (Upper Saddle River, NJ: Pearson Education, Inc., 2003) p. 525. Original version in Rowland T. Moriarty and Ursula Moran, "Marketing Hybrid Marketing Systems," Harvard Business Review (November-December 1990), p. 150.

Endnotes

1. Adopted and modified from Richard Koch, *The Financial Times Guide to Strategy*, 2nd ed. (London: Pearson Education Limited (2000), 50–51.
2. Adopted and modified from Philip Kotler, *Marketing Management*, 11th ed. (Upper Saddle River, NJ: Pearson Education, Inc., 2003), 296; original version in Thomas V. Bonoma and Benson P. Shapiro, *Segmenting the Industrial Market* (Lexington, MA: Lexington Books, 1983).
3. Adopted and modified from Philip Kotler, *Marketing Management*, 11th ed. (Upper Saddle River, NJ: Pearson Education, Inc., 2003), 296; original version in Thomas V. Bonoma and Benson P. Shapiro, *Segmenting the Industrial Market* (Lexington, MA: Lexington Books, 1983).
4. Adopted and modified from Roger J. Best, *Market-Based Management*, 3rd ed. (Upper Saddle River, NJ: Pearson Education Inc., 2004), 278.
5. Adopted and modified from Peter Rea, Ph.D., and Harold Kerzner, Ph.D., *Strategic Planning: A Practical Guide* (New York: John Wiley & Sons, Inc. 1997), 18.
6. Adopted and modified from Peter Rea, Ph.D. and Harold Kerzner, Ph.D., *Strategic Planning: A Practical Guide* (New York: John Wiley & Sons, Inc. 1997) 18.
7. Redrawn from Peter Rea, Ph.D., and Harold Kerzner, Ph.D., *Strategic Planning: A Practical Guide* (New York: John Wiley & Sons, Inc. 1997), 20.
8. Adopted and modified from Philip Kotler, *Marketing Management*, 11th ed. (Upper Saddle River, NJ: Pearson Education, Inc., 2003) 525; original version in Rowland T. Moriarty and Ursula Moran, "Marketing Hybrid Marketing Systems," *Harvard Business Review* (November-December 1990): 150.

Bibliography

"132 Million People Access Web in China." Beijing: *China Internet Information Center*, December 29, 2006.

"The 2003 Slate 60—The 60 Largest American Charitable Contributions of the Year." *Chronicle of Philanthropy*, February 16, 2004.

Adizes, Ph.D., Ichak. *Managing Corporate Lifecycles*. Paramus, NJ: Prentice Hall, 1999.

"Aging Population a Major Problem." *China Daily*, March 12, 2007.

"Aging Population Test Social Security." *China Daily*, December 13, 2006,

"AmCham White Paper: Trade Gap Not the Full Picture." *China Daily*, April 27, 2007.

"Baby Boom." *China Daily*, May 8, 2006.

"Beijing Police Launch Virtual Web Patrol." *On-Line World MSNBC*, June 28, 2007.

Bennis, Warren G. *Changing Organizations*. New York: McGraw-Hill, 1966.

———. "Drucker: A Personal Reflection." *New Management* 2, no. 3 (Winter 1985).

———. Robert Chin, and Kenneth E. Corey. *The Planning of Change*, 3rd ed. New York: Holt, Rinehart, and Winston, 1976.

———. and Burt Nanus. *Leaders: Strategies for Taking Charge*. New York: Harper and Row, 1985.

Best, Roger J. *Market-Based Management*. 3rd ed. Upper Saddle River, NJ: Prentice Hall, 2004.

Booz, Allen & Hamilton. *New Products Management for the 1980s*. New York: Booz, Allen & Hamilton, 1982.

Bork, David. *Family Business, Risky Business*. New York: AMACOM, 1986.

Buchanan, Patrick J. "America in 2050: Another Country." *WorldNetDaily*, March 24, 2004.

———. "Changing America: The United States Population to Double." *Los Angeles Times*, May 20, 2003.

———. *Day of Reckoning*. New York: St. Martin's Press, 2007.

Burke, W. Warner. *Organization Development: Principles and Practices*. Boston: Little Brown and Company, 1982.

Champa, Rudy A. *Strategic Thinking and Boardroom Debate*. Mission Viejo, CA, Critical Thinker Press, 2001.

Chandler, Jr., Alfred D. *Strategy and Structure*. Cambridge: M.I.T. Press, 1962.

Chang, Gordon G. *The Coming Collapse of China*. London: Arrow, 2001.

"Changing America: The United States Population to Double." *Los Angeles Times*, May 20, 2003.

Chen Ming-Jer. *Inside Chinese Business*. Boston: Harvard Business School Press, 2001.

"China's Demographic Dividend to End in 2010." *World Bank*. March 5, 2007.

"China Discloses Giant Bank Fraud." *Washington Post*. June 27, 2006.

"China to Take Decade to be No. 2 Internet Market in Revenues." *Google-Forbes.com*. March 17, 2006.

"China Leading Censor of Net Study Finds." *Tech News & Reviews, MSNBC.com*. April 14, 2005.

Christensen, Clayton M. *Innovation and the Creative Manager*. New York: Irwin/McGraw-Hill, 1999.

———, and Scott D. Anthony. "What Should Sony Do Next?" *Forbes.com*, August 1, 2007.

———, and Kim Peterson. "Sony Screws Up Again With New PS3." *MSN Money*, October 18, 2007.

Clarkson, William. "Drucker: Closing the Theory/Practice Gap." *New Management* 2, no 3 (Winter 1985).

Collins, James C., and Jerry I., Porras. *Built to Last: Successful Habits of Visionary Companies*. New York: HarperCollins Publishers, Inc., 1994.

Collins, James C., and Jerry I., Porras. *Good to Great: Why Some Companies Make the Leap and Others Don't*. New York: HarperCollins, 2001.

Davis, R. C. *The Fundamentals of Top Management*. New York: Harper & Row, 1951.

Donald, Harvey F., and Donald R. Brown. *An Experiential Approach to Organization Development*. 2nd ed. Englewood Cliffs, NJ: Prentice-Hall, Inc. 1982.

Drucker, Peter F. *The Age of Discontinuity*. London: William Heinemann, 1969.

———. *Concept of the Corporation*. New York: John Daley, 1946.

———. *The Daily Drucker*. New York: HarperCollins, 2004.

———. "Driving Change." *Corpedia Education E-Learning Module 8116* (2003).

———. "Drucker on Drucker." *New Management* 2, no. 3 (Winter 1985).

———. *The Effective Executive*. New York: Harper and Row, 1967.

———. *The Effective Executive in Action*. New York: HarperCollins, 2006.

———. "The Elements of Decision Making." *Corpedia 8104*. On-line program (2001).

———. *The Essential Drucker*. New York: HarperCollins, 2001.

———. "The Five Deadly Business Sins." MTS Video No. 3, Ahead of Change Series. London: MTS Publishers, 1999.

———. "The Five Deadly Business Sins," *Corpedia Education E-Learning Module 8108* (2001).

———. *The Frontiers of Management*. New York: Truman Talley, 1986.

———. *Innovation and Entrepreneurship*. New York: Harper & Row, New York, 1985.

———. *Management Challenges for the 21st Century*. New York: HarperCollins, 1999.

———. "Management and Leadership Today and Tomorrow, Part II," Video 4-1. London: MTS Publishers, Ltd., MTS 1996.

———. "Management Power for Executive Success." MTS Video 1. London: MTS Publishers, 1999.

———. *Management: Tasks, Responsibilities, Practices*. New York: Harper & Row, 1973.

———. *Managing for Results*. New York: Harper & Row, 1964.

————. *Managing in a Time of Great Change*. New York: Truman Talley, 1995.

————. *Managing in the Next Society*. New York: Truman Talley, 2002.

————. *Managing in Turbulent Times*. New York: Harper & Row, 1980.

————. *Managing the Non-Profit Organization*. New York: HarperCollins, 1990.

————. *The New Realities*. New York: Harper and Row, 1989.

————. "The Next Society." *The Economist*, November 3, 2001.

————. *Peter Drucker on the Profession of Management*. Boston: Harvard Business School Press, 1998.

————. *The Practice of Management*. New York: Harper & Row, 1954.

————. "Rules for Strategic Alliances." *Corpedia On-Line Program 8106* (2001).

————. "The Successful Acquisition." *Corpedia Education E-Learning Module 8106* (2001).

————. "The Theory of the Business." *Harvard Business Review* (September–October 1994).

————. "You on Me." *New Management* 2, no. 3 (Winter 1985).

————, and Peter Senge. "Leading in a Time of Change." *MTS Video* (1999).

Edersheim, Elizabeth Haas. *The Definitive Drucker*. New York: McGraw-Hill, 2007.

"Edward Jones." Boston: *Harvard Business School*, 9-700-009, Rev. June 15, 2000.

Filley, Alan C., Robert J. House, and Steven Kerr. *Managerial Process and Organizational Behavior*. 2nd ed. Glenview, IL: Scott, Foresman, 1976.

"Firing CEOs Reaches Record High." *Bloomberg News*, September 27, 2006.

Flaherty, John E. *Peter Drucker: Shaping the Managerial Mind*. San Francisco: Jossey Bass, 1999.

Follett, Mary Parker. *Management as a Profession*. New York: McGraw-Hill, 1927.

————, Henry C. Metcalf, and L. Urwick (eds.). *Dynamic Administration*. New York: Harper and Row Publishers, Inc. 1941.

French, Wendell L., and Cecil H. Bell, Jr. *Organization Development*, 2nd ed. Englewood Cliffs, NJ.: Prentice-Hall, 1978.

Fritz, Mark. "Cash Incentives Aren't Enough to Lift Fertility." *Wall Street Journal*, August 17, 2006.

Geus, Arie de. *The Living Company*. Boston: Harvard Business School Press, 1997.

Graham, Pauline. *Mary Parker Follett, Prophet of Management*. Boston: Harvard Business School Press, 1996.

"The Great Firewall of China." *Open Democracy*, May 20, 2005.

"Half of China to Live in Cities by 2010." *China Daily*, November 7, 2006.

Hall, E. "A Conversation with Peter F. Drucker." *Psychology Today*, December 1982.

Harvey, Donald F., and Donald R. Brown. *An Experiential Approach to Organization Development*. Englewood Cliffs, NJ: Prentice-Hall, Inc. 1982.

Herper, Matthew. "The Generic Onslaught." *Forbes.com*, July 7, 2006.

Herper, Matthew. "Threat of Substitute Products Real." *Forbes.com*, July 7, 2006.

Hill, Charles W. L. *Competing in the Global Marketplace*. New York: McGraw-Hill, 2003.

Janis, Irving L. "Group Think." *Psychology Today*, November 1971.

————. *Victims of Group Think*. Boston: Houghton Mifflin, 1972.

"Japan Elderly Population Ratio Now World's Highest." *China Daily & Reuters*, June 30, 2006.

Jay, Antony. *Management and Machiavelli*. New York: Holt, Rinehart and Winston, 1968.

Kanter, Rosabeth Moss. "Drucker: The Unsolved Puzzle." *New Management* 2, no. 3 (Winter 1988).

Kast, Fremont E., and James E., Rosenzweig. *Organization and Management, A Systems and Contingency Approach.* New York: McGraw-Hill, 1979.

Kast, Fremont E., and James E. Rosenzweig. "General Systems Theory: Applications for Organization and Management." *Academy of Management Journal* (December 1972).

Kepner, Charles H., and Benjamin B. Tregoe. *A Systematic Approach to Problem Solving and Decision Making.* New York: McGraw-Hill, 1965.

"Kevin Rollins Stepping Down at Dell." *MSNBC.com,* February 20, 2007.

Kim, Chan W., and Renee Mauborgne. *Blue Ocean Strategy: How to Create Uncontested Market Space and Make the Competition Irrelevant.* Boston: Harvard Business Publishing Corporation, 2005.

Koch, Richard. *The Financial Times Guide to Strategy.* 2nd ed. London: Pearson Education Limited, 2000.

Kotler, Philip. *Marketing Management.* 11th ed. Upper Saddle River, NJ: Pearson Education, Inc., 2003.

Levitt, Theodore. "Marketing Myopia." *Harvard Business Review* (1960); repr. HBR Classic (September–October 1975).

Lim, Paul J. "Putting Your House in Order." *U.S. News and World Report,* December 10, 2001.

"The Man Who Invented Management." *Business Week,* November 28, 2005.

Marks, Michael. *Working at Cross-Purposes: How Distributors and Manufacturers Can Manage Conflict Successfully.* Washington, DC: National Association of Wholesale-Distributors, Distribution Research and Education Foundation, 2006.

"Matching Dell." Harvard Business School Reprint 799-158, June 6, 1999.

"Migration and the Changing Face of Europe." *MSNBC.com.,* June 18, 2007.

Mintzberg, Henry. *The Nature of Managerial Work.* New York: Harper and Row, 1973.

———. "Crafting Strategy." *Harvard Business Review* 65, no. 4 (July–August 1987).

———, Bruce Ahlstrand, and Joseph Josepel, *Strategy Safari: A Guided Tour Through the Wilds of Strategic Management.* New York: Free Press, 1998.

———, and J.A. Waters. "Of Strategies, Deliberate and Emergent." *Strategic Management Journal* 6 (1985).

Moyer, Liz. "A Record Year for Deals." *Forbes.com,* December 21, 2007.

———. "Cost of the Crunch." *Forbes.com,* November 16, 2007.

Nieman, Christoph. "U.S. Businesses for Sale." *New Yorker,* November 20, 2007.

"Only Child Parents Encouraged to Have 2nd Baby." *China Daily,* September 29, 2006.

"Only Child Parents Encouraged to Have Two Kids." *China Daily,* November 10, 2006.

O'Toole, James O. "Peter Drucker: Father of the New Management." *New Management* 2, no 3 (Winter 1985).

Packard, Vance. *The Hidden Persuaders.* New York: David McKay, 1957.

Pascale, Richard T. *Managing on the Edge.* New York: Simon & Schuster, 1990.

Penn, Mark J. "Trendsurfing: The Critical 1%." *MSN.Com.,* August 28, 2007.

Peters, Thomas J. "The Other Half of the Message." *New Management* 2, no. 3 (Winter 1985).

————, and Robert H. Waterman. *In Search of Excellence: Lessons from America's Best-Run Companies.* New York: Warner Books, 1982.

"Population to Peak at 1.5 Billion in 2030s." *China Daily,* June 23, 2006.

Porter, Michael E. *Competitive Advantage: Creating and Sustaining Superior Performance.* New York: Free Press, 1985.

————. *Competitive Strategy: Techniques for Analyzing Industries and Competitors.* New York: Free Press, 1980.

————. *Michael E. Porter on Competition.* Boston: Harvard Business School Publishing, 1979.

————. "What Is Strategy?" *Harvard Business Review,* November–December 1996.

Pritchett, Price. *After the Merger: Managing the Shockwaves.* New York: Dow Jones-Irwin, 1985.

Rea, Peter, Ph.D., and Harold Kerzner, Ph.D. *Strategic Planning: A Practical Guide.* New York: John Wiley, 1997.

Robbins, Stephen R. *Organizational Theory: Structure, Design, and Applications.* 2nd ed. Englewood Cliffs, NJ: Prentice-Hall, Inc., 1987.

————. *Organizational Behavior.* 8th ed. Upper Saddle River, NJ: Prentice-Hall, 1998.

Scarborough, Norman M., and Thomas W. Zimmerer. *Effective Small Business Management.* 7th ed. Upper Saddle River, NJ: Pearson Education, 2003.

Schneiderman, R. M. "Xerox Turns to Burns for Growth." *Forbes.com* April 4, 2006.

"Shanghai Addresses Aging Issue." *China Daily,* June 25, 2006.

Simon, Herbert A. "Administrative Decision Making." *Public Administration Review* (March 1965).

Slywotzky, Adrian, and Richard Wise. *How to Grow When Markets Don't.* New York: Warner Books, Inc., 2003.

"Strong Deal Growth in China." *Price waterhouse Coopers,* December 18, 2007.

Swaim, Ph.D., Robert W. "The Drucker Files: Drucker on the Next Society and China. Part I." *Business Beijing Magazine,* November 2003.

————. "The Drucker Files: Innovation and Entrepreneurship. Parts I, II & III. *Business Beijing Magazine,* January, February, and March 2003.

————. "The Drucker Files: Is a Decision Necessary? Parts I & II." *Business Beijing Magazine,* July and August 2003.

————. "The Drucker Files: Why Your Organization Needs to Be a Change Leader, Parts I & II." *Business Beijing Magazine,* May & June 2002.

————. "The Drucker Files: Strategy and the Purpose of a Business – Parts I & II." *Business Beijing Magazine,* October and November 2002.

————. "The Drucker Files: The Five Deadly Business Sins." *Business Beijing Magazine,* December 2002.

Swift, Mike. "Latinos Projected to be Ethnic Majority by 2042." *Contra Costa Times,* July 10, 2007.

Thompson Jr., Arthur A., and A.J. Strickland III. *Strategic Management: Concepts and Cases.* 13th ed. New York: McGraw Hill Irvin, 2003.

Toffler, Alvin and Heidi. *Revolutionary Wealth.* New York: Knopf, 2006.

"UK Pension Age May Be Raised to 69." *China Daily,* December 1, 2005.

"U.S. Population Growth." *National Audubon Society,* 2006.

Vogt, Richard J. "Forecasting as a Management Tool." *Michigan Business Review* (January 1970).

Welch, Jack. *Jack, Straight From the Gut.* New York: Warner Books, Inc., 2001.

"White Paper: American Business-Trade Gap Not the Full Picture." *American Chamber of Commerce—China* 2007.

"Working-Age Population Set to Decline." *China Daily,* September 1, 2006.

"The World's 50 Most Innovative Companies." *Business Week,* April 18, 2008.

"Zero Population Growth." *Beijing Review,* July 31, 2003.

Index